Writing Children's Fiction

A Writers' and Artists' Companion

**Yvonne Coppard
and Linda Newbery**

Series Editors: **Carole Angier and Sally Cline**

BLOOMSBURY

Bloomsbury Academic

An imprint of Bloomsbury Publishing Plc

50 Bedford Square	1385 Broadway
London	New York
WC1B 3DP UK	NY 10018 USA

www.bloomsbury.com

First published 2013

British Library Cataloguing-in-Publication Data
A catalogue record for this book is available from the British Library.
ISBN: PB: 978-1-408-15687-2
           e-pub: 978-1-472-53533-7
           e-pdf: 978-1-472-53532-0

Library of Congress Cataloging-in-Publication Data
A catalogue record for this book is available from the Library of Congress.

Typeset by Country Setting, Kingsdown, Kent CT14 8ES, UK.
Printed and bound in Great Britain.

Part 3: Write on: writing workshop

Contents

Previous books by Yvonne Coppard

Teen/Young adult fiction

Not Dressed Like That, You Don't!
Everybody Else Does! Why Can't I?
Great! You've Just Ruined the Rest of My Life!
To Be a Millionaire
Jamie and Sooz: Love Hurts

Junior fiction

Copper's Kid
Bully
The Rag Bag Family
Hide and Seek
Simple Simon
Here for a Year? Forget it!
More Madness!

The 'Alexandra the Great' series

What's Cooking, Alex?
Alex and the Ice Princess
Alex in Wonderland

First readers

Don't Let it Rain
The Odd Couple
Tales of Travelers (USA)

Non-fiction for schools

Ten Steps Forward (creative writing in the classroom)
Bully 4 Drama (drama)
Abuse: Sometimes, Families Hurt (personal and social education)
Room for One More: Surviving as a Foster Mum (writing as Beth Miller)

Previous books by Linda Newbery

Young adult fiction

Set in Stone
Sisterland
The Damage Done
The Shell House

Junior fiction

At the Firefly Gate
Catcall
Lob
Nevermore
Polly's March
The Treasure House

First readers/Picture books

Barney the Boat Dog
Cat Tales
Posy

Yvonne would like to dedicate this book to Sophie Quirk, with much love.

Linda would like to dedicate this book to Peter Thomas, an inspirational Head of English with whom she was lucky to work for several years, and who became a valued friend and critic.

Foreword

by Anne Fine, former Children's Laureate

About ten years ago, after a couple of decades of writing for children, I opened a file called *Things I Wish I'd Been Told When I Started*. Writing is in large part a solitary profession, and many authors and would-be authors actually prefer to work alone as they follow the poet Philip Larkin's most basic and sensible advice: 'Sit down and write the book that you yourself would most like to read but no one has bothered to write for you.'

I was lucky. My first novel was a runner-up for a prestigious prize and publication followed. I have been writing ever since.

Sadly, for most writers things are nowhere near that simple.

As the most cursory glance through the contents of this book will attest, the business of writing for young people is beset with important social issues and literary snares. It's not simply a question of what sort of writing they find accessible and appealing. Children's reading has always been monitored by those we might call the gatekeepers: people who choose, or don't choose, to publish the books in the first place, and those such as parents, teachers and librarians who may, or may not, feel inclined to hand them over to the child.

Every now and again along comes some lucky Joe or Josephine who, though oblivious to all the many concerns and pitfalls of the field, settles down to write a book, sees the finished product eagerly accepted, and enjoys great success. But this is rare. And rarer still is the author who can keep the books coming, year after year, and turn what has always been a precarious profession into a happy and productive working life.

The root of success does, of course, have to be talent. Nobody knows quite what it is that makes some people so expert at chiming in with the reading child's capacity to receive, and others so heavy-handed and patronising. And every writer differs in his or her dependence on such factors as memory, observation and intuition. But in a climate where publishers are less and less willing to take a risk on a new author, it makes good sense to know the field. (Robert Louis Stevenson may not have had the adage 'Know Your Market' in mind when he advised would-be writers to 'Read, read, read. Read everything.' But, for a wider range of reasons than ever before, this does remain the very best of advice.)

That's where this book comes in. It covers every single aspect of the field of writing for children. It's in no way didactic. (Cheeringly, as the often contradictory testimonies of those successful authors who have contributed show, there is no one 'right' way to write a book.) But it is useful to be able to learn from the insights and know-how of others.

If I look through that file I opened all those years ago – snippets from newspaper interviews with various writers, scribbled gleanings from conferences, observations from academics, in short, anything I came across that surprised me, interested me, or just rang true to my own experience – I see how much of what I so laboriously gathered over the years could simply have been corralled into a compendium like this.

Why learn the hard way? Why not read it now?

Preface

by Carole Angier and Sally Cline, Series Editors

Welcome to the *Writers' and Artists' Companions*, a brand new series by writers, for writers.

Almost the first thing we discover as writers is how rare it is for our first shining vision to be achieved. As Series Editors our vision was truly shining. We wanted the books to be a joy to read; and to be clear and incisive, yet open to different approaches, for writing is the most individual thing anyone can do. So we chose the best writers we could, asked them to write not singly but in pairs, and had them invite as their guests as many other leading writers in their genre as possible. And magically – our writers have done it.

Writing Fiction for Children is by two superb writers across the genre, Yvonne Coppard and Linda Newbery, with guest contributions from twenty-one top children's authors from both the UK and the US. Among them they cover everything you could wish to know about children's writing – including many fascinating areas we'd never heard of, and wouldn't have been able to ask for (eg. fiction packagers and 'Hi-Lo'.)

As in all the *Writers' and Artists' Companions*, **Part 1** consists of essays on the genre by the two authors; **Part 2** is a wonderful potpourri of tips and tales from their guests; and **Part 3** is a practical guide to writing in the genre, once again by the two authors.

In Part 1 Yvonne and Linda consider such thorny questions as – what is a children's book, or a children's classic? What, indeed, is a child? Should you write for the market, for a particular age? Should you have a message? Should you include all genders, cultures, degrees of (dis)ability? On all these debates and more they manage to be both practical and inspirational, arguing that in the end the best writing comes out of you and what you have to say.

Part 3 starts with story ideas and ends with agents, via dialogue, pace, revision – and much else in between. Yvonne and Linda talk about their own different methods, and open up the dialogue to you: 'Are you a point-by-point planner, a seat-of-the-pants flier? Or, in between, a story grower?' Whichever you are, go for it, they say. And above all, 'Write the story you want and need to write, and have faith that it will find its way.'

Exactly!

Good writing.

Introduction

by Yvonne Coppard

For anyone who had the privilege of an education, at school or elsewhere, books for children have been as much a part of our lives as milk, bread, friendships made and broken, homework, and summers that seemed at once to stretch into eternity yet disappear at incomprehensible speed. We learned fascinating and sometimes unpalatable truths about our world from books, in language we could understand. We were comforted by them before we went to sleep, or bored into stupor by them when they were imposed upon us. We experienced fear and sadness on the page that prepared us for the real thing when we encountered it; we laughed, and thought it over, and adopted and reshaped ideas from books according to our own needs and situations. For those who learned to read easily and well, books were friends, educators, leaders of expeditions into physical and metaphorical places across the universe, through time and space. For those whose reading journey was a lonely struggle up a mountain, the summit always shifting further into the horizon, books were impossible codes with enticing pictures; sources of frustration and dread and shame. Whatever our experience, we have been shaped by books in so many subtle ways.

I think it is possible that fiction for children is the most likely genre of all the books in the *Writers' and Artists'* series to arouse emotion and incite debate, simply because of this wired-in, universal experience. We have all been consumers of children's fiction and are, therefore, all experts with our own opinions of what makes a 'good' or 'unacceptable' book. Those of us who are parents probably have strong views about what must be included in our own children's reading experience – and what must be denied.

We have both taken a love of children's books through into our adult lives, and we do not take for granted the privilege of being able to immerse ourselves in this rich kingdom. We have been lucky enough to be able to make our passion our profession, and we hope to share that passion with you, in the pages of this book. The strength of feeling aroused by childhood experiences of literature came home to us in researching and discussing the history of children's literature, and again when we looked at censorship and at 'classics'. Everyone we spoke to, whatever their background, had a view. 'You have to mention . . .' 'Aren't you going to include . . . ?' 'What about . . . ?' 'Why on earth are you putting that title . . . ?'

Each of us mentions books in her reflections that the other has never come across or long forgotten. We gave up on the original plan to include our own favourite titles – an impossible task, doomed to incite disapproval from ranks of readers for the hundreds of stories we would have to leave out that have an important place in someone's heart.

This decision was vindicated, I think, by the coverage of the opening ceremony of the 2012 Olympics in London. The special place of children's literature was rightly included in the spectacular journey through British history so imaginatively portrayed by director Danny Boyle, scriptwriter Frank Cottrell-Boyce (a guest contributor to Part 2) and thousands of volunteers. There was almost universal approval of the ceremony and of the portrayal of children's literature as one of Britain's greatest triumphs. But public reaction included wails of disappointment about what was *not* included. 'How could they forget . . . ? 'Why didn't they . . . ?' Choose a list of children's classics at your peril; you will never get it 'right'. Any list – whether it's the brief history or present and future classics that we have included in this book, or the list of favourites we left out – can only ever be a subjective selection, not a definitive catalogue. I take heart from that, as proof of the enormous scope and number of great children's books that we have to choose from in such a task.

So, here is how we approached the challenge of trying to encapsulate the world of children's fiction and engage new and established writers in the exploration of why writing for children is so important, and how to practise and improve our art. There are lots of tips for those who wish to write a children's book themselves woven into every section of the book, but we wanted also to inspire readers to discover the world of children's literature, whether or not they plan to write it; we think the experience is worth the journey. Like the authors in all the books of this *Writers' and Artists'* series, we come as a pair, but we are independent individuals with our own views, which don't necessarily coincide. We enjoyed the discussions that our differences sparked. It is possible that you won't agree with either of us. That's what makes the diverse territories of children's fiction such a diverting and entertaining landscape to explore.

Part 1

In 'Reflections', we start by exploring the importance of *story* in our development from earliest conscious thought to cynical, world-weary adulthood; the power of literature to hold, heal or haunt us. It is as children that we learn to read – or learn that this imaginative and educational territory is to be denied us. We must therefore involve ourselves in the developing reading relationship between the child and the book and nurture the 'inner child', the abandonment to the moment, that oils the creative wheels of storytelling.

A look at the current status of children's literature in the book world and in libraries – both areas currently struggling with economic and social forces – leads inevitably to the question of why one would wish to write for children in the first place. We address the commonly held belief that writing for children is somehow easier than writing for adults, and that children's writers are practising their skills in order to move on and write *proper* books one day. We discuss the impact of the growing number of celebrity authors, and offer some positive advice on how to make a start as a children's writer.

The focus then shifts from our personal reflections to an exploration of important themes in writing for children: we have called this section 'Freedom and responsibility in children's literature'. What, exactly, *is* a children's book? What is it *for*? Come to that, what do we mean by 'child', and how does our answer to that question shape our attitudes to children's books? An introduction to the dividing line between juvenile and adult fiction, and a brief history, from the first book specially written for children through to the multi-million international industry we have today, leads us into a discussion of what makes a 'classic' children's book. We look at the rules of engagement for those wishing to write for children, from the need to understand basic developmental stages through to the social and political influences that result in censorship, public debate and social outcry. The various categories of children's fiction are described before returning to the theme of practical advice for making the best possible use of your own talents in writing for children.

Part 2

We invited twenty-one authors whose work we admire to contribute to the book, and were ourselves inspired by what came back. We asked each guest contributor to write a short piece on any aspect of their work and experience that they wished. We thought we might have to ask for changes to pieces where two or more authors had written on the same theme. That didn't happen: each piece features a marvellously individual insight into children's fiction. Most of our contributors are already celebrated authors; some are on their way. Between them, they write for children from early years to young adulthood. They tackle humour; dark tales of blood and revenge; fantasy; historical fiction; serious, challenging issues; and light-hearted observations of the world they see around them. Our contributors need no further introduction: their pieces speak for themselves.

Part 3

Part 3 is the nuts-and-bolts writers' workshop section of the book. Here we have tried to share all the practical advice and skill-building accumulated in our own writing and varied experience of teaching creative writing. We have looked at how to inspire and develop ideas and followed the process through all its component parts, including plot, setting, voice and viewpoint, redrafting, accepting criticism, and a lot more. Top tips based on our experiences and practical exercises to help hone your own skills are included. As with all skills, you get your best results by constant practice.

Throughout the book, we have wanted to spark, or further develop, your own interest in writing for children. We've done our best. Now, it's over to you!

Part 1:
Reflections on writing children's fiction

Reflections

Books we love as children
Linda Newbery

There's something special about the books we love as children. Hard to recapture, it's something we look back on with gratitude, and maybe with a sense of loss. It's probably only as children that we re-read favourite books literally to pieces, and to the point of knowing sections by heart; only as children that we think of fictional characters as our friends and companions; only as children that we live in books. (Unless you're a writer, of course; and as you're reading this, you probably are.) And that phrase 'by heart' is a telling one. We take our favourite books to heart; they become part of us, and stay with us into adulthood. They shape us. If you write, you will often be surprised by echoes from your childhood reading, especially when they come from stories you didn't know you remembered.

More than likely, as an adult, you've revisited a story you loved as a child. You read it differently now. You may be critical; you may even be disappointed. Or maybe you are able to relive, briefly, the joy and the wonder, the immersion in the story, the opening up of imaginative worlds, the relishing of unfamiliar language, the welcome reassurance of good storytelling, that you experienced as your younger self.

Many of us remember with great affection the books that made us readers, or those that made us writers. I owe my early ambition of becoming an author to Monica Edwards, whose stories I read and loved from the age of eight. For the next few years, writing secret chapters and hiding them in my wardrobe, I wanted to *be* Monica Edwards. A great many authors start that way, and one of the big attractions of being a writer for children is that you could, most likely without ever knowing, be that special author for a child somewhere – the first author, maybe, who makes reading fun, or who takes him or her into a different world, or shows the immense possibilities of words and ideas, or gives self-confidence, or creates a character who walks out of the pages.

My first published novel, *Run with the Hare*, was for teenagers. In the twenty-something years since, I've written for all ages, from picture books upwards, and I am now writing adult fiction.

I think the reason I was drawn to writing for teenagers is that there is such enormous scope – nothing you can't write about, although maybe teenage suicide, at least from the viewpoint of the perpetrator, is the last taboo. But it's more than that. Writing about teenagers – and for teenage readers – has a particular potency: for your characters, the next five or ten years of their lives will bring immense change, whether wanted or not. There will be school choices, maybe college or university, jobs, love, sex, friendships, leaving home, becoming independent – and important questions about self-knowledge, values, commitments, priorities. Does anyone face so many drastic life changes as a sixteen- or seventeen-year-old? I hope my adult novel will be enjoyed and appreciated, but I don't think it will have the effect that *The Shell House*, my young adult novel about (among other things) a boy experiencing first sex with a girl but first love for another boy, has had on some of its readers. At the other end of the age range, there is the great pleasure of seeing a young child absorbed in a story, with that rapt attentiveness that excludes the outside world: everything else can wait.

We take it for granted that we can read and write, and that marks on paper or on a screen can translate themselves into scenes and emotions in another person's mind. But let's stop and think about that a moment, because it's a small miracle. Sometimes, for a published writer, it can be easy to sink into gloom, supposing that the book on which you lavished such love and attention has been sucked into a black hole, or pulping machine, or is mouldering in a cardboard box in a charity-shop cellar, and that no one will ever read it. But books have a longer reach than we can know – in time as well as in distance. A story that began as a glimmer in your mind can, once written, live in someone else's imagination. If translated into another language, it can reach readers with whom, face to face, you'd be unable to communicate. Your story springs into life every time a reader finds it and their brain begins the complicated business of decoding marks on paper into sense and feeling. Bringing something to completion and releasing it like a message in a bottle for readers to find is an immense privilege.

The beginning of story
Yvonne Coppard

For me, one of the best rewards in writing is that awe-inspiring moment when a story starts to leave my imagination and take shape in someone else's. It will never again be exactly the same story that I crafted; it will take on a new dimension in the mind of each reader, adding to the stories that already form a part of that reader's life.

Storytelling traditions have been a continuous thread in the history of humankind as far back as we can tell. Deep in a Spanish mountainside, the darkness lit only by the guide's flickering paraffin lamp, I was fascinated to see Palaeolithic charcoal and ochre cave paintings: a fish, a horse, a rudimentary calendar to mark the passing of days.[1] Twenty-five thousand years ago, humans were attempting to communicate something about their world. What was the intention? Instructions for finding a vital food source? A parent's attempt to educate the next generation of hunters? Or a simple, creative impulse to reach out to someone, anyone, in a shared experience? We will never be sure. But this is where story comes from: the drive, the need, to communicate with someone other than yourself. A silent fantasy within your own head is not fully a story until it has been shared. A story grows, develops, explains; it is interpreted anew over successive generations. It needs an audience.

Stories told before there was even a way to write them down sought to explain the world, to bring a sense of order and control to what would otherwise be terrifying chaos: the changing seasons; burning lights across the sky; storms and floods; the unknown territories beyond death. But they were also used to grasp abstract ideas and metaphorical truths for which language is inadequate. In the major religious traditions, story has been and continues to be vital in explaining and affirming faith. Parables, inspiring tales of gods, heroes and saints: they inform, cajole or persuade us into a more enlightened understanding of who we are, and where we fit:

> **"** . . . *story as a mental activity is essential to human thought.* **"**
>
> Mark Turner[2]

Mark Turner, the cognitive scientist, linguist and author (and, coincidentally, husband of award-winning children's author Megan Whelan Turner) believes that story, projection and parable are right at the root of human thought. It is story that sets us humans apart in our ability to communicate with each other. The imagination gives birth to the language that we need in order to share our thoughts and dreams. Turner uses the powerful example of Shahrazad, she of the *One Thousand and One Nights*.[3] King Shahriyar, betrayed by an unfaithful wife, vents his fury on womankind by taking a different virgin bride every afternoon – and having her executed the following morning, before she can betray him. But the stock of virgins is dwindling, and the vizier who has the task of supplying and slaying them is in despair, not least because his own daughter, Shahrazad, is a virgin. Then Shahrazad steps forward to offer herself as the next bride. But she will not die. She will save herself, her father and the kingdom through the power of her stories.[4]

> If I perish, at least my death will be glorious; and if I succeed,
> I shall do my country an important service.

Ah, the confidence of the young and beautiful. It is a high-risk strategy and Shahrazad's father has no faith in it – and yet, being unable to say this to his beloved daughter, he also turns to a story to express his fears.[5] For both Shahrazad and her father, story is the first and last resort when they need to express the deepest levels of human emotion.

This power touches us all. Some children will never learn to read. Visual impairment, a physical or learning disability, lack of educational opportunity or the oppression of war and famine can all make this impossible. Yet stories are still shared, any time and any where, with language or with signs, pictures, grunts and mime. We won't all respond in the same way to the same story, but ultimately everyone who engages with story will find something that speaks to the heart.

The reading relationship
Yvonne Coppard

> *Reading is the sole means by which we slip, involuntarily, often helplessly, into another's skin, another's voice, another's soul.*
> Joyce Carol Oates[6]

It might be obvious, but it is worth conscious consideration: reading is not an instinct. Very few children spontaneously learn to read. Reading can become an intensely tangled and emotional issue: confidence destroyed early rarely returns. Despite nearly twelve years of compulsory schooling, in 2006 a UK Government study found that more than five million adults lacked the necessary level of literacy to function well in everyday life.[7] In 2010 the National Literacy Trust reported that 69 per cent of retail firms and 50 per cent of the manufacturing sector reported serious problems with literacy in their workforce.[8] I believe the power of the fictional world in a young child's development is one that should not be overlooked in our target-centred classrooms.

Oral storytelling awakens and develops the imagination too; pictures inside the head don't need written words, and long ago people managed very well without them. But a relationship with books (whether they are 'real' or downloaded) and the relationships established with those who bring books to you are crucial in establishing the bridge between the story in your head and the stories available in books. Once a child has the message that literacy is beyond him or her; once s/he believes that reading is a huge mountain scaled easily by others but denied to the 'stupid', it's game over. You are among the stupid; you will never 'get it', so why try?

The implications for those trapped in illiteracy go far wider than being denied the pleasure of a good book, or authors not maximising their potential audience. Imagine your own ordinary, everyday life without being able to read: shopping lists; instruction leaflets; official forms and letters; casual requests to 'drop me a note'; letters from absent friends and family; subtitles in films; notes dropped by neighbours or delivery men or handed over at work; every single subject you might need to get a qualification in; the driving test. The *et ceteras* could take us through to next Tuesday. That's why introducing children to stories – and books, those awesome repositories of imagination and knowledge – is crucial to a whole lot more than our ability to sell our work. There is an amazing selection of books for babies available in the Western world: stout, chewable, making a satisfying clunk when dropped on to the floor. Some have covers that can easily be wiped clean of dribble and pureed carrot; some are even waterproof, perfect for reading in the bath.

❝ *In reading, as in eating, an appetite is half the feast.* **❞**
Anon

The power of fiction
Yvonne Coppard

Books for young children should not be objects of reverence. If you want a children's book you can keep for ever, buy two copies and put one away. But the other should be the child's. It is here, in that very first relationship with the book and with the person introducing the book, that the motivation to unlock the written word can take its first steps, or be destroyed.

If you want to write fiction for younger children, an understanding of how they develop and learn is important. An understanding of the emotional power a story can have is essential to writing for children of any age. Reading fiction is about so much more than reading, or books. It is about diving into story, immersing yourself in another world where you can safely explore the unknowable and the fearful without abandoning your comfort zone. It is about family memories, an association of books with snuggling and laughter and safety; it is about treasured stories handed down from generation to generation. A relationship with reading sits at the heart of your school experience and probably influences your take on the world and your ability (or not) to reach your full potential. Reading fiction, research has found, also increases your abilities in social interaction, particularly in perception and empathy.[9]

With a team of colleagues, Keith Oatley, Professor Emeritus of Cognitive Psychology at the University of Toronto, devised fascinating experiments to look at the relationship between reading and social skills. He likens fiction to a simulation of our social world. 'If I am correct, then just as people's skills as pilots improve when they spend time in a flight simulator, so people's social skills should improve when they spend time reading fiction.'[10]

This implies a weighty responsibility, as well as a great joy for those involved in the journey from chewing on books to avidly reading them.

In search of a connection with the 'inner child'
Yvonne Coppard

Many writers describe their creative voice (whether or not they write for children) by reference to what they call 'the inner child'.

I don't personally characterise the creativity that drives me in this way. I visualise it more in terms of an excited puppy (springer spaniel, actually), scampering through the woods off the leash and identifying treasures to explore and occasionally bring back to base. But I do agree that one quality a successful writer should nurture is that child-like ability to observe the world as it is, and to ask questions: why? . . . how? . . . what if? And I do believe this quality has to be regularly fed and watered, in whatever way works best for you, if you are to achieve your best writing. Some writers foster this connection by taking long walks or swimming up and down a pool; some allow time for 'childish' pursuits: jigsaws, games, modelling clay, finger paints. This need to take time out from the driving forces of the adult-centred world is a common theme among writers. It is not 'skiving' or 'dossing'; it is an essential preparation, perhaps to be likened to preparing an itinerary for a complicated journey or browsing several garden centres before choosing just the right plants for your garden.

The joyful abandonment to the moment, the enthusiastic quest for the ultimate answer to 'why?' is where creativity finds a launch pad. If this is the inner child, then the nurturing of this child must be lifelong, without ever coming to maturity. Adult responsibilities blunt and dilute the obsessive focus so characteristic of children. The confidence that there is an answer, that all will become clear in the quest, gradually shrivels into an acknowledgment that life is more mundane than that; it throws up peaks and troughs but very few real answers. We become cynical. Now, you can take that cynicism and let it inform your writing: humorists Will Self, Jack Dee and many more make a good career from their pessimistic, world-weary perspective. We find them amusing because their cynicism resonates with our own. In writing for children, however, you have to try and stay away from the world-weary and the cynical, or you are unlikely to engage your audience.

In Roald Dahl's *Charlie and the Chocolate Factory*, Willie Wonka reveals to Charlie why he launched the 'golden ticket' competition, the prize for which was a visit to his magical, drooled-over palace of children's dreams. He wants to find a child who could take over his chocolate empire when he is too weary to carry on. It has to be a child, he explains to Charlie: 'A grown-up won't listen to me; he won't learn. He will try to do things his own way and not mine.'[11] Here is the epitome of the inner child: intuitive, creative, often boxed and cornered by the rational world. Willy Wonka's factory represents a rejection of adult preoccupations, and it is here where you must live, at least for a part of your working day (not all the time, because you do have to eat and pay the bills).

Albert Einstein reputedly said, 'The intuitive mind is a sacred gift and the rational mind is a faithful servant. We have created a society that honours the servant and has forgotten the gift.'[12] I do not know where creativity lies – whether it be in the intuitive mind, the rational mind or a combination of both. But I like Einstein's distinction. To me, creativity feels like the soft-shelled 'sacred gift'. The harder-shelled hack who deals with agents and asserts a presence with publishers is the 'faithful servant'. Both are gifts to the writer, and both are necessary for success.

Welcome to the world of children's books
Linda Newbery

At the time of writing, there's plenty for the book world to be gloomy about. A 2011 survey by the National Literacy Trust found that one young person in three did not have books of their own, compared to one in ten in 2005.[13] Yet public libraries are under threat; schools' library services are being disbanded; jobs are being lost, and with them the accumulation of years of expertise and experience. There are books, there are readers; but how are the two to meet? School budgets are being cut, and many governing bodies see the library as first stop for making savings. Bookstores give shelf-space to best-sellers, celebrity memoirs, TV chefs and the like at the expense of mid-list authors, with the result that the same few titles appear everywhere. The majority of published books remain invisible, while independent bookshops struggle to survive, unable to match the big discounting found in supermarkets. And the effects of Kindle and other e-readers are as yet un-clear, though book sales are dwindling in the face of e-competition. It's not an easy time – if indeed there ever was one – to make a living from writing.

But let's be positive. In the world of children's books we have the price-less asset of adults whose passion and delight it is to bring children and books together. Parents, librarians, teachers, organisers of book groups, events and the many regional book awards judged by children, volunteers in schools, bloggers from *Mumsnet* to *Guardian Books* online, people running author talks, workshops, family days, competitions and craft activities in bookshops and story museums and at festivals – all these are delighted to get their hands on good new stories, and to see children sharing and enjoying them. The average writer for adults can only dream of such support (and free publicity) as this.

If you succeed in being published, you are likely to find the children's book world a friendly and welcoming place. There may be invitations to visit schools and bookshops, festivals, book fairs, library holiday schemes and suchlike; some of this work will help supplement your income. You may receive the kind of welcome that makes you feel like a celebrity. Children you meet, especially younger ones, won't care that you're not Michael Morpurgo or Jacqueline Wilson; they will simply be thrilled to meet a real live author, someone who works that magic of creating worlds for them to live in.

Recent years have seen a number of awards and incentives for new authors, of which the most prestigious is the Branford Boase Award, given annually to a first-time author. Four of our guest contributors – Bridget Collins, Mal Peet, Meg Rosoff and Marcus Sedgwick – received this prize as a prelude to stellar careers, which gives an indication of its importance in highlighting new talent. The Waterstones Prize is awarded each year for a first or second novel, with shortlisted titles prominently displayed in the bookstores. For those yet to be published, SCBWI (the Society of Children's Book Writers and Illustrators) produces *Undiscovered Voices*, an annual collection of extracts from new work which is widely circulated to agents and publishers; and Chicken House, a leading children's publisher, runs a yearly competition in association with *The Times* newspaper for which the prize is publication.

None of this is meant to imply that the route to publication will be easy. Publishing for children is very competitive, perhaps more so than ever, with numerous universities offering creative writing courses, many of them specialising in writing for children. Graduates from these courses will have a realistic view of the book world and how it works, how to approach agents and editors, and even how to promote themselves. They are thinking of writing as a career; they will have benefited from support and constructive criticism from their peers and tutors, and will know of various organisations that can provide information and opportunities. If you start out on your own, you'll be competing against keen graduates from these courses. Not only are there a great many of them, but they will be several strides ahead in terms of know-how and networking.

However, there's no requirement to take a course as a route to publication. Editors and agents are constantly looking for distinctive new voices, compelling stories and that unmistakable confidence that marks out a real writer. What's on your CV is of secondary interest. If your writing catches their eye, they will be interested in you.

Not everyone can write – more specifically, not everyone can write for children. I've met people who seem keener on being published than they are on writing; who are thinking about publicity and book tours before they've written a word. Then there are the people who want to tell you their plot – in my experience, this never bodes well. Real writers understand that a story is much more than its plot; and no plot, however ingenious and exciting, can compensate for dull writing and inept pacing.

Publishers have cupboards and shelves groaning under the weight of unsolicited typescripts – scripts they haven't asked for, work that hasn't come from one of their own authors or via an agent. These form what is known as the 'slush pile', which gives a fair idea of what editors expect to find there.

Just occasionally those envelopes will contain gems, but most of what's sent in is unpublishable, amateurish, even illiterate, and will be swiftly rejected. No doubt editors of adult books have the same low expectations of their tottering heaps, but children's editors in particular are wearied by stories written by people whose knowledge of children's books is limited to their own reading as a child, or who fondly imagine that because their own offspring/playgroup/nephews and nieces loved this story, it will be an instant hit; or who imagine that their plot is stunningly original, when it provokes nothing but yawns from the publisher's reader who's seen ten like it this month.

Unfortunately, the idea that anyone can write a children's book is prevalent. Later in this section, Yvonne will look at the irritation, for professional authors, of the number of celebrities who turn out a book or two (or have them ghost-written) as a sideline to an acting or singing career. I'm not trying to claim that writing a five-thousand word story for six-year-olds is as taxing as writing a lengthy historical novel requiring months of research. Drawing a cartoon is less demanding than painting the ceiling of the Sistine Chapel, but if you can't draw, you won't be able to do either – your cartoon will be clunky, heavy-handed, unfunny. It won't work. Writing a picture-book text or a first chapter story for young readers requires skill and flair; in fact, writing a successful picture-book text is extremely difficult to accomplish .

Remember, publishing is a buyers' market. If your work doesn't charm or intrigue an editor, there are hundreds of other would-be writers out there. Only your best will stand even a chance of being good enough.

The lost kingdom of libraries

Yvonne Coppard

 When I got my library card, that's when my life began.

Rita Mae Brown[14]

At the time of writing, there is a battle going on in the UK over the fate of the libraries, particularly those smaller branches that have for so many years been part of the centre of rural and suburban life. Even in the big cities, where libraries are more likely to survive, there is a move to make them more 'relevant', as the cost-cutters would have it – more computer terminals, more music CDs and films on DVD; more emphasis on the utilitarian functions of literacy (finding and keeping a job); more of the 'Big Society'[15] spirit of roping in volunteers to keep libraries going rather than 'wasting' money on qualified, chartered librarians. After all, the argument goes, fiction books are cheap enough that people can buy what they want or download them on to their e-readers, and there's no need to search through a pile of reference books once you have mastered Google and the basics of an online search.

Leaving aside the politics, and the sweeping assumptions about how people who are not in well-paid professional posts might live, there is still a lot that has been missed here. Jeanette Winterson quipped in an interview for American Libraries online magazine, 'Nobody's ever going to say, "Can I see the index to your Kindle?" It's so depressing and unsexy.'[16] There is plenty of evidence that people will not give up their libraries without a fight. Our books are a testament to our lives, and whether or not we have the luxury of a personal library in addition to the huge resources of a good public one, a connection with literature seems to be written into our national DNA.

Vociferous opposition from readers and writers alike culminated in 'Save Our Libraries Day' on 5 February 2011. 'Read-ins' were held in libraries throughout the UK. Author Alan Gibbons has thrown himself tirelessly into a leading role in the mission to save libraries from, if not extinction, then certainly a catastrophic loss of access to books for those who have no other realistic way of finding everything books provide.

Gibbons points out that South Korea is a country known for its obsession with all things computer and techno-driven. Yet South Korea is currently building 180 new libraries, and the country tops the international reading league tables (the UK has dropped from seventh to a depressing twenty-fifth place within the last decade).

> *Quite simply, the Koreans understand that individuals who browse and read for pleasure are more likely to be literate than those who do not.*[17]

> **"** *Google can bring you back a hundred thousand
> answers. A librarian can bring you back the right
> one.* **"**
> Neil Gaiman[18]

The contributions of many authors to the campaign have reflected their own debt of gratitude to libraries and librarians in shaping their early love of reading and their subsequent writing careers. Paul O'Grady, comedian, writer and broadcaster, remembers weekly visits with his mother to collect two books a week and, later, finding the essential peace and quiet of the reference library, where he revised for exams without the noise and distractions of home.

Bali Rai, children's author, had no books in his childhood home and the library was his essential point of contact with literature. 'There was no sense that it [literature] belonged to me or people like me,' he says. 'It was my local library that broke down those barriers.'[19]

The place of libraries in the creative heart of a nation is amply summed up by Jeanette Winterson, whose experience of living in a home where contemporary fiction was forbidden makes her a notable example of a writer for whom libraries, and the guiding hand of a librarian, were fundamental: 'It was somebody you could talk to and discuss books with – who just takes it for granted that books are great and that you should want to be here. They don't have to persuade you of anything; they aren't apologising. I found it very calming that I could go into that space and not have any of the troubles or difficulties of home.'[20]

Why write for children?
Linda Newbery

So: why write? And why write for children? Maybe the best and only answer is that you can't *not* write; you feel unfulfilled, lazy, irritable unless you have a project in mind or under way. You have ideas, dreams, questions waiting to be explored. You have a story already unfolding in your head, like the private screening of a film. You want to know what might happen. Beware: it's an addiction. You might never stop. All the writers I know are full of ideas about their current work or the project they're about to start, aiming to make it their best yet. As Stephen King puts it in *On Writing*: 'It's about enriching the lives of those who will read your work, and enriching your own life, as well.' It's about 'getting happy, okay? Getting happy.'[21] Writing, when it goes well, can be exhilarating, fulfilling, exciting, surprising, illuminating, utterly absorbing. If you want to write, you will find a way; no one can take that desire or that ability away from you. You can do it anywhere. It's not like being an actor – you don't have to wait for a casting opportunity. It's not like being a footballer or a gymnast – you need never retire. Age is no handicap, and is even a bonus. For addicts, it's hard to imagine any other life.

As for writing for children: a *Private Eye* cartoon by Steve Way showed two writers meeting at a party. One says, 'I'm an adult author. I deal with going bald and fancying younger women.' The other says, 'I'm a children's author. I deal with good and bad and is there such a thing as innate evil?'[22] This contains the grain of truth that children's fiction does engage with big topics, whether seriously or humorously – consider, for example, Beverley Naidoo's *Journey to Jo-burg*, Patrick Ness's *A Monster Calls*, Morris Gleitzman's *Two Weeks with the Queen* or Frank Cottrell-Boyce's *The Unforgotten Coat*. Cottrell-Boyce said, in an interview on winning the Guardian Children's Fiction Prize, 'I guess that's the good thing about being a children's writer. You try to do something very accessible but substantial as well.'[23]

Interviewed by Sebastian Faulks, Martin Amis remarked, 'People ask me if I ever thought of writing a children's book. I say, "If I had a serious brain injury I might well write a children's book".'[24] This breathtaking disparagement of children's books and the people who write them shows how widely views can diverge. Amis went on, 'The idea of being conscious of who you're direct-ing the story to is anathema to me, because, in my view, fiction is freedom and any restraints on that are intolerable.'

Well, the notion that writing for children requires anything less than total engagement is misguided, not to say insulting, and surely Amis imposes restraints on himself whenever he takes a character's viewpoint; is that a loss of freedom, or a focusing of attention? But I'll resist getting sidetracked, because the point here is who we think we're writing for. It's a question often put to children's authors. Are you writing mainly for yourself? For the child or teenager you once were? For your own children, or for teenagers you know? For the market?

When you come to our guest contributors in Part 2, you may notice that most of them are talking about the demands of the story, rather than whom it's for. David Almond says of *Skellig* that 'it was the culmination of everything I'd done before. And I realised, with a shock of amazement, that it was a book for young people. It was a moment of liberation. I knew that I was growing up as a writer, that somehow I'd come home.' This revelation came from the story itself, and how it needed to be told, rather than from any idea of who might read it. Mal Peet says, 'I treat my readers as equals. The greatest vice is condescension; young readers can smell it a mile away.' And as Caragh O'Brien puts it, 'Writing for yourself isn't whimsy. It isn't the secret to publishing. It's the only thing to do.'

Of course, the term 'children's books' covers such a wide spectrum, from board books for babies to challenging young adult fiction, that we can't lump it all together. Sophisticated teenage novels like Mal Peet's *Tamar*, Aidan Chambers' *The Toll Bridge* and Judy Blundell's *Strings Attached* are indistinguishable from adult fiction, marked only as 'young adult' because their publishers categorise them as such. Writing complex novels such as these is a very different matter from writing a picture-book text, and each has its own demands. If you're writing a text for babies or toddlers, though, you're far more likely to have the possible 'reader' in mind than when you're writing older fiction – how very young children experience the world, what they find funny, absurd, or frightening.

Adèle Geras, who has written more than eighty books for all ages, says, 'The age of your main characters will dictate the language and the concerns of that book'. Obviously some subject matter will rule itself out as unsuitable for young readers, but, as Adèle says, 'even the very youngest child is aware of human emotions: anger, jealousy, fear, rage, love and so forth'. Consider Maurice Sendak's *Where the Wild Things Are*: the magic and power of this story is in its harnessing of universal themes, acknowledging fear of the unknown and making it containable within a recognisable domestic setting.

C.S. Lewis wrote: 'Everything in the story should arise from the whole cast of the author's mind. We must write for children out of those elements in our own imagination which we share with children: differing from our child readers not by any less, or less serious, interest in the things we handle, but by the fact that we have other interests which children would not share with us.'[25] Our contributors make it clear that they aim to do more than to write something acceptable; they want to tell the story in the very best way they can. Whatever you're writing, from picture book to longer novel, it's important to the book's integrity that you find satisfaction in its creation, and that you produce something you're proud of. After all, it will probably go out into the world with your name on it.

In her introduction to the 2012 edition of *Children's Writers' and Artists' Yearbook*, Alison Stanley says that would-be authors should read widely, examine children's magazines and newspaper supplements for current trends, speak to librarians, watch children's TV, etc.[26] Hmm, yes, up to a point. Alison Stanley is a commissioning editor speaking from years of experience, and has no doubt rejected hundreds of stories from writers whose ideas are outdated and stale. Later in this book I shall talk about the importance of knowing enough about the market to avoid wasting your time on something that doesn't fit into publishing categories. But I think too much focus on the marketplace leads to a cynical approach, either copy-catting or trend-predicting.

It's not difficult at present to see that Stephanie Meyer's hugely successful *Twilight* series has spawned hundreds of imitators – the teenage shelves are crowded with tragic, stricken heroines and brooding heroes – and at the time of writing, futuristic dystopias are everywhere, with Suzanne Collins' *The Hunger Games* leading the pack. But set out to follow these trends and you may find that they've rolled on past – publishers' lists reach at least two years ahead, and by the time your typescript lands on an editor's desk they may have commissioned all the paranormal romance or future-world nightmares their lists can support.

On the other hand, editors are always on the lookout for new talent and are often struck by a new voice that seems to have come from nowhere, or a story that's unlike anything they've seen before. Some of the most successful books of recent years have been complete originals – Mark Haddon's *The Curious Incident of the Dog in the Night-Time*, for example, or David Almond's *Skellig*, or *The Ghost's Child* by Sonya Hartnett. The editors weren't looking out for these books, but they recognised something outstanding when it came along.

New writers never do come from nowhere, of course – they come from what they've loved reading, from the books that have shaped them. To my mind, the most interesting writers haven't devoted themselves to the children's bookshelves and a methodical identification of what readers want – readers rarely do know what they want, until it arrives in front of them – but are likely to be influenced by a diverse range of authors and styles from the reading they've done for themselves. My own suggestion is to familiarise yourself a little with the market, and then ignore it. I agree with Patrick Ness' view that 'I don't think you should give readers what they want. You should make readers want what you give them.'[27]

As I've heard Philip Pullman put it, in order to succeed you need three things: talent, luck, and determination.[28] And, as you can't decide to be talented or lucky, determination is the only one of these you can put to practical use. You will certainly need determination and a measure of self-belief if you're going to succeed in the crowded and fast-moving world of children's publishing. Yvonne and I hope in this book to ease your progress, to give you realistic expectations of the marketplace, and to help you to make the most of your talent and enthusiasm.

Writing for children is easier, isn't it?
Yvonne Coppard

Natalie Babbit, the American author and critic, dispenses straight away with the myth that a story for children will be simpler or 'easier' in style.[29] She asks us to compare the opening sentences of two classic twentieth-century stories. First, in the adults' corner, we have *A Farewell to Arms* by Ernest Hemingway (1929): 'Now in the fall the trees were all bare and the roads were muddy.' Compare that with the opener to a classic children's tale, Rudyard Kipling's *Just So* story, 'How the Rhinoceros Got His Skin' (1902):

'Once upon a time, on an uninhabited island on the shores of the Red Sea, there lived a Parsee from whose hat the rays of the sun were reflected in more-than-oriental splendour.'

Enough said?

I think there is some merit in the requirement of a happy ending when it comes to the very young. The picture book that kills off Mummy in a night-time robbery and shows beloved Teddy thrown into the fire by enraged Daddy would be a cruel trick indeed. Most of us would agree that such a book should not easily find a publisher, however free the market forces. But I do have on my shelves an undeniably attractive picture book sent to me some years ago for review about a brother and sister living in Pompeii at just the wrong time for happy endings.[30] The children survive the volcano but their home, friends and family are all wiped out. I struggle to imagine the young child for whom this might be an appropriate gift, but it's an appealing and informative book just the same.

Lemony Snicket's *A Series of Unfortunate Events*, with dire warnings from the author himself *not* to read the awful account of the violence and misery endured by the newly orphaned Beaudelaire children, became a global success. More recently, I was shocked at the ending of John Smelcer's *The Trap*, a beautifully written story about a young man searching for his grandfather in the frozen wastes of Alaska. No spoilers, but have a hankie ready. Children I talked to about this story were sometimes angry – 'It shouldn't have ended that way, I didn't like it' – but they recommended the book to their friends nonetheless, and wanted to read it again themselves. The same children read Hans Christian Andersen's *Little Match Girl* and *The Steadfast Tin Soldier* and declared them to be 'a bit sad, but good'.

Tiny children are tender and inexperienced in the ways of the world. They deserve a gentle introduction to the perils they may encounter on their journey through life. But by the time they reach junior school, children are more knowledgeable, and much tougher, than adults think. They have almost certainly experienced the horror of bullying, whether directly or as an on-looker. They have negotiated the choppy waters of friendships that are made and betrayed, the humiliation of not being on the list of the chosen for the soccer team or the birthday party. The scales have dropped from their eyes and they have seen their parents or other significant adults for what they are: not omniscient, not omnipotent, only flawed humans who get it wrong sometimes, just as they do. No wonder, then, that children revel in tales of violence and disorder. What else is going to help them explore, safely and often with humour, the issues and disappointments life throws into their path with no warning?

Children's fiction doesn't need an overt educational or moral mission; it doesn't need to be 'for' something. All children's stories offer a learning experience, because children are by definition rather short on experiences, and will soak them up wherever they can find them. So I believe your duty as a children's writer is to throw yourself heart and soul into the story and not allow yourself to be constrained by what you 'ought' to be writing. Of course there are limits to your target audience's physical or developmental capacities. These may moderate your choice of vocabulary and steer you away from the exploration of concepts that are too abstract to be understood by younger readers. But these constraints are fewer in number, and less powerful in a child's life, than the gatekeepers and censors would have us believe.

When are you going to write a proper book?
Yvonne Coppard

One of the most frequent questions asked of writers in casual conversations is 'Have you had anything published?' The question seeks to define, I suppose, whether you are a 'proper' writer rather than an unsuccessful amateur. But Dr Seuss and J.K. Rowling both struggled on through multiple rejections before the Cat in the Hat and Harry Potter became two of the best-loved characters of modern times.

Just as, according to some philosophers, a tree falling in the forest makes no sound unless there is someone there to hear it fall, the question implies you are only truly a writer when a mainstream publisher has recognised your talent – and this is true for all authors, of course, not just those who write for children. With many agents receiving over a thousand manuscripts a week, and no chance of reading them all, you will stay saner and happier if you see being published as the icing on the cake, rather than the cake itself, and try to add as many strings to your bow as you can. A canny punter in a book shop once advised Helena Pielichaty, past Chair of the Children's Writers and Illustrators Group in the Society of Authors, and a well-established children's author of some thirty-two titles, 'You know what you wanna do, don't you? You wanna be like that Michael Morpurgo . . . '

Julie Sykes, author of the *Fairy Bears* and *Silver Dolphins* series, told me of her frustration when the builder working on her house extension kept interrupting her working day to chat through the open window. She was reduced to crawling, commando-style, through the house to avoid him. When her husband asked the builder not to disturb Julie while she was working, he said, 'Isn't it about time your wife got a proper job?' Politically incorrect, certainly, but an attitude with which writers, especially those who write for children, are unfortunately familiar.

Once you have established that you are indeed a proper *writer*, it's important to show that you have aspirations to write a proper *book* one day. 'Are you planning to write anything for adults?' 'Do you *just* write children's fiction?' These are not (usually) meant to be offensive questions. But I have heard authors quietly grumble a counter-question into their coffee: 'Would you ask a paediatrician if he is planning to become a proper surgeon one day?'

There is a public perception, quite widespread, that children's fiction is the easier option, or that it is akin to an apprenticeship, a journey towards the real thing. Can't hack it as a writer for adults? Have a go at children's literature. It is not a helpful approach to children's fiction to see it as a staging post. Such a view demeans children's authors but also, and more importantly, it suggests that children should not expect the best, that the standards to be striven for are not as high as those which apply to the adult world. Child readers are different, not inferior: they need books that are engaging in their own right, not signposts to some greater artistic endeavour. As Peter Hunt says: 'Children's books are different from adults' books: they are written for a different audience, with different skills, different needs and different ways of reading; equally, children experience texts in ways which are often unknowable . . . To say that, for example Judy Blume is not as good as Jane Austen, is like saying that this apple is an inadequate orange because it is green, and that oranges are innately superior anyway.'[31]

The way a child views the world is certainly less experienced, usually less cynical. But adults are brought up short often enough by the wisdom of a child to know how important a contribution to thinking a child can make. From the boy who saw that the Emperor's new clothes were a nonsense, to eleven-year-old Nkosi Johnson, who spoke so movingly at an international AIDS conference not long before his death from the disease,[32] children are paying attention to what goes on around them. They are learning and analysing the information gained from their observations; they are formulating judgements about the world and those who hold sway within it. Stories are a powerful part of that, and it would be nonsensical to expect that what children absorb from books and other vehicles of creative thought will have no influence on their development and world-view as adults. One day, many of those children will determine how we 'experts' will be dealt with in our dotage. For this and for so many other reasons, they deserve the best we can provide.

In recent years the growth of celebrity children's authors has done little to correct the misguided perception that writing for children is easy. The natural career progression of fame, whatever its original source, is increasingly to have a go at a children's book (and an autobiography, of course). The ready-made fame of the authors, although totally unconnected to the world of books in itself, means the books are guaranteed to become best-sellers, even though a significant number were not even written by the celebrity whose name appears on the title page.

> *I don't sit there with a typewriter and write it . . . I don't have time for that.*
> Katie Price[33]

Some of the celebrity authors who write their own material may well have made it anyway, on literary quality alone. Comedian David Walliams (*Mr Stink*; *Gangsta Granny*; *Billionaire Boy*) claims that he haunts bookshops, watching to see people's reactions to his work. His passion for writing shines through in his enthusiasm as a judge of BBC Radio 2's annual short-story competition for children. Walliams has discovered a new creative outlet that he thinks may even eclipse comedy for him in the future. No sour grapes should fall his way, surely. But what of the celebrity who employs someone else to devise and write a children's book, lending only his or her name to the endeavour: can this be a proper book?

Linda Chapman, a prolific author of a range of children's fiction in her own right, including the popular *Unicorn* series, has also ghost-written celebrity books. She explains how it works: 'Usually, you'll meet with an editor. The editor has already devised an idea or the outline of a story that will suitably reflect the image the celebrity is aiming for. You're unlikely to meet the celebrity personally – but make sure you like him or her. Don't choose someone with a reputation you wouldn't want to be linked to. The celebrity may or may not wish to see and comment on your draft, and may or may not read the finished book.'

It's easy to make disdainful comments about ghost-written books, but they are a useful source of income for hard-pressed authors struggling to make a living. You write for a flat fee rather than the more chancy royalty on your book's cover price. Publication is guaranteed; the necessary promotion that will get your book noticed is already a done deal. I share the irritation expressed by Linda earlier about this. It might be envy or sour grapes (we writers are prone to both) but it is difficult to restrain a sigh at the mushrooming celebrity trend in children's books. They are always something *else*, something *additional* to the author's main, 'proper' career. Their source is too often a desire to take advantage of the prevailing market appetite for celebrity rather than a passion for writing for children. I worry that it teaches us all, young readers included, to judge literature not only by its quality, but also by the shelf footage allotted in bookshop and supermarket, or perhaps the beauty or fascinating back story of the author.

If you want to write for children, that's the kind of thing you're up against. It might not be wise to give up the day job until you're confident you can make it, but don't be put off. A good book is still a good book, whether it's written by the brashest reality TV star or the most passionate MA graduate in Creative Writing.

Most professional writers barely scrape a living, and have to take on other jobs to make ends meet. But, like Linda, I don't think I've ever met one who wants to stop and do something else instead. It might be more and more difficult to get past the hurdles, the gatekeepers, the censors and the prevailing markets before you find and reach your audience – but that's probably why you bought or borrowed this book.

Socrates disdained the written word; he believed that writing words down killed them off.[34] Writing, he said, is like a painting. It cannot be questioned, cannot respond; it only says the same thing, over and over. Any idiot can make his own interpretation without challenge, and his interpretation might be the exact opposite of what the writer intended. For Socrates, oral debate was the highest form of communication. Over two thousand years later, those who cannot read or write are universally at a disadvantage, and passionate campaigns are being fought to save libraries. Now, in the twenty-first century, the enemy is the Kindle, the e-book, the computer download complete with movable this and speaking that: bite-sized literature for a byte-driven age. There are those who think the book may not even survive, although I bet they are the same people who said the video would kill off the cinema and the introduction of commercial television would make the BBC extinct within a generation. I think the pleasure of holding a real book and opening it with real hands will be with us for a while yet.

Notes

1. The Cueva de la Pileta, near Benaojan, Andalucia, Spain.
2. Mark Turner, *The Literary Mind*, Oxford University Press, Oxford, 1998, p. 12.
3. Ibid.
4. This collection, over centuries, of folk tales, mainly from West and Southern Asia has as its common 'frame' the story of King Shariyar and his wife Shahrazad.
5. A donkey tries to show off his superior intelligence by advising an ox how to manipulate their master into giving the overworked ox a day off. The donkey's ploy is indeed successful: the master stops using the ox for the work, but sends the donkey to do it instead.
6. Quoted in *Open Page*, 16 December 2011 flcenterlitarts.wordpress.com
7. Sandy Leitch, *Prosperity for All in the Global Economy: World Class Skills* (Leitch Review of Skills), London, 2006 hm-treasury.gov.uk/leitch. Crown Copyright.

8. *The New Scientist,* 28 June 2008.

9. Djikk, Mar, Oatley et al., *Journal of Child Psychotherapy and Psychiatry,* University of Toronto, vol 42, p. 241.

10. *Review of General Psychology,* vol. 3, p. 101.

11. Roald Dahl, *Charlie and the Chocolate Factory,* Puffin, London, 2007, p. 185.

12. Although this remark is often attributed to Einstein as a direct quote, it is actually a paraphrase by Bob Samples, a Christian apologist, in *The Metaphoric Mind: A Celebration of Creative Consciousness,* 1976.

13. C. Clark, J. Woodley and F. Lewis, *The Gift of Reading in 2011:* Children and Young People's Access to Books and Attitudes towards Reading, 2011, www.literacytrust. org.uk/assets/0001/1303/The_Gift_of_Reading_in_2011.pdf

14. See www.goodreads.com/10383

15. United Kingdom Prime Minister David Cameron's term for rebalancing government and community responsibilities for social welfare.

16. *American Libraries,* 13 March 2012.

17. Alan Gibbons, in *Why do Libraries Matter?* paraxis.org

18. Quotation seen woven into a carpet in a library in Canberra, Australia.

19. Online interview: readingagency.org.uk/media/05-authors-speak-out-for-libra/

20. Jeanette Winterson, online interview, 3 March 2012 americanlibrariesmagazine. org/columns/newsmaker/interview-jeanette-winterson

21. Stephen King, *On Writing,* New English Library, New York, 2001.

22. *Private Eye* cartoon by Steve Way (date of first publication unknown).

23. Frank Cottrell-Boyce, interviewed by Susanna Rustin, *The Guardian,* 27 October 2012.

24. Interview in *Faulks on Fiction,* BBC2 TV, February 2011.

25. C.S. Lewis, 'On Three Ways of Writing for Children', in *Of Other Worlds: Essays and Stories,* Geoffrey Bles, London, 1966.

26. Alison Stanley, 'Getting Started', in *Children's Writers' and Artists' Yearbook 2012,* Bloomsbury, London, 2011.

27. Patrick Ness, addressing the Society of Authors (Children's Writers and Illustrators Group) Conference, *Joined-Up Reading,* Reading University, September 2012.

28. Philip Pullman was talking about writing but was also referring to his novel *The Firework-Maker's Daughter,* in which Lila discovers that she needs to dedicate the Three Gifts to the Fire-Fiend so that he can give her the Royal Sulphur without which she'll never become a firework-maker. She comes home empty-handed, or so she thinks, and despairs because she didn't know she had to take gifts. But it turns out that she did: she brought him her talent, her courage (or determination), and her luck. No two of those are any good without the third, and the only one you can do anything about is determination.

29. Natalie Babbit, in P. Hunt (ed.), *Understanding Children's Literature*, Routledge, London, 1999, p. 24.
30. C. Balit, *Escape from Pompeii*, Francis Lincoln, London, 2003.
31. P. Hunt (ed.), *Understanding Children's Literature*, Routledge, London, 1999, p. 4.
32. The International AIDS Conference, Durban, South Africa, 2000.
33. Comment by Katie Price during the launch of her *Angel Uncovered*, as reported in *Daily Mail* online, 22 July 2008.
34. In Plato, *Phaedrus*, c. 360 BCE.

Freedom and responsibility in children's literature

What is a children's book?

Linda Newbery

> *Where the children's story is simply the right form for what the author has to say, then of course readers who want to hear that will read the story or re-read it, at any age.*
>
> C.S. Lewis[1]

If there is a dividing line between children's and adult fiction, it's one that is increasingly blurred, with titles such as Mark Haddon's *The Curious Incident of the Dog in the Night-Time* and Jennifer Donnelly's *A Gathering Light* leading the trend for books included on both teenage and adult lists. Titles such as Françoise Sagan's *Bonjour Tristesse* and Alain-Fournier's *Le Grand Meaulnes* might have been published as 'crossover' novels had such a thing existed at the time of publication. These titles all have characters in their teens, but it's more than the main character's age that determines where a book sits on the shelves.

There are books in which child characters are of central importance but which clearly aren't children's books: Ian McEwan's *The Cement Garden*, for example, or Henry James' *The Turn of the Screw*, or more recently Emma Donoghue's *Room*, with its five-year-old narrator. Classics such as William Golding's *Lord of the Flies* and Harper Lee's *To Kill a Mockingbird* are frequently read by fourteen- and fifteen-year-olds, but aren't children's books. It's not even a question of the story being told from a child's viewpoint: Rose Tremain's *The Way I Found Her*, narrated by thirteen-year-old Lewis, isn't a children's book, and neither is Michael Frayn's *Spies*, or L.P. Hartley's *The*

Go-Between. In these novels the reader sees over the heads of the child characters, with adult understanding. There is a distance between narrator and reader, a gulf of experience and knowledge.

On the other hand, there are children's books with adult main characters. Aidan Chambers' *Dying to Know You* has a seventy-four-year-old narrator, and Eleanor Updale's *Montmorency* stories are notable for not including children in central roles.; Kenneth Grahame's *The Wind in the Willows* has a cast of animal characters, all of whom appear to be adult.

If we try to impose a rule, we will instantly find exceptions. Some books are obviously for children, while the older teenage novels, featuring characters approaching adulthood, bestride the fence, if there is one, between children's and adult fiction. And there are some books that defy classification, among them one of my favourites, a small gem by the German author Reinhardt Jung called *Bambert's Book of Missing Stories*. Its main character is a sad and lonely man called Bambert who lives alone at the top of a tower. To assuage his loneliness, he writes stories and sends them out into the world, attached to balloons; he trusts that his stories will reach their readers and find their way back to him. A ten-year-old could read this book, but alongside the trusting innocence of its main character there is an adult sadness at its heart. It achieves the rare feat of appealing equally to children and to adults, in different ways.

Philip Pullman's *His Dark Materials* trilogy works similarly, combining a page-turning adventure story with deeper explorations of faith, morality, and the meaning of life and death, drawing on a familiarity with stories and how they work which will resound more with adult readers than with children. This, of course, makes for a book (a trilogy in this case) worth re-reading. Revisiting books enjoyed in childhood can bring a special kind of nostalgia, recalling the wonder of first reading while opening up new aspects of the story and new responses to the questions it poses.

Mostly, though, books for children or teenagers will fall into well-defined categories. You need to be aware of these, and preferably, when you start out, to fit into one of them. Often on writing courses and at other book events I've met people whose idea of what they're writing is so vague as to be completely impractical. A story 'for all ages, really' will only work if it's as brilliant as *Bambert's Book of Missing Stories* – and most books aren't. A series of ten books which plans to follow the main character from age six to sixteen 'so that readers can grow up with the character' is ambitious but unlikely to find a publisher.[2] A densely-written 100,000-word tale of talking animals in a toy cupboard is mismatching form and content, showing little awareness of child readers. Yes, there are the exceptional books for which rules don't matter, and maybe yours is one of those. But it will look more professional, when you approach publishers or agents, to have an idea of who you're writing for, and where your book might sit on a children's list.

So – what do you want to write? You may not even need to ask yourself that question. You may be an illustrator with a desire to write your own picture-book texts; at the other end of the spectrum, you may be setting out to emulate writers like Meg Rosoff and Mal Peet, who are at the tipping point between young adult and adult fiction. It's unlikely that you'll set out with no idea at all. But, as we go on to look in more detail at the range of books that appear on children's lists, it will become apparent that with such diversity we are hardly talking about the same thing. A board book for babies is a very different proposition from a substantial six-book series for twelve-year-olds. In fact, board books won't be included in the categories that follow, because they can't be described as 'fiction' – most are concept books, involving colour or shape recognition, counting games and the like. They are very specialised, not as easy as you might think, and some don't even have authors, but are produced in-house by the publishers or stem from an idea by an illustrator.

Children's literature – a brief history
Yvonne Coppard

There is no agreed starting point for children's literature, owing in part to the lack of an agreed definition about what it is. The history of children's literature is woven from a complex balance of tensions between education, religion, politics, power, social cohesion and shifting theories of child psychology and development. When stories were swapped and shared within a strong oral tradition, there was little division between adult and child consumers of story.

Few people were literate, and in the absence of money or the printing press (which first appeared in 1476) it would be difficult to consider any kind of fine distinction between one type of audience and another.

> **"** *The definition of 'children's literature' lies at the heart of its endeavour.* **"**
> Karin Lesnik-Oberstein[3]

Where the dominant cultural ethos is patriarchal, ultra-conservative or auto-cratic, or where basic freedoms are repressed, literature often takes on the utilitarian function of legitimising the control of the ruling elite (be it the British Empire, white supremacists or the Taliban). The first priority is therefore not to tell a story that will nurture the imagination, but to imbue young hearts and minds with the 'right' attitudes and behaviour to support and sustain the society in which they live – and to know their rightful place in the pecking order. In liberal, progressive, post-modern cultures, the child has developed a status which is at least equal to that of adults (many parents would claim their children have more rights and more power than they do). So the history of children's literature is enmeshed within the history of each individual society that embraces it. Like story itself, definitions shape-shift to fit the audience, and the audience in turn shape-shifts to fit its own historical and cultural context.

The legend of Robin Hood surfaced around the mid-fifteenth century,[4] and Thomas Malory's *Morte d'Arthur* a bit later (1486). These were popular with children and adults, but there is no evidence that they were stories told or written especially with children in mind. In the US, one of the first books 'especially prepared for North American youth' was *Spiritual Milk for Boston Babes*, published in London in 1646. Many scholars believe that *Orbus Pictus* by Jan Amos Comenius (1658), an illustrated information book, published in Bohemia. was the first book to be designed especially for children. At around the same time in France, Charles Perrault (1628–1703) was gathering oral traditions and old stories to blend into his fairy story collection *Tales of My Mother Goosey*: the popularity of his versions of *Sleeping Beauty*, *Cinderella* and *Little Red Riding Hood*, among many more, endures to this day.

With the advent of the printing press came a flourishing market for books of all kinds, and a growing interest in reading as an educational tool for children, especially stories and historical tales that could help to mould their moral and patriotic values. But in 1744 John Newbery published *A Little Pretty Pocket-Book*, along with a free gift: a ball for boys, a pincushion for girls. This may have marked the start of the growing tide of books that were not just for instruction, but leisure books, owned and read outside the classroom.

The eighteenth century was a time of intellectual enlightenment in Europe: John Locke (1632–1704) and Jean-Jacques Rousseau (1712–1778) were prominent preachers of the gospel of knowledge as the route out of poverty, moral turpitude, ignorance and despair. For Locke, education was vital from very early childhood. In 1693 he published *An Essay Concerning Human Understanding*, in which he claimed that the child is like a *tabula rasa* – a blank slate, waiting to be written on. In *Some Thoughts Concerning Education*, Locke exhorted parents to observe their children carefully, so that they could understand their natural inclinations and guide them on the right path, since 'the minds of children [are] as easily turned this way or that as water itself'.[5] But the child should also have liberty; learning should be infused with a sense of independence. Locke may not have used the word 'manipulative' in his manifesto for educating children, but his advice was to make whatever had to be learned into sport or play so that the child would choose to learn it.

Rousseau, who was himself largely self-educated after a turbulent, motherless childhood, claimed that education started even before birth. Like Locke, he favoured an independent learning approach. In 1762, he wrote: 'Let him know something not because you told it to him but because he understood it for himself.'[6] But Rousseau also emphasised the importance of truth in educating a child. He was vehemently against what he saw as the elaborate lies of fairy stories and myths.

Adults . . . speak differently in fiction when they are aware that they are addressing children.
Barbara Wall[7]

It was in this context that Maria and Richard Lovell Edgeworth published their *Practical Education, Or, the History of Harry and Lucy* in 1780. This book encouraged children to take charge of their own education in order to make a useful contribution to their world.

The first half of the nineteenth century brought us *Snow White, Cinderella, Hansel and Gretel, The True Bride* and the like, courtesy of Jakob and Wilhelm Grimm. Like Perrault in France, the brothers Grimm gathered oral traditions and tales spun over the years to weave their own storytelling magic in Germany. Hans Christian Andersen in Denmark was gaining great popularity across Europe with his own reshaping of oral tales and traditions into *The Emperor's New Clothes, The Princess on the Pea, The Little Match Girl* and *The Snow Queen*. In Britain, Lewis Carroll wrote *Alice's Adventures in Wonderland*. The heroine of the story is a child, but the subversion of logic and the embrace of nonsense as a literary form, with its own narrative structure and internal logic, may have been instrumental in the growing popularity of the fantasy genre that followed. In the US, L. Frank Baum's *The Wonderful Wizard of Oz* (first published in 1900) became a phenomenal international success. It remains one of the best-known and loved stories in the US, spawning more than a dozen sequels and referenced by many authors in their own writing.

Merchandising of characters and titles was one of the big developments of the twentieth century. *The Tale of Peter Rabbit*, by Beatrix Potter (1902), was notable because Potter herself designed a Peter Rabbit doll. It is unlikely that she anticipated the plethora of china, toys, christening and baby gifts, towels and bedlinen, nursery decorations and so on that would attach themselves to her characters. At about the same time, Boel Westin notes that in Sweden – where children's literature had traditionally been rooted in a desire to shape moral, well-mannered children – a cultural shift started to move things on a little as 'children's literature began to respond to the needs of children rather than adults'.[8]

By the time the 'swinging sixties' came along, 'teenagers' (still a relatively new breed) were experiencing things their parents had never encountered. Perceptions of the boundaries between 'child' and 'adult' were no longer easily identifiable. Television gave developing minds access to information and cultural influences beyond the experience of previous generations. Accessible and effective birth control took the fear out of sexual exploration. The concept of 'family' was on the move. As parental authority began to wane in the real world, the portrayal of parents in contemporary children's fiction also shifted. They became less powerful, less deserving of the respect and obedience of their children. There was, of course, already a long tradition of the powerful child in children's literature. Fairy stories and classic novels are littered with orphans, wicked stepmothers and timid or ineffectual fathers.

John Rowe Townsend, in his excellent history of children's literature, *Written for Children*, argues that the rise of the 'young adult' novel is linked to inter-generational shifts in society. 'More and more fictional parents were useless to their children or even positively vicious.'[9] This reflected the real world, where adults felt less sure of their entitlement to tell young people what to do, and the younger generation were less inclined to listen and take notice. Townsend charts the rise of the young adult novel from the 1950s, when Beverly Cleary's *Fifteen* broke new ground in 1956, with the heroine Jane's first experiences of dating and desire. Fifty years later this is a very tame read, and the boundary-pushing baton has been carried forward by the likes of Melvin Burgess (*Junk*, known as *Smack* in the US, and *Doing It*) and William Nicholson (*Rich and Mad*). All four books have been banned by more than one righteously indignant authority concerned about the 'corruption' of childhood.

Joanna Nadin, creator of *Rachel Riley* and *Buttercup Jones*, beautifully observes the tension between embarrassing and/or boring parents and their more adventurous children.[10] Jacqueline Wilson's books often feature children having to take on responsibilities beyond their years, protecting younger siblings or reversing the parent/child role with a hapless or sick parent.

But children have been in difficult circumstances throughout history. They did not move seamlessly from twelve-hour days in mills and factories to the comforts of the 1950s family hearth. Their experiences were rarely reflected in the stories about and for them, but those experiences have been well documented by political agitators and social historians. In the twenty-first century dark and difficult themes once considered suitable only for 'young adults' have increasingly found younger and younger audiences.

What is a children's book for?
Yvonne Coppard

> *We read to find out more about what it is like to*
> *be a human being, not to be told how to be one.*
> Penelope Lively[11]

The children's author has a complex challenge in seeking to communicate the power of story. The adult novelist may intend to shape thoughts and attitudes, to exert a moral influence. As readers, we might be enticed into learning about the world, ourselves and others. Alternatively, the author may seek only to entertain, which is a noble enough ambition in itself. With children's fiction there is often an added expectation of a duty to do something else – something in, with and under the story: to teach, perhaps, or to proclaim a moral message that will help to mould the child. At the root of this expectation is a debate about what a child actually is, and what a child's book is for.

So what is a child, exactly?

Jacqueline Rose (1984) claims that the whole concept of a 'child' is flawed, since 'children are divided by class, race, ethnic origins, gender etc.' She concludes that the term 'child' is an artificial construction that authors and critics invented to meet their own needs.[12] The age at which children assume adult responsibilities in different parts of the world is a clue to the shifting territory inhabited by the 'child' concept. Even the physical boundaries have a habit of moving: our twenty-first-century children are taller, heavier, stronger and tend to reach puberty earlier than ever before.

In literature, both for children and for adults, there are recurring themes in the portrayal of children. The child can be a child of Nature (*The Jungle Book; The Secret Garden*) or the Rescuer (*The Lion, the Witch and the Wardrobe; The Subtle Knife; The Last Dragon Slayer*). He or she is often the narrator and the observer of the adult world (*David Copperfield; The Curious Incident of the Dog in the Night-time; The Lovely Bones*) and may have to endure abuse and cruelty before the required triumph over adversity (*Harry Potter; Cinderella; The Kite Runner*).

In most cultures, there is a magic age when an adult is created. For some, adulthood is conferred automatically, overnight, simply by living long enough to see dawn on the appropriate birthday. For others, there are preliminary tests or ritualised requirements to prove the child worthy of the move into the adult world. But in wealthy Western cultures, a child necessarily inhabits a subsection of what we call childhood, moving through the ranks in an orderly manner from baby to toddler, infant to junior, on to pre-teen, teen, young adult. The author for adults must find an audience that shares an enthusiasm for the chosen genre, be it historical novels, vampires, science fiction or any of the other popular genres. The author for children must decide not only what kind of fiction he or she wishes to write, but also what kind of child is to be the audience. The final hurdle is the recognition that while books for adults are bought by those who will read them, this is not generally true of children's books. They are more likely to be bought by parents, teachers, librarians, friends and relatives. Those adults (and perhaps particularly parents and teachers) often require the book to do more than 'only' tell a story.

Just as there can be no independent, unchangeable definition of 'child', so story itself is a shape-shifting mystery. Shakespeare's heroes and Malory's tales of Arthur survive through the centuries, taking on and absorbing modern interpretations. Story and audience mould themselves to each other and to the historical and cultural context in which they are read (or viewed on film and television).

What is a children's classic?
Linda Newbery

What do we mean by a 'classic'? It's one of those terms people use freely without a clear idea of what it means, whether referring to cars, music, architecture or literature. Does the term denote longevity, or adherence to conventions, or work of enduring quality? In children's books, *Alice's Adventures in Wonderland*, *The Wind in the Willows*, the *Winnie-the-Pooh* stories, *Charlotte's Web*, *The Secret Garden* and C.S. Lewis' *Narnia* stories are among the titles that spring to mind; they are books that many adults remember fondly and buy for their own children, ensuring that the stories pass on to new generations. Just behind them sit books from the 'golden age' of children's publishing from the late 1960s to the early 1980s: Nina Bawden's *Carrie's War*, Michelle Magorian's *Goodnight Mr Tom*, Philippa Pearce's *Tom's Midnight Garden*, Ian Serraillier's *The Silver Sword*, *Flambards* by K.M. Peyton and Rosemary Sutcliff's *The Eagle of the Ninth* – stories which absorb the reader completely into the worlds they create, making the characters' predicaments seem real and urgent. Alan Garner's *The Owl Service*, published in 1967, marked a high point in multi-layered storytelling, and certainly deserves to be remembered.

Which of today's books will last into the future is hard to predict, although Philip Pullman's *His Dark Materials* trilogy is surely guaranteed longevity, as are David Almond's *Skellig*, Celia Rees' *Witch Child* and Michael Morpurgo's *War Horse* – and the *Harry Potter* series. Luck plays its part, as so often. Winning a major prize such as the Carnegie certainly helps to establish a good book as great, though this in itself is no guarantee of long life, as a glance at the award archive will confirm; some of the winning titles have stayed with us, while others, and the names of their authors, have faded from view. Historical and fantasy stories probably have the edge here, because novels which are firmly rooted in the real, present-day world have to slip into the hinterland of seeming dated before they are far enough in the past to become historical.

Becoming a classic seems to involve a degree of chance, and, for some very prolific writers, it also requires one book to stand out from the rest of their work. I can think of a number of highly gifted writers who have been so prolific and dependable that they're almost taken for granted: Gillian Cross, Anne Fine, Robert Westall, Jan Mark and Geraldine McCaughrean, for example. Collectively, these excellent writers have won all the big prizes several times over, and their works are reliably engrossing, original, readable and thought-provoking – but which Gillian Cross book will be the one to last into the future, and which Westall, Mark, Fine or McCaughrean? Perhaps writers known for just one book, series or character have the advantage.

Many stories lauded in their time now seem intolerably racist or sexist, or make class assumptions which jar with today's readers. Yvonne will look at the books of her childhood in which dutiful obedience was the clear expectation of girls. *What Katy Did* by Susan Coolidge is a good example. Katy's exuberance on the faulty garden swing is punished by a spell as an invalid, during which she must learn to copy the uncomplaining role of saintly Cousin Helen. Casual racism sat alongside imperialism in the *Biggles* books by W.E. Johns, in which anyone of foreign appearance is described as 'slant-eyed' or 'swarthy' and is regarded with suspicion. Hugh Lofting's *Doctor Dolittle* stories contained frequent references to 'coons', 'niggeresses' and 'greasy natives'. English-born but later emigrating to America, Lofting was awarded the prestigious Newbery Medal (the US equivalent of the CILIP Carnegie Medal) for *The Voyages of Dr Dolittle* in 1922. The books are still in print, with new editions as I write (in 2012), though there have been several revisions to remove the offending terms, and Lofting's illustrations, with their crude racial stereotypes, have been replaced. New Kindle editions of the *Biggles* stories were also released in 2012, so if one definition of a 'classic' is a book that goes on being printed, both Dr Dolittle and Biggles fit the bill.

In forty or sixty years' time, will popular children's books of today attract the kind of criticism now heaped on Hugh Lofting and W.E. Johns? Will attitudes confidently held today come to seem misguided and outdated? Will environmental irresponsibility be the new racism, with scorn directed from a more enlightened future age at references to the use of fossil fuels, or casual meat-eating? It's an intriguing prospect. Surely, though, readers of the next generation will be bemused by the wave of pinkness and sparkliness which currently pervades series fiction for young girls, and which seems such a backward step from the move to gender equality in the 1980s.

All the titles above are novels for the core nine-to-twelve section of children's books, with a couple edging into teenage; but of course there are younger books that deserve classic status, such as Julia Donaldson's *The Gruffalo*, *Rosie's Walk* by Pat Hutchins, *Dogger* by Shirley Hughes and *Gorilla* by Anthony Browne. In a crowded field it is hard to predict which current writer-illustrators will be spoken of in such company. The best-loved picture books tend to be those comfortably shared by children, parents and grandparents, and – crucially – those which will stand multiple revisiting. *Guess How Much I Love You* by Sam McBratney is a well-loved favourite, but picture books don't have to be pastel-coloured and reassuring; *Where the Wild*

Things Are by the late Maurice Sendak has a very different kind of appeal that has lasted since its publication in 1963. The highly decorative, allusive work of Jane Ray, so perfectly suited to folklore and retellings, will surely be around for years to come, even though the trend at present seems to be for sketchier, looser work which is seen as more child-friendly. Jane Ray could be put into the same category as Geraldine McCaughrean and Gillian Cross, having produced so much beautiful, highly accomplished work that it's hard to single out one of her books for particular praise.

So what makes a classic? An important criterion is that it's a book that can be re-read several times and will still seem fresh and even surprising. As Italo Calvino wrote, 'A classic is a book that has never finished saying what it has to say', and 'Every re-reading of a classic is as much a voyage of discovery as the first reading.'[13] It needs to speak to all times, not only its own. War stories such as *War Horse, The Silver Sword* and *Goodnight Mr Tom* are of interest not only as period pieces, but for engaging readers of all ages with the dilemmas and predicaments of the central characters, their losses and loyalties and demands on their courage. Most children will respond to the idea of being relatively powerless, of having to fit their own plans and priorities into a world controlled by adults. Conversely, they enjoy the notion of being power*ful*, as in many a fantasy story, when children have special powers and talents and enjoy freedoms which would seem improbable in the real world.

Wouldn't every children's writer love to produce a classic? If only we knew how, or what it is. Starting to write *Lob*, I knew that I wanted it to have a classic or timeless feel. I had in mind an essential seriousness, combined with playfulness, and a sense that although the story is set in the modern world, it had the weight of tradition behind it, acknowledging its debts to the poetry of Edward Thomas and the folklore figures of the Green Man and Lob Lie-by-the-Fire. But will *Lob* be around in ten years' time, or twenty? My lofty aims have probably fallen into the gap that awaits every writer between intention and finished story.

Yvonne Coppard

I like Mark Twain's definition: 'Classic: a book which people praise but don't read.' A classic children's book is one that has enduring appeal over several generations. They are books you keep and treasure, and read to the next generation, and the next. A classic book is about a story and characters that have the scope for each generation to approach and interpret afresh, against a different historical and sociological landscape. The *Winnie-the-Pooh* stories are good examples of this – the original stories with drawings by Ernest Shepard have given way to the Disney incarnation in my grandchildren's generation, but the characters endure and the stories have just as much resonance as they ever did. Where better to learn the values of humility, kindness and staying true to your friends than sitting round the honeypot with Pooh Bear? Who can more clearly demonstrate the value of always looking on the bright side of life than Eeyore, the doleful donkey?

The treasured classics among my family and friends include Frances Hodgson Burnett's *The Secret Garden* and *The Little Princess*, although the stories became known via film versions long before the texts were tackled. The tales of Beatrix Potter would not fit my 'classic' definition: while they were all the rage when my daughters were young, few children would recognise more than a couple of the characters, and part of their appeal is their quaint old-fashioned flavour. Their day seems to have passed – for the moment. But I am a firm believer in the circle of life, and hope Beatrix Potter's stories will be 'rediscovered classics' one day.

Classics of the future?
Yvonne Coppard

There are so many possible classics of the future on my shelves that deserve to be mentioned; I can only share some thoughts about a small selection of them. There are books that I believe have the look of classics right now but which will not endure through generational shifts and changing times. I think it's much harder to pick out classics of the future for older readers, as tastes diverge much more in adolescence and the drive to be free-thinking and independent of previous generations will influence literature as it influences everything else. Many of the best-sellers in this decade are dystopian, supernatural, darkness-versus-light fantasies, but I am not sure how many will survive into another generation. Increasingly, the internet and exposure to world travel and immigration are teaching us more about complexity; good and evil are not easily identifiable as opposites. So perhaps the likes of the *Harry Potter* books, Pullman's *His Dark Materials* trilogy and the *Twilight* series may not be devoured so readily in the future.

For me, the enduring classics are likely to include *The Very Hungry Caterpillar, Where the Wild Things Are, Gorilla* and *The Gruffalo.* These are books that, like *Winnie-the-Pooh,* speak to the universal condition of man, in a language both toddlers and the adults who read to them can understand and respond to. Moving on from picture books, Roald Dahl and Anne Fine capture what is likely to be timeless in childhood experience, and Francesca Simon's Horrid Henry seems to be moving into the space once occupied by Richmal Crompton's scruffy William.

The canon of Jacqueline Wilson will surely find a place in the history of literature; she persuaded us to accept that children are not immune from the big issues of which it was thought they had no awareness at all. My personal choice for teenagers would include titles that marked some kind of watershed moment in the development of the teen/young adult novel. I would definitely want to see Linda Newbery's *The Shell House,* Anne Cassidy's *Looking for JJ,* Tabitha Suzuma's *A Note of Madness* and Anthony McGowan's *The Knife That Killed Me.*

I think the popularity of historical novels will continue, and would hope that the meticulous research and storytelling power of Mary Hooper's *Fallen Grace,* Mary Hoffman's *David* and Celia Rees' *The Fool's Girl* will be enjoyed by my great-grandchildren. However, I am content to wait and see, anticipating with relish the raft of titles undiscovered so far, written by authors as yet unknown. Perhaps one of them will be you. This is one of the things that makes writing children's fiction so exciting.

Who are children's books for?
Linda Newbery

To reach its audience of children, a book has to pass through the various 'gatekeepers' we've referred to earlier, all of them adult: commissioning editors, librarians, teachers, parents. These interested parties have varying aims: commercial, or educational, as well as a wish to provide entertainment and enjoyment through reading.

C.S. Lewis' remark, 'I am almost inclined to set it up as a canon that a children's story which is enjoyed only by children is a bad children's story,'[14] is widely quoted. It is also challenged, on the grounds that a children's book should not need the validation of adults to prove its worth, and that children should have a literature which is uniquely their own. Visiting schools is a good way of finding out what's currently a word-of-mouth favourite (at the time of writing, *The Diary of a Wimpy Kid* is everywhere). Concern about boys' reading in particular has led to the widespread production of books with immediate appeal, fast-paced action, high-octane adventures and/or wacky humour. Distinctive marketing of series, too, has become ever-important.

Just as the democratisation of reading generally has grown exponentially through websites, blogs and Amazon reviewing, children's opinions on the books they read are given increasing importance. There are now innumerable regional awards in which children vote for their favourite titles. The first and biggest of these is the Red House Children's Book Award (formerly the Children's Book Award) administered by the Federation of Children's Book Groups, and organised through the 'testing' and ranking of hundreds of books each year. Reviewing and the awarding of prizes is no longer the sole preserve of adult critics and specialists.

Leila Rasheed wrote recently that 'As a children's author, you should want to be loved rather than admired.'[15] Some authors – Michael Morpurgo, Patrick Ness and Eva Ibbotson, for example – manage to achieve both. Yvonne and I both take C.S. Lewis's statement to mean that good children's literature can't be produced in a patronising way, and that honesty and integrity should not be compromised for the sake of crowd-pleasing.

Breakthrough books and authors
Linda Newbery

To become a 'classic', a book has to reach beyond the specialist world of children's books to reach the public at large. There are significant books that haven't achieved this and yet have been tremendously important to other writers and to the development of literature for young people. Some of the books I'd put into this category are by Aidan Chambers, Robert Cormier and Jill Paton Walsh, influential writers, in their different ways, at the teenage end of children's fiction. These three set a high standard for intelligent, thought-provoking, challenging fiction for older readers. Aidan Chambers' *Break Time*, *Postcards From No Man's Land* and *This is All*, Robert Cormier's *I Am the Cheese* and *After the First Death*, and Jill Paton Walsh's *Goldengrove*, *Unleaving* and *Fireweed* have, between them, influenced many another writer.

Alan Gibbons is one of many admirers of Cormier: 'He never flinched, applying a scalpel-like intelligence to intellectual manipulation, racism, trauma and physical and emotional damage.' Gibbons singles out *Heroes* and *Tunes for Bears to Dance To* as particularly admirable. Jill Paton Walsh's lyrical writing is shown at its best in the linked pair, *Goldengrove* and *Unleaving*, coming-of-age novels with complex explorations of philosophy and morality, while *Fireweed* is one of the finest war novels for teenagers.

Aidan Chambers, a Hans Christian Andersen laureate, has been an important standard-bearer for writers including Celia Rees and myself. Celia, who first came across him while teaching in the 1980s and looking for novels for her older teen readers, told me, 'His novels *Break Time, Dance on My Grave, Now I Know*, were unlike anything else I'd read – uncompromisingly honest in subject matter, unpatronising, utterly devoid of clichés and, above all, wonderfully innovative in the way the narrative unfolds. His books dealt with difficult themes and were not easy reads. He was writing for older teens caught between children's books and fully adult fiction. He was making a persuasive and powerful case for challenging, cutting-edge literature – just for them.' These authors have produced outstanding, original, important work: yet I think few non-specialists would mention their books if asked to name classics for young readers.

While on the subject of breakthrough books, I must mention *Riddley Walker* by Russell Hoban. Though published for adults rather than on a teenage list, it has decisively made its mark on young adult fiction and is the defining post-apocalypse novel for many writers and readers. Patrick Ness has described it as 'one of the most extraordinary books of the last fifty years',[16] acknowledging its influence on his award-winning *Chaos Walking* trilogy and especially his creation of a distinctive language and voice for his main character, Todd.

The rules of engagement
Yvonne Coppard

> *The good ended happily, and the bad unhappily.*
> *That is what fiction means.*
> Oscar Wilde[17]

Common definitions of children's literature, even in recent years, have been too narrow to encompass what young readers are up to, both in and out of the classroom. Such definitions concentrate on books – problematic in itself, with the growth of internet downloads and e-publishing. Where do we place the reference books and dictionaries that children dip into for school work or for pleasure? What about cartoon collections, and joke books?

It's hard to ignore the constraints that present themselves when you are a children's author. Your audience is unpredictable, developing, vulnerable. Every breath, every encounter, is potentially a new learning experience. It should not surprise us when attempts are made to use literature to shape and mould impressionable minds. Improving, cautionary or moral tales direct you to your place, and ensure you stay there.

Many of the great classics that were put into my hands as a child – *Little Women; Anne of Green Gables; Pollyanna; The Secret Garden* and *What Katy Did* – were undoubtedly tinged with the hope of teaching me how to be a dutiful daughter/pupil/citizen. I loved these books dearly. Did they shape my aspirations to become one of these models of decorum and cheerful servitude? I bet they did, at least a bit, although aspiration and reality turned out to be very different things.

Healthy, happy children lap up stories about their peers in terrible situations just as keenly as those for whom it is experience, rather than imagination, that colours their response to the story. Books cannot help but open doors for us onto other worlds and other experiences. Children chortle at portrayals of hopeless adults whose children have to rescue or educate them – and empathise with children forced to take on serious adult responsibilities in families torn apart by divorce, bereavement, mental illness and abuse. Here we see another power at the disposal of a good story: it can accompany your painful, solitary journey, showing you that you are not alone and that children like you the world over suffer, and survive.

Many of the beloved classics of the English-speaking world, especially for younger children, are underpinned by a philosophy that the book has to be more than 'mere' entertainment. For young children there is a growing expectation that a 'good' book must boost literacy, or explain what will happen on the first day of school, or when parents split up, or when you go to the dentist. It should model certain pleasing traits and attitudes; good behaviour usually triumphs over bad. For older children, the 'gritty' novel taps into the darker side of childhood experiences and the message becomes more about what a book should NOT do, rather than what it should. There are occasional outrages and high profile bans from schools and libraries (often involving Melvin Burgess).[18]

In 1973, Joan Aiken insisted that she would not purposefully incorporate moral messages into her work because 'children have a strong natural resistance to phoney morality. They can see through the adult with some moral axe to grind almost before he opens his mouth.'[19] But Rosemary Sutcliff, writing in the same publication, said: 'I am aware of the responsibility of my job: and I do try to put over to the child reading any book of mine some kind of ethic.'[20]

Is there a formula that will give your children's book a better chance of success? Linda has explored the distinction between 'a children's book' and 'a book about children' and also looks at what kind of book becomes a children's classic. When I start a new book for children, I am aware of some basic expectations. For example, children's books will be shorter, written in a simpler style with a linear plot where events happen in a logical order. Further, they are supposed to be optimistic in tone and end happily. It seems to me though, that attempts to define what children's literature should be are a bit like the hopes and expectations parents have for the children themselves: unreliable and more honoured in the breach than the observance.

Writing for a multi-gendered, multi-cultural world
Yvonne Coppard

There has been a mountain of useful and interesting research into the difference between boys and girls when it comes to reading development and choices of material as they grow. Traditionally, girls have consistently scored more highly than boys in reading tests. A report by Professor Keith Topping of Dundee University throws some light on this.[21] He found that there are significant differences in reading preferences. He confirmed the widely held belief that boys prefer to read non-fiction; he also found that they have a clear preference for the less challenging, easy to read books. This preference strengthens as they get older, with the most marked difference between boys and girls being seen between the ages of thirteen and sixteen (the crucial pre-GCSE years).[22]

As the mother and grandmother of a purely female tribe, I have little direct experience of the stereotypical assertion that girls read a wide selection of stories but boys will only read about football, violence or computers. Observations from my time as an English teacher would, I suppose, indicate that this was broadly true. Yet enthusiasm from both genders for Roald Dahl's books shows no sign of waning, though he jumps from male to female characters with ease.

In my early teaching days, it was hard to find novels and plays that dealt with the world as it really was in my part of inner London: a chaotic ethnic mix of races and cultures and socio-economic backgrounds with widely diverging aspirations and horizons. *Swallows and Amazons* didn't fit, not in this part of the Thames reach. The search for novels that reflected my students' real lives (*and* that were on the 'approved' list, *and* that were available from the central purchasing service in boxed sets of thirty) was a constant frustration. There were black and Asian characters in some of the books (and occasional suggestions of other colours and cultures), just as there were occasionally stories about children with a disability, or an unusual distinguishing feature of body or background. But these were characters who were bullied or downtrodden in some other way. There was usually a plucky white friend who refused to follow the gang, who stood up for the 'weird' kid and often paid a hefty price. It was disturbing. It was something that should have been addressed a lot sooner than it was and I think we still have a long way to go before we can say that the literature to which our children have access is truly inclusive.

Such issues are emotive, and the range of questions is so vast that I have neither the space nor the knowledge to attempt a proper exploration in this book. I follow the arguments as they arise with interest. But whenever I think about the relevance of all this to the writer, I return to the same question. Should we write deliberately to fill a gap on a particular sales shelf: 'boys', 'girls', 'eight-to-twelve' and so on? Should we deliberately aim to tick enough boxes to be deemed 'inclusive', by ensuring that our characters reflect the widest variety of cultures and ethnicity? Should we count the number of disabled or overweight or short-sighted children we have included in our stories?

It makes me feel uncomfortable, that idea, maybe because I have read so many stories where the conscious effort to be 'inclusive' gets in the way. Instead of immersing yourself in the story, you find yourself counting: at least one of every skin tone, at least one disability, the whole range of sexual orientations and a few single parents (both genders, naturally). Throw in a couple of parents with an 'alternative' lifestyle and you have it covered, surely.

Rather than picturing the 'target audience' I'd go for an embedded understanding of how children live and where they come from. I always advocate wide reading and research into the 'target' audience; I will be doing just that, in our later workshop section. But it is not at all contradictory to know your audience, and yet write first and foremost the story that is waiting to be told rather than the story that will fit the slot determined by market forces. You can't write decent fantasy if you've never particularly liked it, however much of a gap in the market there might be; you have to stay true to yourself and your own gift. If you write about real people, and you have observed the world around you, then characters of all sorts of colours and distinguishing features will be allowed in, naturally and at their own pace.

My novels are predominantly seen as 'girls' books', but I didn't consciously intend that to happen. I wrote the story that I had in my head, and the characters who were telling the story were female. My homespun thumbnail research into my readers, which is based on conversations with audiences in schools and at literature festivals, is that girls are more likely to read stories where the central characters could be either gender, and boys tend to prefer stories that have a boy at the centre. I have written only two books with a central boy (*Simple Simon* and *To Be a Millionaire*) and I did receive more letters from boys than was the case for the other books. But how much of this is to do with marketing decisions and packaging ?

A University in Texas is currently conducting a three-year research project with pre- and early-teen students who struggle with reading.[23] Nearly two hundred students have been given an e-reader to use for a session each day in school, loaded with twenty-five classics across various genres. In the half-way results, the team found attitudes to reading had become markedly more positive among the boys, but there had been a decline in the enthusiasm shown by the girls. One of the reasons identified for this e-book preference among boys was that no one can tell their reading level or their choice of book. The voice-to-text option was also valued among students for whom English is not the first language. As I said earlier, reading is about so much more than simply *reading*.

The power of the cover is indisputable; in the bookstore it is the first thing that attracts browsers and entices them to look inside. So why do we swamp our shelves with pink, sparkly covers that still carry the old message, whether we like it or not: *not for boys, unless you want to be a girlie*? I will be very interested to see what effect e-readers, where the title is more likely to draw interest than the cover, have in the reading choices of future generations.

Inclusiveness in children's fiction

Linda Newbery

Bob Dixon, in his two-volume work *Catching Them Young*, published in 1977, robustly challenged the assumptions of class, racial and gender superiority which he saw as prevalent in children's fiction. He made the startling claim that 'Much of the material in children's books is anti-social, if not anti-human, and is more likely to stunt and warp young people than help them to grow.'[24] He attributed part of the blame to criticism of children's fiction – 'much of it is still at the spiffing-good-yarn-for-twelve-year-olds level. Shallow responses of this kind won't do any longer.' In his study, he points to crude racial stereotyping, class superiority, subservient roles for girls and macho ones for boys in works such as *Thomas the Tank Engine*, the *Janet and John* reading scheme, the stories of Enid Blyton and the *Biggles* books of Captain W.F. Johns.

One story Dixon attacks is Enid Blyton's *The Little Black Doll*, published in 1937. A black-faced doll is disliked by his owner, Matty, who considers him black and therefore ugly. The other toys don't like him either, so he runs away and is befriended by a fairy. When he sets off in the rain to fetch a doctor for the fairy, who has fallen ill, he finds that all his blackness has been washed off, and that underneath he is pink. Returning to Matty with his pink face, he now finds himself accepted both by her and by the other toys. Dixon comments, 'It would be difficult to find a story more psychologically destructive, to white as well as to black children.'[25]

Admittedly, criticising *The Little Black Doll* is by now the equivalent of shooting fish in a barrel. We have moved on considerably since 1937 as both society and attitudes have changed, and literature is no longer the preserve of white middle class writers – but it's instructive to look back and see what was once considered acceptable, and from a writer whose popularity has scarcely waned. The copy from which Dixon quotes was a 1965 reissue, and in 1976 the story was published again, by the Collins imprint Armada, in a collection of Blyton stories. Revisions had been made in what Dixon calls 'a confused attempt to give this story a face-lift'.[26] When Sambo returns home the other toys have decided to accept him; this time, wishing he was still black, they rub his face with ink. As Dixon points out, this tones down the racism of the original but still puts Sambo at the whim of the other toys. It is difficult to credit that by 1976 such a morally flawed story could be seen as worth salvaging.

Change was already well on the way by the time Bob Dixon embarked on his project. Traditionally, until well into the sixties, fantasy and historical fiction were the mainstays of children's fiction, with realism seemingly stuck in a time-warp. As a child, I remember being bemused by the world of board-ing schools and servants inhabited by so many fictional children, and by the supposed poverty their families endured while somehow maintaining tennis courts and ponies. As John Rowe Townsend put it, these were stories of 'com-fortable bourgeois life, written it seemed by comfortable bourgeois adults for comfortable bourgeois children'.[27]

The 1960s saw this literary conservatism challenged by the publication of *Goalkeeper's Revenge* by Bill Naughton, *Gumble's Yard* by John Rowe Townsend, and (not on a children's list, but quickly acquiring word-of-mouth notoriety with teenagers) *Up the Junction* by Nell Dunn. By the early 1970s, Leila Berg was producing the *Nippers* series for early readers (including her own *Fish and Chips for Supper*) – easy-to-read stories which featured working-class characters and settings. In a letter to the *Times Educational Supplement*, Leila Berg explained: '*Nippers* are written in the belief that every child needs to be able to look at a book or hear a story and feel "That's me!" This is what every middle-class child has done practically since babyhood.'[28]

Leila Berg faced opposition to her project, on the grounds that children were being given what they already knew and that the vocabulary of the stories was impoverished and limiting, but the series became firmly estab-lished. (Such an argument seems to suppose that children will read only one kind of book, rather than choose from the range available as they gain in confidence.) By the time Gene Kemp's *The Turbulent Term of Tyke Tiler* won the Carnegie Medal in 1978, urban realism was here to stay. Eve Garnett's *The Family from One End Street* had won the Carnegie as early as 1937, but this book is regarded as condescending and patronising by John Rowe Townsend, Bob Dixon and other commentators: members of the Ruggles family are seen from outside, and clearly know their place.

Other changes took longer. Eileen Browne, in *Carousel* magazine, explains how the picture book she produced in 1986 with Tony Bradman, *Through my Window*, filled a much-needed gap in the market. 'I was living in the Finsbury Park area of North London – an area of great diversity, with friends, neighbours and colleagues from many ethnic backgrounds. There, I ran a junior youth club which included children from Jamaican, Turkish Cypriot and African families. I'd illustrated picture books for many years and used to give them out as prizes. The children loved to pore over the illustrations . . . there was a seminal moment when one of them said, "Put us in your books", and I realised how important it was for them to see pictures of themselves.'[29] In the 'Jo' stories (*Through My Window* led to two more books) Jo has a black mother and a white father, and the illustrations show children and families from a range of ethnic backgrounds and racial mixes.

The attraction of such books as these is that the characters are simply there, as part of the mix of people a child might meet at school or in the community. But, as Eileen Browne says, her book 'should not have made history in 1986. It should have been typical of many picture books for young children.'[30]

For a while, particularly back in the 1980s when 'issues' fiction was prevalent, especially for teenagers, it seemed that books about black or Asian characters were invariably about racially motivated conflict and prejudice. Malorie Blackman has related that when she began to write fiction, people often expected her, as a black author, to write about racism. Though initially resenting the assumption that this would be her automatic choice of subject, she eventually did: turning racism on its head, in the series beginning with *Noughts and Crosses*, set in a society where to be black is to be superior, and to be white is to belong to a deprived underclass. *Noughts and Crosses* includes the memorable scene in which Callum, a white boy, needs a sticking plaster for a cut and can only find dark brown ones – such a simple but telling detail, much commented on, making most white readers realise that they have never considered that plasters are coloured pink to match pale skins. In a *Guardian* interview in 2008, Malorie said that as a child she never read stories with black characters in them; her first was Alice Walker's *The Color Purple*, which she read at the age of twenty-three.[31]

The notion of every child being able to see her- or himself in books extends beyond skin colour, of course. Scope, a charity working with disabled children, launched its 'In the Picture' campaign to address the effective exclusion of disabled children from children's literature. Artist Jane Ray was on the steering committee, and support has come from many well-known writers, including Jacqueline Wilson, who says: 'I think it's very important to include disabled children in books in an ordinary, everyday kind of way. I feel that they should be simply part of the story, as characters in their own right – funny, friendly, feisty, downright naughty, whatever!'[32]

One of the guiding principles of 'In the Picture' is that 'Images of disabled children should be used casually or incidentally, so that disabled children are portrayed playing and doing things alongside their non-disabled peers.'[33] Disabled children don't have to be the focus of the story; nevertheless they can be present, as part of the social mix.

Illustrations, particularly of crowd scenes, can easily show a range: children with physical disabilities, in wheelchairs, children who are overweight – even something as commonplace as children wearing glasses, whether or not this is referred to in the text. Gone are the days when the wearing of spectacles automatically signified braininess or geekiness, often accompanied by a nickname such as 'Specky', 'Goggles' or 'Prof'.

However, there is sometimes resistance from publishers' sales and marketing departments. One of my writer friends fought – and lost – a battle to have a child in a wheelchair shown on the jacket for a story with such a child as one of the main characters; the publishers insisted that the image would deter readers. Which readers? This seems to create a category of readers not in wheelchairs, or readers who don't know any wheelchair-users and don't want to think about them. Are wheelchair-deniers the only readers who count? It is interesting to speculate on who is being privileged, and on what grounds.

Turning to a different aspect of body image, I wish that photographic models on teenage covers didn't almost invariably have the appearance of airbrushed supermodels, with styling often at variance with the period in which the story is set. Put a less-than-beautiful face on the cover, and the book remains on the shelf – that seems to be accepted thinking. Do we – or children – really want to read only about people blessed with exceptional good looks? And don't we, in any case, prefer to 'see' the characters for ourselves?

In *Reading and Righting*, the author, journalist and critic Robert Leeson writes of the moves to counter prejudice of various kinds in children's books. He describes the hostility met by the organisation Librarians for Social Change, set up in the 1970s to combat 'the more despicable manifestations of injustices such as racism, sexism and ageism' in children's books, and also the founding of The Other Award in 1975 to highlight 'non-biased books of literary merit', with subsequent winners including Jan Needle, Farrukh Dhondy and Gene Kemp.[34] Both organisation and award received criticism for social engineering and what would now be termed 'political correctness' at the expense of freedom for writers.

In his survey of literature of the 1970s and 1980s, Peter Hunt comments, 'It is interesting to see that the religious/didactic element in children's books has been replaced by a movement to be "politically correct" – socially and racially aware. This need has been answered by hundreds of books clearly designed to be bibliotherapeutic (or, if we are cynical, to exploit the market).'[35] In the *Carousel* article referred to above, Eileen Browne recalls the mixed response to her book in the US, with one librarian calling it 'a form of social anarchy' and another accusing it of using 'a children's medium for a political issue'.[36]

Such accusations have not gone away. So where does this leave you, the author, or would-be author? Yvonne has already outlined the dilemma. It can be a difficult line to tread, especially if you are writing a story set in the real world. Single-parent families and step-siblings are now as frequently found in children's fiction as they are in life, but try to shoehorn in too many ingredients and you will be, at best, trying too hard and, at worst, cynically trying to cover all bases, as Peter Hunt suggests. On the one hand, tokenism is no substitute for genuine engagement with your characters' lives and concerns. On the other hand, a minor character's dyslexia or obesity does not have to be of major importance to the story; true inclusiveness means that such things are part of life, not needing to be 'tackled' or treated as an issue.

It could be argued that it's the responsibility of the publisher to include a range of ethnicities and situations on their lists; individual authors obviously can't be expected to cover everything. But the need for inclusiveness is something to be aware of. Are you making assumptions about class, age, ethnicity or body image that may not be shared by your readers? And if so, are you risking shutting some readers out?

Peter Hunt (a novelist as well as an academic) played an interesting trick in his 1989 novel *Going Up*, which made me backtrack. The story follows two teenagers, Tom and Sue, in their first year at university. Some chapters into the book, Sue is outraged when one of her new friends suffers a racist insult, and it was only then – because Hunt had not mentioned it – that I realised the friend was black. I felt wrong-footed, as no doubt Hunt intended, by the realisation that I see characters I'm reading about as white, unless alerted otherwise by name, situation or description. It made me wonder whether black readers see fictional characters as black, and mixed-race characters imagine them as mixed-race, unless specifically told otherwise. And of course this can work to the author's advantage – but only when there are no illustrations.

In looking at the notion of inclusiveness, we are touching on an aspect of writing for children which is not experienced by writers for adults: that of responsibility to our readers. Yvonne has discussed this earlier, and you may feel it to a greater or lesser degree, depending on genre and the imagined age of your readers and whether or not there are illustrations; but such notions will affect the assessment of your work by critics, librarians, teachers and parents, the 'gatekeepers' of children's fiction.

Although, as usual, there are exceptions at the older end, few writers for young people would choose to end a story in which the protagonist is left completely without hope, for example;[37] or to write a novel about anorexia in which the sufferer obstinately refuses all advice and treatment, or to convey the thoughts of an overweight girl with low self-esteem who commits suicide. (Teenage suicide is, as I mentioned earlier, the last taboo; which is not to say that it shouldn't be handled, but few writers would venture inside the head of a successfully suicidal main character.) The writer for adults needn't have these constraints in mind, or worry about the possible effect on the reader. Perhaps that's what Martin Amis meant.

Censorship
Yvonne Coppard

As I noted above, there are rules of engagement that I believe must be borne in mind when writing for children. This is not the same as censorship, although the boundaries are rather blurry. Linda, for instance, has written about the lack of inclusivity apparent in some books in the past that were based on ignorant and offensive assumptions that marginalised whole communities of children.

In her autobiography, Jeanette Winterson recounts how she hid books under her mattress. Her adoptive mother forbade her to read fiction, believing it to be a work of the devil. When Jeanette's mother eventually found the books, she burned them.[38] It was an extreme, private form of a censorship that has always dogged the arts, and nowhere more tenaciously than in the world of children's literature.

> *Don't join the book burners. Don't think you are going to conceal faults by concealing evidence that they ever existed. Don't be afraid to go in your library and read every book, as long as that document does not offend our own ideas of decency. That should be the only censorship.*
> Dwight D. Eisenhower[39]

A bewildering variety of people embrace censorship, particularly when it comes to children: nursery workers, teachers, parents, publishers, librarians, retailers, TV and radio programmers, reviewers, awards panels . . . to name but a few. All feel the need to decide what is and what is not 'appropriate' for the targeted age range. Can there ever be any hard and fast definition of what 'appropriate' might mean? Children of the same age in countries around the world come in unique packages, with experiences and skills and knowledge and vulnerabilities that are theirs and theirs alone. Even in one country, how does any label accommodate all this? Take the discussion to a world forum and it simply can't be done.

In Britain, the cultural base for censorship appears to be slightly different from that in the USA, despite the widespread assumption that we share a common language and cultural heritage. In the UK, books are subject to the censorship of booksellers, publishers, school librarians and parents. Unless a book really hits the panic button (usually on grounds of religion, race or sexuality), censorship tends to be sneaky, almost shamefaced. But in the US there seems to be a more direct (and more vocal) wielding of censorship power across a wider community base. A groundswell of opinion among school boards, parents, politicians and child experts can quickly lead to identifying a book that allegedly poses a threat to children.

In 2012, it was found that one in five UK parents avoided telling fairy tales to their children, citing the violence, the 'scariness' or the politically incorrect overtones (usually gender-based).[40] Censorship decisions around the world illustrate the curious complexity of human history and interaction that some-times unites and sometimes divides us. International peace envoys would do well to bear that in mind, and avoid children's literature as a topic of conversation in their search for common ground between the nations. Anna Sewell's much loved classic Black Beauty (1877) was banned in South Africa under apartheid because the regime judged it to be an allegorical tale of the struggle for black rights; they also objected to the association of 'black' with 'beauty'.

Phillip Pullman's trilogy His Dark Materials was accused particularly by fundamentalist Christians in the US of being an attack on God and religious faith. Melvin Burgess' Junk (1996) tackled drink, drugs, prostitution, life in a squat, imprisonment . . . and the vitriol which greeted the book's publication illustrated that however enlightened and sophisticated we think Western society has become, we're still not ready for such a bleak if realistic appraisal of how some young people's lives can unfold.

Another preoccupation that the adult world imposes on children's litera-ture is an obsession with the 'innocence' of children. They are to be protected from 'knowing' about 'sex' – a term usually defined quite vaguely and very widely, often encompassing a refusal to teach children the names for parts of their own bodies, and those of differently-gendered friends. Adult embar-rassments, borne from a knowledge of foul deeds not shared by any but the most abused children, only fuels the child's longing to explore these forbidden literary fruits.

> " . . . *Little Red Riding Hood reflects men's fear of women's sexuality – and of their own as well.* "
> Jack Zipes[41]

Just two generations back, elderly friends and relatives assure me, many children learned about sex early on because they shared sleeping quarters with parents and a succession of baby siblings. Yet in our supposedly more enlightened and sophisticated age, anything that hints at sexual activity (or the supernatural, or both) is guaranteed to lead to a wave of bans. The storm created by *Jenny Lives with Eric and Martin* (1981) was matched a decade later by the reaction to *Daddy's Roommate* (1991), both stories portraying homosexual parents. Another decade, and we haven't moved on so much: in 2009 William Nicholson, author of *Rich and Mad* (which I enthusiastically promoted as a fabulous young adult title exploring pertinent issues for teenagers today), had his invitation to speak at the Manchester High School for Girls withdrawn, after protests from parents.

Judy Blume's *Forever* (1974) has an iconic place in the literary memories of many British and American women who were teenagers in the 1970s and 1980s. I came across my own daughter's copy, with all the 'sex bits' carefully listed in pencil on the frontispiece. Cheerfully, without a shred of embarrassment, she explained that her list of references saved time for her group of friends who were passing a selection of 'rude' books around. 'We don't have to keep going through the book to find the sexy stuff, Mum; we can turn to the right page whenever we want to.' Having done much the same thing at a similar age, in secret, with D.H. Lawrence's *Lady Chatterley's Lover*, I was hardly in a position to disapprove (although that didn't stop me). Needless to say, *Forever* was not received enthusiastically by children's libraries or parents, but it was lapped up by readers who were, unfortunately for the censors, capable of voting with their feet and paying with their own money.

I don't advocate shoving explicit sexual images and stories into the faces of young people. Advertising, merchandising, fashion, popular TV series and the tabloid press already provide more education about the sleazy side of sex than children's literature ever could. But let's not confuse the noble endeavour to protect a child's innocence with our own paranoid prissiness, either. More than twenty years ago, I was shocked to learn that one of my books, *Not Dressed Like That, You Don't!* was deemed by the Chief Librarian on my own childhood patch (Hillingdon Borough Libraries, to name and shame) to be 'unsuitable' for general release. It sat beside Judy Blume's *Forever* under the counter, available only at the request of already-corrupted children who had prior knowledge of its existence. To this day, I have no idea what led to that decision. I have read and reread the book, which shows the diaries of a teenage girl and her mother, side by side. It was supposed to be humorous, not ground-breaking. I have opened the book at random, searching for something that might have been read out of context, but it remains a mystery. I wish I had felt able to challenge the librarian at the time, but I was young and inexperienced and didn't want the wrong kind of publicity. I could picture the headline: '"My Porn Books Should be Available to Children!" Declares Local Author.'

Censorship remains a hot topic in children's literature, and perhaps rightly so. Young minds need to develop, young imaginations need to fly, unfettered by the nightmares that knowledge beyond their years will impose. But when you have a look at who bans what, and why, and where, you begin to wonder whose view is right and, more importantly, whose view should prevail.

The last week in September is traditionally 'Banned Books Week' in the US. Libraries and booksellers across America draw attention to the injustices of censorship by hosting events that encourage people to challenge bans on books, highlighting them with lots of publicity and reading them in public. It is an idea taken up in the UK. Islington libraries in London have mounted a banned book event.[42] Swansea Library Service in Wales came up with the ingenious publicity stunt of wrapping fifty banned books in brown paper, so that library visitors would not know what they had until they opened the package. How astonished they were to find that books they had studied in school, or read to their own children, were regarded as dangerous and unsuitable once they crossed geographical or cultural borders.

The list of banned books is astonishing, and so long that it can't be shared in totality here. But as well as the titles mentioned above, it includes:

Aldous Huxley's *Brave New World*, Mary Shelley's *Frankenstein*, *Blubber* (Judy Blume again), anything to do with J.K. Rowling's *Harry Potter*, and – one of my own favourite books, a staple on the GCSE[43] English Literature syllabus – Harper *Lee's To Kill a Mockingbird.* I choose these examples from an extensive list to illustrate the simple point that censorship of literature is both idiotic and doomed. These books have all survived to become huge best sellers, classics of their time – and, some of them, blockbuster movies.

Notes

1. C.S. Lewis, *Of Other Worlds: Essays and Stories*, Geoffrey Bles, London, 1966, p. 24.
2. The *Harry Potter* stories do of course see Harry grow from child to adolescent – but the phenomenal success of that series is impossible to replicate, certainly not by copying.
3. Quoted in P. Hunt, *Understanding Children's Literature*, Routledge, London, 1999, p. 15.
4. The first mention of Robin Hood is possibly a passing reference in *Piers Plowman* (late thirteenth century). Most of the tales about him come from the fifteenth century, appearing first in oral tradition or ballads before finding their way into written tales: *Robin Hood and the Monk; The Lyttle Geste of Robyn Hoode; Robin Hoode his Death; Robin Hood and Guy of Gisborne; Robin Hood and the Curtal Friar* (West, 1996, p. 506).
5. In this 1693 essay, Locke exhorted parents to watch their children and note their natural inclinations so they can mould and steer their children on the right path. Compare the twenty-first-century variation of this idea: 'follow your dream'.
6. Jean-Jacques Rousseau, *Emile, or On Education*, 1762.
7. Inglis, 1981, p. 101 in P. Hunt (ed), *International Companion Encyclopaedia of Children's Literature*, Routledge, London, 1996.
8. Westin, 1991, p. 7 in *International Companion Encyclopaedia of Children's Literature*, Taylor and Francis e-library, p. 22.
9. John Rowe Townsend, *Written for Children*, Penguin, London, 1987.
10. The *Rachel Riley* series and *Buttercup Mash*, Oxford University Press, Oxford.
11. Interviewed on BBC2, date unknown.
12. J. Rose *The Case of Peter Pan: The Impossibility of Children's Fiction*, Macmillan, London, 1984.
13. Italo Calvino, 'Why Read the Classics', translated by Patrick Creagh, essay in *The Uses of Literature*, Harcourt Brace Jovanovitch, San Diego, 1986.
14. C.S. Lewis, op. cit., p. 24.
15. Laila Rasheed, on an authors' messageboard.
16. Patrick Ness, quoted in 'Whole Truth for Teenagers: Patrick Ness's Novels have Attracted Acclaim, Awards – and Censure', an interview by Nicolette Jones, *The Independent*, 24 June 2011.

17. *The Importance of Being Earnest,* first performed 14 February 1895.

18. *Junk,* 1996; *Smack,* 1999; *Doing It,* 2006: Andersen Press, London.

19. 'Purely for Love' in V. Haviland (ed.), *Children and Literature: Views and Reviews,* Bodley Head, London, 1973.

20. 'History is People', op. cit.

21. Keith Topping, *What the Kids are Reading,* Dundee University, 2012.

22. General Certificate of Secondary Education, the national gateway exams in England and Wales for employment and further education, taken at ages fifteen to sixteen.

23. Southern Methodist University, Texas.

24. Bob Dixon, Preface, *Catching Them Young 1: Sex, Race and Class in Children's Fiction,* Pluto Press, London, 1977, p. xiv.

25. Ibid.

26. Ibid., p. 111–12,

27. John Rowe Townsend, *Written for Children,* 3rd edn, Penguin, London, 1987.

28. Leila Berg, 'Language of Nippers', letter in *Times Educational Supplement,* 15 December 1972, p. 14.

29. Eileen Browne, 'Making Picture Book History: The "Jo" Books', *Carousel,* no. 51, Summer 2012, p. 4.

30. Ibid., p. 5.

31. Malorie Blackman, interviewed by Alison Flood, *Guardian,* 10 November 2008.

32. www.scope.org.uk/campaigns/inclusion and participation/disabled-children-books

33. *In the Picture* website www.childreninthepicture.org.uk

34. Robert Leeson, *Reading and Righting,* Collins, London, 1985, p. 138.

35. Peter Hunt, *An Introduction to Children's Literature,* Oxford University Press, Oxford, 1994, p. 149.

36. Eileen Browne, op. cit., p. 5.

37. A notable exception is *I Am the Cheese* by Robert Cormier, Random House, London, 1977.

38. *Why Be Happy when You Could Be Normal?,* Grove Press, New York, 2011, also available for Kindle.

39. Commencement address at Dartmouth College, Hanover, New Hampshire, in 1952.

40. BBC2, 14 February 2012.

41. J. Zipes (ed.), *The Trials and Tribulations of Little Red Riding Hood,* Routledge, London, 1993.

42. www.islington.gov.uk/libraries

43. See note 22.

Categories in children's fiction

by Linda Newbery

Picture books

To anyone who hasn't given it much thought, picture books might seem to offer an easy entrée to children's publishing; all you need is a simple story told in few words, and an obliging friend who can draw. On writing courses, I've occasionally met students who think they'll start with picture books and 'work their way up' to longer texts. The reality is very different. It is much harder to place a picture book with a publisher than the newcomer may expect. Books in this format are expensive to produce, because of the colour illustrations; publishers will usually only invest in a text if they are confident of selling foreign rights to offset their initial costs. Picture books are like jokes – they work or they don't. No publisher will bother with a picture book they think is quite good or mildly pleasing; they've got to love it, and be excited by its possibilities.

Many picture books are produced by a writer-illustrator – Anthony Browne, Mini Grey, Emily Gravett – but there are also opportunities for writers who aren't artists to produce the texts, with well-known pairings such as Michael Rosen and Quentin Blake, Michaels Morpurgo and Foreman, Sue Heap and Nick Sharratt. The mistake frequently made by beginner writers is to assume that they need an artist friend to do the pictures. The quickest way to put off an editor is to send your text accompanied by amateurish artwork, and even competent illustrations will reduce the already slim chance that your text will be accepted. An artist unfamiliar with the picture-book format may well assume that the illustrations simply show what's referred to in the wording, but many picture books – famously, *Rosie's Walk* by Pat Hutchins[1] – subvert this, creating enjoyment as the reader 'discovers' what the text seems not to know.

It's possible, of course, that your friend is a major undiscovered talent, but usually the editor and/or art director will want to make the pairing of author and illustrator. Art editors often visit student degree shows to find new talent, so they may already have artists for whom they need a suitable text. Alternatively, the publisher may offer a contract for a text and only afterwards find the right illustrator.

There's a freshness and excitement to this matching of text and artist, because your text is likely to be transformed into something you couldn't have imagined. It's not uncommon for the author and illustrator to work quite separately, never meeting, or at least not until the book is well under way. Illustrator Korky Paul prefers not to know the author's ideas, but to bring his own interpretation to the text. In *The Fish Who Could Wish*, it was Korky's idea to show the setting as an Amazonian rain forest; there is no verbal reference to this in John Bush's text.

The design of picture books is of crucial importance. Sometimes the writer's role will be limited to the provision of text, which the artist and designer will then make into a book; sometimes writer and artist will work as a team. It's as well to be aware that picture books are usually produced in a 32-page format, giving twelve or fourteen double-page spreads. Even if you're not going to illustrate your own story, it would be valuable to have some idea of design, of the appearance, size and variety of text, the flow across pages, the creation of a surprise when a page is turned. I like to think of it as writing a playscript, and a very minimal one; the words give cues to the artist, and to the reader.

Although I've suggested earlier that you shouldn't study the market too slavishly, I think a would-be picture book writer *does* need an awareness of the form and its possibilities. Otherwise, it's too easy to think that a picture book is just a simple story with cute illustrations, and to underestimate the subtlety and excitement offered by this format. The Illustration Cupboard's website[2] shows a range of work from artists past and present, and of course there's nothing so enlightening as sitting down to read books for yourself or sharing them with a young child to see what catches and keeps attention.

In terms of length, picture books can range from no words at all (for example *Clown* by Quentin Blake) to more substantial stories such as *Dogger* by Shirley Hughes. A thousand words would be on the long side, edging into the next category – first readers. Many picture books have only a hundred words or fewer, and within so short a span not a single word must be wasted. There is no need to explain what will be shown in the pictures – for example, if someone is startled, a picture will do better than a word.

Publishers sometimes say that rhyming texts are difficult to sell in foreign editions, but many of the most successful books do depend on rhymes – *The Gruffalo*, to name one of the best known. Rhymes, rhythm, repetitions and patterns can provide enjoyment in the reading aloud, and in the rereading which is essential to the life of a picture book.

So what sort of idea will make a picture book? Often the idea is a very simple one, the fun coming from absurdity or accumulation of detail. Julia Jarman explains how *Big Red Bath* came about:

> All my stories are a mix of real life and imagination, as is children's play, and this story was inspired by the fun and games in my bath-room. I do have a big red bath and my grandchildren love to play in it. There's riotous splashing, hide and seek with bubbles and imaginative play with toys. New to writing for the very young, I used an old favourite, John Burningham's *Mr Gumpy's Outing*, as a model. There's repetition and alliteration and onomatopoeia and a similar structure as a sequence of animals jump in the bath, but also rhyme, which just happened. I pictured my story as fourteen double-page spreads, with a question at the end of many of them, upping the all-important 'what happens next?' element. The crazy climax was inspired by the fact that the real bath has clawed feet like a bird's. So what if it could fly? Of course I had to bring them all safely home. Finding the right rhythm was key, and the right names for the children, not the same as my grandchildren's. I knew I wanted my story to bounce, so once I had 'Ben and Bella in the big red bath' – those Bs are crucial – I was away!

Such stories as *Big Red Bath* are often read at bedtime, so excitement is tempered by a return to normality and a sense of calm at the end. Very young children can engage with the stories before they begin to recognise words, learning to predict, to enjoy the sounds and the rhythms.

Picture books often use animal characters to depict emotions in a way that makes a direct or acceptable appeal to a child. *Owl Babies* and *Guess How Much I Love You* are famous examples of this, while Susan Varley's *Badger's Parting Gifts* and *Always and Forever* by Alan Durant and Debi Gliori are consoling stories for a young child faced with the ageing or death of a relative.

Included in the picture-book category are lift-the-flap and pop-up books, some of them very complicated. Storytellers who specialise in such 'paper engineering' include Robert Crowther, whose titles include *Pop-Up House of Inventions* and *Most Amazing Hide-and-Seek Alphabet Book*. Production of such books is very specialised, the cut-outs planned so that they will initially fit on a flat sheet of card, and robust enough in book form to endure many a raising and re-folding – hence the term 'engineering'. If this is where your interest lies you are probably an illustrator first and a writer second; or, if a writer, you have an idea which lends itself to pop-up treatment. There are plenty of how-to guides on the mechanics of paper engineering.

First readers and young series

These are short illustrated stories, complete books, usually divided into chapters. For a young child, this may be the first experience of a story written in chapters, which should preferably make instalments for reading aloud by an adult. Notionally these stories would be targeted at readers of about three to seven, with length and content reflecting that span – ideal stories for children to share with adults, to begin to read aloud, and to enjoy alone as they gain confidence. In fact, the readership of these books stretches farther than publishers may realise. Older children who struggle with reading and baulk at a longer book are often attracted to these short, manageable stories.

There may be stand-alone hardbacks and gift editions but many of the books in this category are slim paperbacks, usually with illustrations on most pages to avoid putting off young children with unbroken expanses of text. Some may have illustrations in colour, but most are in black-and-white. In this category there are many character-led series, and some publishers have an imprint specifically for this format, such as Corgi Pups at Transworld and Bananas at Egmont. Commissioning editors may provide guidelines about length and style – for instance, the Banana books are subdivided into three age groups, and sometimes use speech balloons in the illustrations. Other publishers produce character-led mini-series.

Some of the most commercial series for this age group are the work of several authors – *Rainbow Magic*, for instance, published by Scholastic, which runs to hundreds of titles. Among the writers for this series (and also for *Animal Ark*, for slightly older readers) are authors who are established in their own right, but who are subsumed under the Daisy Meadows pen name for this purpose.

In terms of length, these stories range from about a thousand words at the younger end to five or six thousand, though publisher briefs may vary. Much longer, and we're moving into the next category.

So: what will work? There's a lot of wacky humour and fast-paced action in series for this age group, but Anne Fine offers good advice in the *Children's Writers' and Artists' Yearbook 2012*: 'Does it sound mad to say that plots can be overrated? And never more so in books designed to be read aloud to the young . . . Children love to identify with someone or something in the story – it doesn't really matter what. It could be another child, or a puppy, or even a lost pebble' (as in one of her own stories, *It Moved!*).[3] Too much action, at the expense of character and feeling, can leave the reader (of whatever age) feeling indifferent. We'll look more at the shape of stories in Part 3, but Anne Fine's point is a crucial one. A story might hinge on a simple problem and resolution, but above all the child must have someone to engage with, whether human or animal.

Linda Chapman, a specialist in this age group with eight series currently in print as well as others she has ghost-written, differentiates between series consisting of linked but separate stories and those which develop with each story leading to the next. With the first kind, she plans the 'world' of the setting but starts off with no more than rough ideas for the initial three stories. For stories linked in a progression, more detailed initial planning is needed: the outline of each story, and how it contributes to the overall arc of the plot. Linda says, 'Usually with this type of series, there are six books and there is a format to each one – the characters will find something or achieve something in every book. I plan what that will be, and how the characters and their relationships will develop.' Linda adds that the stories within a series shouldn't feel too repetitive: 'For example, in each *Skating School* series I vary where the action took place – sometimes it's in the school, sometimes in the gardens, sometimes out in the countryside.' As Linda Chapman often has several series running concurrently, she needs to be well-organised and methodical. 'Approaching a publisher, I usually have a very detailed plot for the first two books along with three sample chapters, short outlines of books three and four, then suggestions for how the series might develop.'

When familiarising yourself with this type of story, look at the possibilities in the ways text is presented – although there's usually less freedom than in the picture-book format, stories can still use illustrative material in the form of notes, envelopes, posters, signs and handwriting, and in the case of the Banana Books, speech balloons. For instance, if your character comes across a sign warning DANGER – KEEP OUT! or sees a poster about a lost dog, it can be shown in a picture. Such variety helps to break up the text and make it approachable to a young reader.

Anne Fine's point about reading aloud is important, too – and this doesn't only apply here, but to all kinds of writing. These stories are very likely to be read to a child at bedtime and, like picture books, they can make great play with rhythm, rhyme, alliteration and repetition, all of which make repeated readings enjoyable.

There are such things as stand-alones in this category, but they're in a minority – partly, I think, because the books are so slim that their spines are not easily seen on bookshelves, whereas a line-up of four, six or eight books with the same design is more noticeable. An outstanding exception is *Storm*, by Kevin Crossley-Holland, which was published in the Banana Books series and was awarded the Carnegie Medal in 1985. This is the only occasion on which a book for such young readers has won the Carnegie. More recently, the very popular *Mr Gum* books by Andy Stanton have won awards, but on the whole series books for this age group go unnoticed by judging panels.

The advance (the initial fee paid by a publisher – more on this later) is likely to be small for a book or series of this type. However, there are compensations. Books for this age group are in great demand, once published; they are frequently borrowed from libraries, earning Public Lending Right; they are usually in inexpensive paperback, so sales at school and library visits can help your book to reach readers quickly.

Fiction for the seven-to-nine age group

This is an important area, but one which seems to be undersupplied. Several times recently I've heard publishers say that they're looking out for good novels and series for this age group, but that quality stand-alone titles in particular are hard to find. Michael Thorn, who runs the ACHUKA website, commented when choosing titles for a July 2011 round-up: 'What strikes me when I make selections for this category is the overwhelming preponderance of what I can only describe as funny and frothy reads . . . Oh, how much Dick King-Smith is missed!'[4] Marcus Sedgwick, in a *Guardian* review, commented on the need for one-off alternatives to the plethora of 'My-sparkle-pony-wish-fairy-dinosaur' series which currently dominates younger fiction.[5]

It should be said that all age-ranging is approximate, and perhaps never more so than in this area, where some children will be reading the younger series described in the previous category, others devouring substantial junior novels such as the longer *Harry Potter* books, or even moving into teenage fiction. But, in very general terms, we're talking about novels written in short chapters, in length roughly 10,000–25,000 words, and usually illustrated.

I can appreciate the difficulty for children and parents when trying to find suitable books. Most libraries and bookshops divide children's books into Picture Books, Young Stories, Junior Fiction, and Teenage. Looking for seven-to-nine books in my local library, they were hard to find between two bigger and better-stocked categories. It's not surprising that adults choosing for children return to the familiar names of Roald Dahl, Enid Blyton, Jill Murphy, Dick King-Smith, Hilary McKay and Francesca Simon – often going for titles and authors they remember from their own childhood.

Jon Appleton, from Hodder Children's Books, explains that 'it's crucial to provide books which bridge the gap between picture books and longer novels. Parents, teachers, librarians ask for them.' But he adds that 'It's difficult to publish stand-alone titles for this age group.' Like other editors, he notes 'shelf presence' as a reason for the lack of stand-alones; as mentioned above, a single slim book, displayed spine-out, gets lost on the shelves. However, there is a place for the illustrated, beautifully designed book which will command attention.

It seems that here is a gap waiting for good new authors to fill it – so if you're starting out, and feel that you can write for this age group, it's well worth considering. The children's book market as a whole is a very crowded one, but in this slot your work may receive a particularly warm welcome from critics and buyers.

Junior fiction

We're moving now into the core area of children's publishing – stories for pre-teenage readers between nine and twelve. I can remember when there was a notional length of 40,000 words for this age group and 60,000 words for a teenage novel, though that has changed with the phenomenon of *Harry Potter* and the discovery that quite young children can cope with books of 450 pages or more. Fantasy fiction, in particular, is often quite chunky.

This age group crosses from top primary into the early years of secondary school. There are still plenty of series to be found; very popular at the time of writing are fast-paced adventures aimed primarily at boys, including the hugely successful *Alex Rider* novels by Anthony Horowitz, the *Young Bond* books by Charlie Higson and the *Cherub* series by Robert Muchamore, all of which are welcomed by teachers and parents wanting to encourage reluctant boy readers and are widely promoted in schools and libraries. At the top end of this age group is what publishers sometimes term aspirational fiction for pre-teens, or 'tweens': stories aimed mainly at girls who are starting to become interested in boys and fashion. Examples are Jo Cotterill's *Sweet Hearts* series, the *Ally's World* sequence by Karen McCombie and *Artichoke Hearts* by Sita Brahmachari, a recent winner of the Waterstones prize.

Stand-alone novels are more common here than in the categories previously mentioned, and there are numerous authors – Michael Morpurgo, Anne Fine, Geraldine McCaughrean, David Almond – who only write stand-alones (although David Almond has recently published *My Name is Mina*, a 'prequel' to his highly acclaimed *Skellig*). In this section you will find every kind of genre: adventure, mystery, animal stories, fantasy worlds, historical, supernatural, humour, retellings of myths and legends.

There is such variety and scope within the nine-to-twelve category that it's hard to give useful practical advice. For that, move on to Part 3, where we'll be covering various aspects of writing effectively.

Teenage and young adult fiction

Teenage fiction has had its ups and downs over the last thirty years or so. Before the 1970s, it hardly existed – there was nothing between children's fiction and adult books. John Rowe Townsend wrote in 1965 that 'Teenage fiction is an American speciality.' In the 1970s the author and editor Aidan Chambers, seeing the need to bridge this gap, launched the *Topliners* series with Macmillan. Broaching the idea, he was told (incredibly as it seems now) 'by all sorts of people – publishers, librarians, booksellers – that there was not only no market for teenage books but that no writers worth their muse would want to write them.'[6]

Soon, however, UK writers such as K.M. Peyton, Jean Ure, Jill Paton Walsh and Aidan Chambers himself joined pioneer Americans S.E. Hinton, Kathleen Paterson, Judy Blume and Robert Cormier in the creation of fiction for and about adolescence. There was a tremendous surge in the 1980s as every major publisher brought out a distinctively branded teenage list, rapidly followed by a slump as the sales figures failed to match those of younger fiction. In recent years, though, the teenage market has burgeoned, with Stephanie Meyer's *Twilight* series achieving cult and crossover status, followed more recently by *The Hunger Games*. As is often pointed out, the major children's prizes tend to go to books for teenage readers: both the Costa Children's Prize and the Carnegie in 2011 were won by teenage dystopian novels

(*Blood Red Road* by Moira Young and *Monsters of Men* by Patrick Ness) and the shortlists are frequently dominated by older fiction.

The terms 'teenage' and 'young adult' seem to be used interchangeably, certainly as far as bookshop and library shelving is concerned. In the States and Australia, though, young adult fiction is regarded as a separate category, and is treated with as much seriousness as fiction for adults. The blurring of the terms does lead to confusion, and to good books being overlooked. In UK bookshops, the teenage shelves more often than not contain books for the younger end, the 'aspirational' novels referred to in the previous category and the numerous sparkly girly series – with the unfortunate result that many readers of fourteen or fifteen give up looking at the teenage shelves, finding the books there too young for their tastes. This means that they're likely to miss excellent novels of adolescence such as *Postcards From No Man's Land* by Aidan Chambers or *Life: An Exploded Diagram* by Mal Peet. Most libraries and some bookshops now place the young adult shelves alongside general fiction, kept well away from the children's section with its floor cushions and baby books, to encourage teenagers to browse.

There are many attractions to writing for teenagers – not just the prospect of getting a film deal or being the next Stephanie Meyer. (It's as well never to think of yourself as the next anyone, but to develop your sense of what kind of writer *you* are.) One of those attractions is that the scope and length of a young adult novel can lend itself to anything you want to write about. Main characters in their teens (and their readers) will face enormous changes over the next ten years, whether they want to or not, and this opens up all kinds of possibilities even if what you're writing has an ordinary domestic setting. It's a time for shaping attitudes, sorting out priorities, finding goals and ideals, having wild and impractical ambitions, falling in and out of love, needing and earning money, discovering that adults are fallible – all those coming-of-age things that have proved so fruitful for writers past and present.

It helps either to remember being a teenager or to be in close touch with some. Meg Rosoff wrote, in a *Guardian* booklet on *How to Write Books for Children*, 'If you can remember what life was like when the world seemed to be perpetually out of focus, when the sort of issues that interested you were existentialism, sensation, falling in love, and the shape of the universe, you're probably halfway there.' She concludes: 'My best advice is to write fiercely. Your audience craves intensity, passion, catharsis, sex, extreme experience, philosophy, relationships, hallucinatory revelations.'[7]

Short story collections

Collections of stories are usually grouped by theme, as in Tony Bradman's anthology *Under the Weather*, focusing on climate change; *Unheard Voices*, compiled by Malorie Blackman to mark the two-hundredth anniversary of the abolition of the slave trade; *The Truth is Dead*, Marcus Sedgwick's compilation of stories which look at alternative versions of history; and *Next*, Keith Gray's collection about the after-life. Single-author short story collections are rare. The late Jan Mark was a specialist, and Anne Fine has published several, but it would be surprising for a first-time author to interest a publisher in a solo effort. However, there are other opportunities. Sometimes a compiler or publisher will notify agents, writing organisations and publications about a forthcoming anthology on a given theme, and invite submissions; this could be a way into first publication. The brilliant Siobhan Dowd was first published in a Tony Bradman anthology, *Skin Deep*; realising her talent, Bradman put Dowd in touch with his own agent, and she went on to publish four novels to great acclaim.

It's worth looking out for short-story competitions, as these can lead to publication (not necessarily in book form – maybe in magazines or on websites): something to add to your writing CV, and the chance to catch the eye of an agent or editor.

Graphic novels

In recent years there has been a new interest in graphic novels – stories told in 'comic-strip' format, told primarily through drawings. Comics, too, are making a comeback, led by *The Phoenix*,[8] a high-quality weekly production which features seven stories in each issue, some in serial form, others as one-offs.

Graphic novels have been with us for a long time, from the westerns and romances of the fifties and sixties, produced as small-format magazines and seen as a throwaway form of reading, to the more substantial *Tintin* and *Asterix* series. *Maus* by Art Spiegelmann, a concentration camp story characterising the Jews as mice and the Nazis as cats, was a key book in establishing the graphic novel, showing that its potential reached beyond its usual confines. A younger and more comforting story is one of the best-known, Raymond Briggs' wordless *The Snowman*.

Now, graphic novels for children and teenagers have become part of the mainstream, representing ways of storytelling which are at once traditional and innovative. The vibrant energy and boldness of graphic novels is an attraction to artists from various backgrounds, including, notably, Manga. Some devise their own stories, while others are paired with writers.

This is one field where a study of the market will definitely be helpful – it's an innovative field, full of possiblities and reaching out to a wide readership. Look, for instance, at *MeZolith*, written by Ben Haggarty and illustrated by film concept artist Adam Brockbank; *Good Dog, Bad Dog* by Dave Shelton; and *The Invention of Hugo Cabret* by Brian Selznick. As well as stories originally appearing in this form, there are adaptations of novels, such as the Anthony Horowitz *Alex Rider* series, Charlie Higson's *Silver Fin* and classic plays in the *Manga Shakespeare*.

Fiction packagers

I'd seen the numerous *Animal Ark* stories by Lucy Daniels, but hadn't realised that 'Lucy Daniels' was a multiply-split personality until, at a conference a good few years ago, I found myself having coffee with three of her. The *Animal Ark* series, published by Hodder, is the product of a company called Working Partners, as are many other phenomenally successful series for children of all ages, including *Rainbow Magic, Beast Quest, Dinosaur Cove* and others which have sold in their millions. Another 'fiction packager' is Hothouse, which lists *Darke Academy* and *Spell Sisters* among its many series.

The three authors I met over coffee were all successfully published under their own names, but supplemented their income and filled gaps between projects with the 'Lucy Daniels' books. (Shhh . . . many a young reader would be deeply disillusioned to find out that Lucy Daniels is not a real person, especially as the fiction is maintained on the Hodder website that she lives in Yorkshire and is busily writing her next book.) John Crace, investigating the phenomenon of more than five million sales in the UK alone, wrote in the *Guardian*: 'The list of Animal Ark authors reads like a Who's Who of children's fiction. Sue Welford, a Whitbread prize nominee, Jenny Oldfield and Helen Magee, all of whom are names in their own right, have done a turn as Lucy Daniels. In Jenny Oldfield's case, she has done dozens of turns, and the reason is simple: money. A three-to-four-week spell spent writing a 25,000-word Animal Ark manuscript can net the author over £20,000 in royalties and foreign rights.'[9]

Working for a fiction packager is very different from working directly with a publisher. Karen Ball, who is Head of Editorial at Working Partners as well as writing fiction under her own name, explained this to me:

> The commissioned author follows a detailed storyline that's been brainstormed in-house – which means that the copyright for the book or series belongs to Working Partners. WP pays an advance and passes on part of their royalty earnings to writers, who will be provided with detailed editorial support throughout the process.

The benefits for the author are, she says, that

> the writing can go relatively quickly because the painstaking plotting has already been done for you. This makes WP projects ideal for fitting around other commitments – and your confidence can be significantly boosted as you bring your creative talents to a team experience. A successful series with WP can also help raise your profile and act as an introduction to new publishers, with long-term benefits to your career.

Working Partners recruits both established and new authors to join their team of writers. At the start of each project, plot outlines are given, and writers invited to send in a sample of three chapters which flesh out the bones. If chosen, the writer is given an advance, and although their name won't appear on the cover, they will be credited inside the book. The website[10] gives very clear pointers as to what the editorial team is looking for.

Clearly this wouldn't suit everyone. You'd be writing someone else's story, about someone else's characters; you wouldn't be allowed to deviate from the agreed plot or take the story in an unexpected direction. This may put you off from the start, or you might tire of working in this way. On the plus side, you'll never be stuck for a plot or fear that your novel is falling to pieces. You will pick up tips about structuring, plotting, maintaining tension etc., that may be useful in your own writing. And, as John Crace points out, the financial returns – if you are involved in a very successful series – could be significantly more than you could expect as an unknown author publishing under your own name.

Leila Rasheed is one author who enjoys the combination of writing for Working Partners alongside the books she writes under her own name. She told me that deadlines are tight: 'I had about three months to write each book, and they were about 35,000 words each. I was sent a very thorough plot outline but still problems cropped up and had to be solved. My own writing had to go on the back burner while I prioritised this.' However, what Leila appreciates is 'the feeling of being professional, writing to a brief. It feels like work, employment, in a way that writing my own books doesn't. Writing my own books is different, feeding my need to be creative; writing a Working Partners book feeds my need to be useful, employed. It's nice to work as part of a team after spending a lot of time writing on my own. I would also say it's a good way to try out writing a new genre or for a new age range.'

Educational publishing

It can be confusing to work out who's who in this area. There are publishers who specialise in producing books for schools and colleges (examples are Pearson and McGraw Hill), while others, such as the Oxford University Press, publish both for the mass market and for education. Sometimes an educational publisher is part of a larger company or group: for example Wayland and Franklin Watt are divisions of Hachette, and Heinemann is part of Pearson, which in turn is part of the Penguin group.

Some educational publishers produce only information and non-fiction, and of course vast ranges of such books are required by schools. But we're talking about fiction here, so have a look at who publishes what.

There are two main areas which may be of interest to the fiction writer. First: reading schemes, such as the *Oxford Reading Tree* published by the

Oxford University Press, are linked to National Curriculum levels and are carefully graded and structured. The second area is the production of novels which support the National Curriculum, for instance the A&C Black *Flashbacks* series: short, accessible novels set at various points in the past, to engage junior-age children with reading and at the same time to show what it was like to live in a certain period.

In either case, publishers will issue precise guidelines regarding length and reading ability, so it's not a good idea to write a whole story on spec and send it off; instead, find out the name of the editor responsible for the series and ask what he or she is looking for. Again, there are many authors who supplement their writing income by writing for the educational market: *Oxford Reading Tree* has Geraldine McCaughrean, Martin Waddell, Pippa Goodhart and Sue Gates among its contributors, and Philip Pullman, early in his career while working as a middle-school teacher, wrote a book of word games.[11]

'Hi-Lo'

In recent years, books for reluctant or unconfident readers have come to be known as 'Hi-Lo' – meaning high interest and readability catering for low levels of reading skill and vocabulary. Such books have always been available, mainly through educational publishers, but have traditionally had a rather off-putting 'textbooky' appearance, drawing attention to their remedial purpose or with covers that looked too childish for teenagers to be seen with.

Barrington Stoke has been the specialist leader in this field since 1997. It's an independent, Edinburgh-based publishing house, dedicated to producing stories by top authors which look like mainstream publications. 'We commission new stories from authors who our readers' peers will be reading,' says editor Vicki Rutherford. 'This way our readers will be reading books by the same authors as their friends, which we hope helps them avoid the social stigma around not being able to read so well.'

The stories range from five to nine thousand words. Considerable care is given to every aspect of production, from the use of cream paper, easier on the eye than white, and of a specialised dyslexic-friendly font, to the trialling of stories with readers of the appropriate age and lengthy discussions with the authors to iron out any difficulties or possible misunderstandings. Contributors include Catherine Johnson, Beverley Naidoo, Terry Deary and Jeremy Strong, and popular teenage authors Bali Rai, Keith Gray and Kate Cann.

Writing for this market is more difficult than it might appear. The risk of writing a story so minimally is that it can read more like a plot synopsis than a fully realised novella, with the result that the reader feels hustled through on fast-forward. It takes a skilled writer to get the balance right – maintaining emotional power and involvement while using a relatively simple vocabulary and sentence structures.

Although it's unlikely that Barrington Stoke would take on a book by a first-time author, other publishers of 'Hi Lo' may do so. This is another way for writers, once published, to extend their range and become known to a wider selection of readers.

Writing for more than one age group

One of the most enjoyable things about writing for young people is that there can be enormous freedom. If you've been working hard on an 80,000-word novel, it can be refreshing to spend time experimenting with a picture-book text, or writing a humorous poem. Authors for children have, traditionally, enjoyed a far greater right to roam than writers of adult fiction.

However, this seems to have changed since I was first published in the late 1980s. Then, when I looked at the big names in children's books – Michael Morpurgo, Berlie Doherty, Margaret Mahy, Geraldine McCaughrean and Jan Mark, for example – it was notable that those authors wrote for various age groups. It seemed almost that the mark of a career author was to be versatile enough to produce a challenging teenage novel and a picture book in the same year, often with a first reader and a junior novel in between, or maybe a retelling, and with no loss of quality. A first reader by Jan Mark, a picture book by Margaret Mahy or a retelling by Geraldine McCaughrean would have all the wit, relish for language and attention to detail that made their longer novels so distinctive.

The change has come about, I think, through the influence of marketing departments, bookshop buyers, and the demise of Ottakar's and Borders, which has left Waterstones and W.H. Smith to dominate high-street book-selling. This may seem to be moving some distance away from an author's decision to write one kind of book rather than another. But there is strong competition for space on bookshop shelves, and a survey will quickly show you the importance of 'branding'. Jacqueline Wilson's career took off when she was matched with illustrator Nick Sharratt for The Story of Tracy Beaker; from then on her books have had a distinctive 'look', recognisable from yards away. In recent years, some of the authors who have established themselves most quickly – Robert Muchamore, for instance, or Lauren Kate, and of course Stephanie Meyer – have been given their own branding. Readers know what they'll get from a Robert Muchamore book, or a Rick Riordan, or a Jean Ure,[12] and once they've enjoyed one, will be keen to devour the rest. It works, clearly, because those books are everywhere.

So publishers and marketing departments do tend to encourage authors to stay where they're successful, and not go meandering off to different sections of the shelves.

This is not to say that you can't still write for different age groups. I do, and it's one of the things I enjoy, and wouldn't want to change, not least because my visits to schools and libraries are so varied, talking to everyone from reception classes to adults. The drawback is that my books aren't all shelved in one place, and because they come from different publishers, they don't share a 'look'. The result is that I'm not known for any one thing.

It will be up to you to decide – and, of course, sales and popularity aren't everything. But at the start of your career, when you approach publishers, it would be unwise to express a desire to follow your teenage dystopian novel with a rhyming picture-book text or a book of silly poems. A publisher taking you on will certainly want more than one book, but they will want to 'place' you firmly in one area, and start building your image.

Branching out, if that's what you want to do, can come later – Vivian French, one of our contributors in Part 2, enjoys the opportunities that come from being versatile.

Notes

1. Rosie the chicken goes for a walk around the farmyard. The words simply state that she walks around the yard and back home; but the pictures show that she is being stalked by a fox. The fun for the reader is the mismatch between text and illustrations – Rosie never sees the fox, which is thwarted at every turn. She returns to her roost with only the reader aware of the dangers she has skirted. Or did Rosie know all the time that the fox was there? The story permits more than one interpretation.

2. See www.illustrationcupboard.com

3. Anne Fine, 'Writing Books to be Read Aloud', in *Children's Writers' and Artists' Yearbook 2012*, Bloomsbury, London, 2011.

4. Michael Thorn, ACHUKA website www.achuka.co.uk, 3 July 2011.

5. Marcus Sedgwick, *The Guardian*, 22 July 2012, p. 14.

6. Aidan Chambers, 'Alive and Flourishing: A Personal View of Teenage Fiction', in *Booktalk*, Bodley Head, London, 1985.

7. Meg Rosoff, 'How to Write Books for Children', Guardian News and Media, London, 2008.

8. *The Phoenix* is the brainchild of David Fickling, of David Fickling Books, and was initially launched for a trial period as *The DFC*, with its first issue including a story by Philip Pullman. Several of the stories first published in *The DFC* are now available as graphic novels.

9. John Crace, 'If You Knew Lucy', *The Guardian*, 22 March 2000.

10. See www.workingpartners.ltd.co.uk

11. Philip Pullman, 'Using the Oxford Junior Dictionary', in *A Book of Exercises and Games*, Oxford University Press, Oxford, 1979. Co-edited and illustrated by Ivan Ripley, this was republished as 'Using the Oxford Illustrated Junior Dictionary' in 1995.

12. Jean Ure is not a new arrival and has not always had her current 'look'. She was one of the foremost authors for teenagers when teenage fiction began to take on its own identity in the 1970s, and wrote a number of challenging young adult novels, including *Plague 99*, *The Other Side of the Fence* and *If it Wasn't for Sebastian*. *See You Thursday* became a trilogy about Marianne and her blind boyfriend Abe, a pianist. More recently she has specialised in 'pre-teen' novels and series, with jackets and illustrations by Karen Donnelly.

Becoming a writer

by Linda Newbery

Think of yourself as a writer

On school and library visits, I'm often asked for tips for young writers. I list three, the first of which is, 'Think of yourself as a writer.' (The second and third: 'Write something every day, even if it's only for ten minutes' and '*Never* throw anything away.')

If you think of yourself as a writer, and if you *do* write, you're a writer.

Over the years I've seen a good many books about the nuts and bolts of writing, which seem to imply that if you put all the bits together correctly you'll produce a satisfactory book, rather in the way you might build an Airfix model or bake a cake. Recently I was given a book which sweeps all such advice aside, with the caveat that until you learn to think as a writer, you can study technique as exhaustively as you like, but it won't help you in the slightest. That book is *Becoming a Writer*, by Dorothea Brande, an American author and editor, and was first published in 1934. It immediately struck chords with me, as it has with many others.

Dorothea Brande talks about 'writers' magic'. So does Stephen King: 'Writing is magic, as much the water of life as any other creative art. The water is free. So drink.'[1] And you will find plenty of direct or oblique references to this special magic in the guest contributions in Part 2. I don't mean it in a whimsical way, and nor do Brande, King or our contributors; but writers' magic is the crucial ingredient and will sustain you through difficulties, rejection and other setbacks. Without it, writing is just a job of work,

Finding this writers' magic isn't like turning on a tap. Sometimes you have to wait, as author Jenny Alexander explains: 'You have to make yourself receptive and hold that position, even though that period can feel like an uncomfortable hiatus, but when you do, you get exactly the inspiration you need.'[2] This chimes with notions in Buddhist teachings and Gestalt therapy of the 'fertile void'. During what may appear to be a period of mental dullness or barrenness, ideas are gathering and coalescing, waiting for their time to emerge. Hilary Mantel, twice winner of the Man Booker prize, says: 'I used to think when I set out that doing the research was enough, but then the gaps would emerge that could only be filled by imagination. And imagination only comes when you privilege the subconscious, when you make delay and procrastination work for you.'[3]

Referring to what we would today term left-brain and right-brain activity, Dorothea Brande stresses the importance of developing both sides of your personality – almost training yourself as if you are two people. She refers to the unconscious (not subconscious) mind, and how writers need to be in touch with it, as well as acknowledging the more rational, orderly conscious mind. She uses the term 'genius' – not as the defining quality of a paragon, but as the transforming insights we all have in some degree.

Many writers are aware of these different ways of thinking – and, in fact, of not-thinking, of dreaming, or going into a state described by Brande as light hypnosis. If you haven't experienced this for yourself, it may sound pseudo-mystical. But look at our guest contributions and see how often they reveal that they don't feel fully in control of what they're writing; how ideas and connections slowly surface and reveal themselves. David Almond refers to the 'shock of amazement' as he realised what he was writing. Caragh O'Brien talks of the 'obsessed, fascinated pleasure of being lost in my own mind'. Mary Hoffman says that once you have found your 'muse', you must be alert and receptive to its visits. Anthony Browne's most successful ideas are 'those that come organically, and I have learned over the years that to consciously try and pluck an idea from nowhere is futile,' and for Frank Cottrell Boyce, 'If you just dive in, you get what you never imagined.' There is definitely something going on here which is beyond the control of the conscious mind; tuning into it is one of the greatest pleasures of writing.

We will, of course, be spending time with nuts and bolts, the writer's toolkit, in Part 3. But first, let's concentrate on what's really important: thinking of yourself as a writer, and learning to take care of the part of yourself that does the writing.

Nurturing your creativity

Picasso famously said, 'Every child is an artist. The problem is how to remain an artist when he grows up.'[4] Creativity is not an asset handed out to some lucky people and denied to others; we all have it. Julia Cameron, author of *The Artist's Way*, says that she does not so much teach creativity as help people to let themselves be creative. Tutoring residential courses, I've noticed a kind of collective sigh as people relax into the week's routines – in committing to the course, they have given themselves permission to devote the next few days to their writing. There is a lot of guilt attached to writing by people (that is, most people other than professional writers) who face the daily demands of work and family life – as if it's a self-indulgent squandering of time that should be spent on more dutiful activities. (If you become a published writer, this will soon change to feeling guilty when you're *not* writing.)

The Artist's Way is a course in unlocking creativity, starting with the writing of *Morning Pages* (Dorothea Brande also recommends this). Write three pages, by hand, as soon as you wake up, about anything that comes into your mind, and for no one's eyes but your own. The aim is to free yourself from what Cameron describes as 'our own internalised perfectionist, a nasty internal and eternal censor, who resides in our (left) brain and keeps up a constant stream of subversive remarks that are often described as the truth . . . "You call that writing? What a joke. You can't even punctuate. If you haven't done it by now you never will. You can't even spell. What makes you think you can be creative?" And on and on.'[5]

It's so easy to put yourself off writing altogether if you listen to this inner censor. Of course, you need a critical eye as well as the creative urge that makes you want to write – but that will come later. If you haven't written anything, you can't improve it. We will talk more about revising and improving your work in Part 3; but in the initial stages you need to remind yourself that no one need ever see what you've written, unless you choose to show them. It doesn't matter if it's flawed, clumsy, inadequate, trite. You are writing. Like practising yoga or dancing, the more you do it, the more natural it will seem.

Giving a shape and a discipline to your writing day may seem to be at odds with the remarks above about imaginative freedom, but even if you have to fit your writing around the demands of paid employment you are likely to find that some kind of routine works for you. Getting the best out of your brain means knowing when it works freely and when it's at its most sluggish, and shaping your day accordingly. If this means setting your alarm clock half an hour earlier in order to squeeze writing time into your schedule, so be it. (I used to do this while working full-time as an English teacher.) Or maybe you're a late-night person who can work into the early hours – in which case you should set aside half an hour, or even less than that, during which time you will write. Of course you can do more if you feel like it, but you should make this pledge and stick to it unless prevented by something drastic. Either way, you are training your brain, in effect, to be productive at certain times of day. Having a routine makes it easier.

Maybe you're lucky enough to have a room of your own for writing, in which case you can create a suitable ambiance – using noticeboards, music, favourite or relevant objects on your desk. Some writers make special compilations of music to suit the book they're working on.

Be careful what you read. Some writers avoid fiction of any kind while they're writing fiction themselves. Other writers' styles, especially, the rhythm of their prose, can be infectious (Cormac McCarthy and David Almond are two authors I would definitely avoid while writing; their distinctive rhythms are so seductive). Dorothea Brande recommends that not only should you avoid fiction, but also abstain from films, drama, poetry, theatre – anything that involves words. All your verbal energy and interest should go into your writing.

Beware of talking about the book you're writing (unless to a tutor or writing buddy – and even then, you may prefer to wait until the first draft is complete). Terence Blacker has written, 'Never, if you write fiction, talk about your work in progress . . . once the steam is let out of a story through talk, it can never be recovered. When a would-be author tells you every turn of the novel they are planning, you know they will never write it.'[6] The story you're writing should be a well-kept secret between you and yourself. Others may know something about it – possibly an editor, if the work has been commissioned – but make them wait. This is partly because talking about a story reduces it to plot, and any story reduced to plot will sound trite, even risible. Even as you talk about your plot you will hear the life draining out of it.

While you're writing, consider keeping the book world at arm's length. There are few things more daunting than being confronted with news of other authors' six-figure advances, glittering prizes, multiple-book deals, film adaptations, blanket publicity campaigns, festival appearances, translation into twenty-six languages, and the like. Unless you have an exceptionally generous and equable temperament, reading all this stuff – so readily available, every day of the year, on Facebook, Twitter, blogs and websites – can fill you with a deep sense of inadequacy and pointlessness, and the misleading notion that every writer other than yourself is being rewarded, feted and admired. Don't go there. Or, if you must, at least wait until you've written your quota for the day. You are writing what you're writing, and trying to make it as good as it can be. You're not trying to compete with every other author.

Nearly every writer experiences feelings of hopelessness from time to time: when the work isn't going well, when writing is drudgery, when you ask yourself whether the world really needs yet another book, when you'd rather tidy your sock drawer or confront your tax return than grapple with the stodgy mess that is your novel. In itself that's no bad thing: doubt is the necessary partner to ambition, and unshakable confidence suggests arrogance and inflexibility. But to keep your doubt in its place, it's best not to feed it by looking for distractions that will make you and your work feel worthless.

If you are gregarious, needing encouragement from others, there are numerous online message-boards and group blogs for writers, offering insights into writing methods and techniques. Every year, a scheme called NaNoWriMo (National Novel Writing Month) sees participants commit themselves to writing a 50,000-word novel during November. 'Make no mistake: You will be writing a lot of crap. And that's a good thing. By forcing yourself to write so intensely, you are giving yourself permission to make mistakes. To forgo the endless tweaking and editing and just create. To build without tearing down.'[7] There are forums and discussions, tips and strategies. For some people, it helps to know that they're not alone; this literary boot camp can turn your project from being vague and time-unlimited into something achievable.

If you're going to stick with writing, you need to find out how best to nurture your creative side, and – equally important – how to protect it from disillusionment and deflation.

Writing and 'flow'

Emotional Intelligence, a term now in common use, was a new concept when Daniel Goleman published his book of that name in the mid-nineties. His premise was that skills such as empathy, understanding and social awareness are at least as important as IQ, and better predictors of success in various areas of work and enterprise. Part of emotional intelligence – and happiness – is to experience 'flow'.

This idea will be easily recognisable to writers, musicians, academics, athletes, artists, craftspersons and others engaged in engrossing occupations. Most writers know the occasional (I stress occasional) feeling of emerging in a state of bewilderment or euphoria from page or screen, blinking in the light of the real world, unsure how much time has passed since they sat down. But what is interesting is the analysis of 'flow' and the conditions which create it. Goleman describes 'flow' as 'a state in which people become utterly absorbed in what they are doing, paying undivided attention to the task, their awareness merged with their actions. Indeed, it interrupts flow to reflect too much on what is happening – the very thought "I'm doing this wonderfully" can break the feeling of flow . . . And although people perform at their peak while in flow, they are unconcerned with how they are doing, with thoughts of success or failure – the sheer pleasure of the act itself is what motivates them.'[8]

Goleman draws on research by Mihaly Csikszentmilhalyi, a psychologist at the University of Chicago, who explains that 'People seem to concentrate best when the demands on them are a bit greater than usual, and they are able to give more than usual. If there is too little demand on them, people are bored. If there is too much for them to handle, they get anxious. Flow occurs in that delicate zone between boredom and anxiety.'[9]

We are lucky as writers in that we naturally inhabit that 'delicate zone'. We don't have repetitive days at the office. We never write the same book twice; we are always trying to push ourselves, to write a better story than we've written before. Csikszentmilhalyi tracked two hundred painters in their careers after art school, finding that 'it was those who in their student days had savored the sheer joy of painting itself who had become serious painters.

Those who had been motivated in art school by dreams of fame and wealth for the most part drifted away from art after graduating.'[10]

If you have experienced 'flow', you will want, even crave, that sense of joy and exhilaration again. It will arise from the new challenges you set yourself – from giving yourself permission, giving yourself time, letting your brain do what it does, and from simply getting stuck in.

> *You will never turn a bend in the road and find happiness waiting for you at the end of the journey as if it were a city . . . happiness is the road itself and you must walk it.*
> Michael de Larrabeiti [11]

Stephen King again: 'Writing isn't about making money, getting famous, getting dates, getting laid, or making friends. In the end, it's about enriching the lives of those who will read your work, and enriching your own life, as well. It's about getting up, getting well, and getting over. Getting happy, okay? Getting happy.'[12]

What works for us
Linda Newbery

- For each novel, I use my study noticeboard to build up a collage of words, pictures and colours, evoking the atmosphere and setting of the story. (Admittedly, this can become rather too absorbing: almost a project in its own right.)

- The most important part of my routine is to write first thing in the morning, early. This makes me feel positive, the story taking shape in my mind from the moment I wake up. I then return to it several times during the day.

- A story is a puzzle to be solved, in terms of how to work it out for myself and how to present it to the reader. I start off with questions but only some of the answers; new questions arise as I write.

- For that reason, I never make a complete plan – what I like is to start with good ingredients.

- Even at the planning stage, I like to dream a bit. For days, weeks – or months if I'm working on another project – I don't write anything down at all, but let the ingredients marinate in my mind. As soon as I start to write brief notes for myself, something is lost. I have to get it back through writing the story.

- I trust my brain to solve problems while I'm not looking, and usually while I'm not at my desk, but swimming, driving, gardening or half-asleep. When this starts to happen, I know the story is really starting to live. Until then, it's work.

- I *never* show my work to anyone until the first draft is finished.

Yvonne Coppard

- I start with a vague idea of plot and the central character(s).

- I work on the characters until I know them so well they are completely real to me.

- Although I plan carefully what I *think* is going to happen, I have learned always to be prepared to change along the way.

- Engaging in mindless physical activity really works for me: a long walk, swimming lengths, cleaning *all* the windows in one go – I do this especially when things are slow or I have become stuck at some point in the book, as it restores energy levels and lets my brain get on subconsciously, without interference.

- I write the first draft as quickly as possible; I circle anything that needs to be checked ('How do you spell . . . ?' 'Didn't I say this character died in Chapter Two?' etc.) and go back later to mop up all the fiddly things. In the first draft it's important not to stop the creative flow that Linda talked about earlier.

- After I think I've finished the final draft, I set it aside and get on with something else for a couple of weeks (or more, if no deadline is looming). Then I go back to read it again, with a fresh eye, before declaring it to be finished and celebrating.

- There is definitely a time to stop drafting and let your baby go out into the world; for me, if I have done all of the above and still only changed a comma here and a tiny detail there, it's time to let go.

Notes

1. Stephen King, *On Writing*, Hodder, London, 2012, p. 327.
2. See also Jenny Alexander's website http://jennyalexanderbooks.wordpress.com
3. Hilary Mantel, interviewed by Stuart Jeffries, *The Guardian*, 18 October 2012.
4.. Pablo Picasso, quoted in Laurence J. Peter, *Peter's Quotations: Ideas for Our Time*, Bantam Books, New York, 1977, p. 25.
5. Julia Cameron, *The Artist's Way*, Souvenir Press, London, 1994, p. 11.

6.. Terence Blacker, in *The Author* (journal of the Society of Authors), Summer 2012, p. 75.
7. See National Novel Writing Month website www.nanowrimo.org
8. Daniel Goleman, *Emotional Intelligence*, Bloomsbury, London, 1995, p. 91.
9. Ibid., p. 92.
10. Ibid., p. 93.
11. Michael de Larrabeiti, 'The Plane Tree and the Fountain', in *The Provençal Tales*, Pavilion Books, London, 1988.
12. Stephen King, op. cit., p. 326.

Part 2:
Tips and tales

Guest contributors

David Almond

In 2010 David Almond was presented with the Hans Christian Andersen Award, the most prestigious honour for a children's writer. His novels, which include *Skellig, Kit's Wilderness, Clay* **and** *My Name is Mina*, **have won the Carnegie Medal, the Whitbread Children's Book Award, and the Smarties Gold Award. He has recently published an adult novel,** *The True Tale of the Monster Billy Dean.*

I never planned to be a children's writer. I was an educated grown-up adult. I'd write books for educated grown-up adults. And so I did, for several years, with varying degrees of failure and success. Then a new story, *Skellig*, started telling itself in my head. As I wrote it down, I knew that it was the best thing I'd ever done, that it was the culmination of everything I'd done before. And I realised, with a shock of amazement, that it was a book for young people. It was a moment of liberation. I knew that I was growing up as a writer, that somehow I'd come home.

Children themselves are like stories. They're growing things, in a state of flux. They know they don't know everything yet, they still have a degree of wildness in them, and they welcome stories in many forms. So the children's book world is a place of great experimentation. Look at a children's book department – long books, short books, books filled with text, books with no text at all, marvellous blends of word and image, books in weird shapes and sizes, books that flash and books that squeak.

And children leap free of the categories we try to impose on form. Tell a child the story of *Hansel and Gretel* and pretty soon they'll be tiptoeing through the house as if it's a forest, whispering and shuddering as they approach the gingerbread house. So the story on the page moves fluently into drama, movement, song.

I love the fact that all children are writers themselves. They understand the difficulties in writing and they want to share its joys. They ask questions that get right to the heart of it all. Like the girl who fixed me with her eye and said, 'How do I turn all the mess in my head into straight lines on the page?' Or the boy who edged towards me and whispered, 'But what does it really feel like, when you're writing well?' Both questions came from people who were clearly engaged in the driven passionate process of making stories, of getting words to work.

I've sometimes been asked if, as a children's writer, I feel artistically confined? No. Before, I thought of myself as simply a prose writer. Now I also collaborate with illustrators and make picture books. I work in the theatre and help stories come to life on the stage. It still feels very new, and at the best of times it also feels weirdly ancient. Writing for children reminds us that yes, books are literature. They stand neatly on shelves alongside other books. But they're profoundly attached to the voice telling tales as darkness falls. Writing for children reminds us that the black mark on the white page is also a sound, a vision, a thing that moves in the mind and that can move the senses and the body. It reminds us of storytelling's roots. The writer is linked to the tellers of tales in ancient caves. Some try to say that writing for children is a minor marginal activity. Don't believe them. Writing for children sits right at the heart of our culture, and always will.

Malorie Blackman

London-based Malorie has written over fifty books and has won numerous awards, including the Smarties Silver and the Young Telegraph. She is perhaps best known for *Noughts and Crosses* (listed in the BBC Big Read Top 100) and *Pig-Heart Boy*, which won a BAFTA when adapted for TV. Malorie also writes for film, TV and theatre.

For the majority of writers, writing is a solitary, lonely profession. One of the prerequisites of being a writer is a love of one's own company. Yes, discussing ideas with friends, family and editors can be fun, illuminating and productive; when it comes to turning initial ideas into something publishable, well, that's another story altogether.

After many years in the computing industry, I decided I wanted to be a writer but didn't have a clue where to start. Someone suggested I try a writing workshop; I bit the bullet and applied for a Ways into Writing course, which was swiftly followed by a Women Writers workshop. At that stage, I wasn't quite sure of my preferred genre or target audience. A couple of short courses later, I finally found the one that made me think, 'Yes, this is it. This is where I belong.' It was a Writing for Children workshop.

It took me a couple of terms even to pluck up the courage to share my writing in a workshop. The encouragement and straight talking of Carol, my Ways into Writing tutor, eventually sorted out that dilemma. One day, when once again I had declined her offer to read my work out loud, Carol said, 'Malorie, d'you want to be a writer?'

'More than anything else in the world,' I replied.

'Then you need to s∗∗∗ or get off the pot,' came her reply.

That was some of the best advice I've ever had in my life; it made me find the courage to start reading my work out loud for others to criticise. More than that, it encouraged me to take risks with my writing, to be unafraid of the personal, the painful, the downright strange! That's the beauty of a good workshop – a truly supportive atmosphere where there is no feeling of censure or disapproval.

Elizabeth Hawkins, my wonderful Writing for Children workshop tutor, used an incredibly clever ploy. We had to bring in our work, typed or neatly written, for someone else in the workshop to read. Then, as the writer, you were not allowed to speak until everyone else had finished critiquing your work. It forced each of us to properly listen to what was being said. We couldn't leap in with cries of, 'You misunderstood what I meant!' As Elizabeth pointed out, our words had to stand on their own legs; we wouldn't be there to explain them to each of our readers.

I recommend workshops and writing classes to anyone serious about becoming a writer. Friends and family will tell you what they think you want to hear. Fellow writers in workshops will tell you the truth as they see it. Writing may be a solitary activity for most of us, but creative writing work-shops make it less so.

Valerie Bloom

Valerie Bloom was born in Jamaica but came to the UK in 1979. She won acclaim as a poet, and performs widely in Britain and the Caribbean. Her first novel, *Surprised by Joy*, was a poignant story about a young girl struggling to get to grips with the culture shock and shattered expectations of moving from Jamaica to England. Val is based in London but travels widely across the world.

My first book was a mistake. I should have done my research, read all the books on how to get published. Instead I looked up the address of a small publishing house in Ealing, bundled up my handful of poems and headed off to London. I strolled into the publisher's office without an appointment and thrust the papers under her nose saying, 'I've written these poems. Would you like to publish them?'

The only defence I have is that I was young and newly arrived from the Caribbean. I believe it was sheer astonishment that prompted her, after a brief perusal, to say yes.

No mention had been made of a deadline. So when, on the eve of my holiday in Scotland, I had a phone call asking for the manuscript, you can imagine the panic I was in. I sat up all night writing poems and mailed them the next morning before going off on holiday. That first book of poetry was written in Jamaican 'Patwa'. The publishers weren't Jamaican and editorial input was negligible. I'm pleased to say I no longer have a copy of that edition in my possession; I hope nobody else does either.

That experience taught me to edit meticulously. I have probably gone to the other extreme as I now find it difficult to send off a manuscript, always feeling it's not quite finished. Being a poet, I find it easy to prune my prose. (Though this could owe something to the hours I spend pruning my hundred or so bonsai.) The problem I have is knowing when to stop. With the poems, I have the handwritten drafts in my notebooks, so I can easily reinstate something which should not have been taken out. The novels are a bit more unwieldy to chop and change.

My poetry impacts on my prose in other ways too. For the most part, I take the same care in getting the right words in the right places as I would with a poem (which is another reason the books take so long to finish). It took several days to get the opening paragraphs of the last book right.

A novel, as in the case of my latest book, might start life as a poem. The snapshot of the native Caribbean people's encounter with Columbus, which was *Three Ships*, was enlarged to become *The Tribe*.

I have always been a bookworm. Give me a sniff of a book and I'm good for nothing until I've finished it. So when I'm writing, I have a policy that I will not look at another book until mine is finished. This proved to be a tad problematic when I was writing *The Tribe*. Being a historical novel, it required copious amounts of research, and sure enough many precious hours which should have been spent plotting, drafting and redrafting, were spent devouring information. It was four years before the novel was finished. Striking a balance between research and writing is something I have yet to master.

Probably my biggest drawback is procrastination. If I could conquer that, be less of a perfectionist, be less easily distracted with gardening, cooking . . . I bet I could be a great writer.

Tim Bowler

After studying Swedish at university and working in forestry, Tim Bowler became a full-time writer, known for gripping and atmospheric teenage novels. *River Boy* won the Carnegie Medal in 1998, and since then his titles have included *Starseeker*, *Frozen Fire* and *Buried Thunder*. Tim is currently writing an eight-book urban thriller series, *Blade*.

I've been writing since I was five. I live in a small Devon village with fields, moor, sea and solitude within easy reach. My workroom is an old stone outhouse ten minutes' walk from my home. It's sparse, cobwebby and eccentric but I like it. The only sound I hear when I'm working is birdsong and the occasional snort of horses in a nearby stable. It's a perfect place to write stories.

I'm passionate about stories. They're strange, magical things and they work upon us like alchemy. The best stories travel with us through life. They become part of our spiritual bloodstream. They move us, entertain us, shock us, transform us. I mostly write about teenagers. I find them fascinating. They're not children or adults but a species all their own with more voices in their heads than a choir. A teenager is a child falling asleep and an adult waking up and there are profound changes taking place within each individual. Writing about teenagers means empathising with those voices and those changes, and with the teenager you yourself once were.

Writing is a deeply personal activity. There's no one right way to do it, just the way that works for you. I always start from characters and settings. If these are strong enough, I find the plot reveals itself to me as I go along. Many writers devise a plot first but that doesn't work for me because I find the act of writing throws up my best ideas. I try to make sure something is happening on every page. I want readers to miss sleep, miss meals, miss everything to go on reading. The best books for me are the ones that cut deep. On the surface is a gripping narrative that keeps the reader hooked, but running underneath like a subterranean stream is the real story, the heart and essence and hidden meaning of the thing.

To students of writing I would say: just go for it, give it everything, take risks. You can't really fail with this. If the story doesn't work, start again. You don't have to show your writing to anybody until you're ready. When you think you've got nothing worth saying, write another page. If that's no good, write another. You've got self-doubts? Join the club (every writer I know is in it), and write another page, and then keep on. Sooner or later the good stuff will come. But you've got to put down the words. You can't edit what you haven't written. So be bold and get busy. You have stories inside you that no one else can tell.

Anthony Browne

Anthony Browne is internationally renowned as an author/illustrator, and has received, among his many honours, the Hans Christian Andersen Award and the Kate Greenaway Medal. He was Children's Laureate from 2009 to 2011, during which time he promoted the importance of books and illustration for children. Anthony's best-loved works include *Gorilla,* *Zoo* **and** *Voices in the Park.*

In the best picture books there is often a mysterious gap between the pictures and the words, a gap that is filled by the child's imagination. Sometimes the illustrations will tell a slightly different story from the words, by suggesting what the character is thinking or feeling. Sometimes they may even contradict the text. The way an illustrator places characters in a scene, uses colour, light and shade, free or controlled paint, can tell us far more of the story than the words.

For me a book always starts with a vague idea, or sometimes just an image. The most successful ideas are those that come organically, and I have learned over the years that to try consciously to pluck an idea from nowhere is futile. Often several fragments of an idea stay latent in my head for some time before they mature, gradually coming together to form something more coherent. Once cultivated, the idea is rarely in the form of a short story, or a poem, or even a series of pictures. The best way to describe it is like the idea for a film. The story is played out in my head in a series of frames and scenes, and rather than there being a divide between the words and the pictures, the two components are inseparable.

Throughout the formation of the idea my mind operates in much the same way as a film director. When children ask me how I make a picture book, I often tell them to imagine they have been lent a video camera and asked to film a day in their life. They could shoot every moment for an entire twenty-four hours. The film would cover every banal detail of their existence during this period. It would be interminable for everybody, except perhaps the most ardent of *Big Brother* fans. A film director reduces this material into a reasonable length, keeping the essentials and discarding the rest. To do this the filmmaker creates a storyboard: a series of rectangles each containing a rough drawing which represents a frame in the film. Its purpose is to provide a visual map of the entire movie at a very early stage of production. It is simply the first and most basic way for the director to express his idea.

I do exactly the same thing when I plan a picture book. I draw out a series of twenty-four rectangles (representing the twelve double-page spreads that form a typical picture book), and fill them with very rough drawings and scrawls of text. In my case the rectangles represent the pages in the book, but I'm still thinking in filmic terms at this stage. In my mind there is a kind of animation to the idea, and I view my storyboard almost exactly as a filmmaker would. Rather than the fixed pictures they will eventually become,

I view the boxes as scenes from the story, with a clear sense of progression through time.

Using this method, the pictures and the words are devised together. The relationship in a film between the visual images and the verbal dialogue is crucial to its success, and I consider this relationship to be of equal importance in a picture book.

Anne Cassidy

Often dubbed 'Ruth Rendell for Teenagers', Londoner Anne Cassidy is a prolific author of crime fiction for Young Adults. Her many books include the *East End Murder* series and the acclaimed *Looking for JJ*, which was awarded the Book Trust Teenage Prize and was shortlisted for both the Whitbread Children's Book Award and the Carnegie Medal.

A grisly murder, a mystery, a teenager involved. These are the features of many of my novels for young adults.

I was the main character in my first book for young adults, *Big Girls' Shoes*, in 1990. I was Brenda: too tall, awkward, hated my family and school. Almost everything about the book was autobiographical. It was set in the mid-sixties, when I was a teenager. The family in the book were mine. My mother, well dressed, a shampoo and set every Saturday; my father, a betting man, a blue collar worker, quick to lose his temper. My best friend, the boy I loved, the school I went to, were all in this novel. People told me to write about what I knew and I did.

But I also knew one very important thing. Every book, whether it's for teenagers or adults, needs a gripping story. So, in *Big Girls' Shoes*, the two teenagers overhear a murder during a phone call; it's this murder that propels the story of the book. I wove fiction into autobiography. In subsequent novels the fictional element got larger and the autobiographical strand lessened. But even in my most recent book, *Heart Burn*, I am the main character's mother, a fussy woman who is over-anxious about her children. The plot, though, is entirely fictional.

Crime fiction is perfect for teenagers. Each book has a mystery that has to be solved. Characters have to be quickly established and are drawn into some dangerous situations. The idea that evil has penetrated our lives, and that we must find the courage from somewhere to fight it and put the world back to rights, fulfils a human fantasy that dates back to a time long before crime fiction. In young-adult crime novels the teenager is the centre of the story; the character has to be real and recognisable to the reader. Everyone has their own faults and sorrows and desires. The crime that is committed throws all this into disarray and the teenager must do things alone: find information, deal with dangerous people, uncover a mystery.

In *The Dead House* Lauren was the victim of terrible violence that wiped out her mother and baby sister. She saw the killer. When she revisits the house in which it happened she begins to remember the face of a clown, a children's party entertainer who was around at the time of the murders. It shakes her conviction about what she saw and the whole mystery opens up again. Who killed her mother and sister? Lauren has to face up to the past and put the world to rights.

Writing crime fiction for teenagers means that you can also be topical. Many of the crimes I write about are based on things that I read in newspapers: knife crime, drugs, abductions, murder. *Looking for JJ* was triggered by newspaper stories of ten-year-old children killing other children.

These are dark subjects with big themes. Young adults are hungry for this kind of fiction.

B.R. Collins

B.R. (Bridget) Collins trained as an actress after leaving university, and attended Arvon courses on her way to being published. Her first novel, *The Traitor Game*, a tense juxtaposition of fantasy and reality, won the Branford Boase Award and was followed by a psychological thriller, *A Trick of the Dark*. Bridget's most recent publication is *The Broken Road*, set at the time of the Children's Crusades.

A little while ago I was on a bus with a group of schoolkids. I'd taken out my earphones – I love eavesdropping – and I found myself actually blushing. My goodness, their language. I had rarely heard such inventive, extreme, hilarious obscenity. I sat there, my cheeks burning, trying not to laugh, making mental notes. When it comes to strong language, thirteen- to fifteen-year-olds beat us adults hollow. They were teaching me words I didn't know.

But I couldn't put any of them in a book. Not if I wanted those kids to be the target audience.

Things are changing. In my first book, my characters did speak the way they would have done if they were real. There were a lot of f-words. Most of them weren't gratuitous. And the ones that were gratuitous weren't that gratuitous – honest . . . I loved my publisher for letting me keep them. It meant that the book didn't have to be coy or squeamish. It seemed to me that if I was going to be honest about the things that happened to my characters, it didn't make sense not to be honest about the way they spoke. All those f-words might make a few parents wince – but they were true.

Yes, things are changing.

My most recent book didn't have any f-words in it to start with. It did have the s-word, the p-word, an a-word, various b-words and the word 'turd', which I didn't even realise was swearing. As I was redrafting, my editor emailed me to ask if I'd consider taking them out.

Well, not really, I said. It's set in the Middle Ages, I said, it's really important to me that those earthy, physical things have a real presence in the book. The vulgarity has to be there to counterbalance the spirituality, you see. If I can't be coarse I can't be lyrical, either. And – well, those words aren't even very strong, are they?

Hmm, I see what you mean, she said. But would you mind taking them out anyway?

So I sighed, and took them out. Of course I did. It took me a long time and a certain amount of ingenuity. ('Urinate'? Too clinical. 'Have a pee'? Too childish. 'Make water'? Yeah, scraping the barrel there . . .) But I managed it. Out with the s-words and b-words, in with 'scumber' and 'cods' and 'cullions', not to mention 'skit' and 'skite', which mean exactly what they sound like. Thank God for the OED. I don't know what I would've done if the book hadn't been set in the Middle Ages.

The sad thing is, my publishers are probably right. Young-adult books may be read by teenagers, but apparently they're mainly bought by the gate-keepers – the librarians and teachers. Most of them probably don't mind the odd obscenity – but some do. And we want them to buy our books too. Swearing is a luxury we can't afford.

I really miss that a-word, though.

Frank Cottrell-Boyce

Born in Liverpool to an Irish Catholic family, Frank Cottrell-Boyce is an acclaimed screenwriter, novelist and actor as well as a children's author. His debut novel for children, *Millions*, was adapted from his screenplay of the same name, and won the 2004 Carnegie Medal. Frank was later commissioned to write the sequel to *Chitty Chitty Bang Bang*, released in October 2011 with the title, *Chitty Chitty Bang Bang Flies Again*. Working with Danny Boyle, Frank was the scriptwriter for the spectacular and highly praised opening ceremony for the London 2012 Olympic Games, in which children's books played a prominent part. That was a great year for Frank, as he was also awarded the Guardian Children's Fiction Prize for *The Unforgotten Coat*.

Lots of writers – include some of the greatest – say they need to know how it ends before they can start. I even heard Alan Garner once say he always knew the last sentence before he began. Psychologically of course it makes perfect sense to be able to visualise the finish line before you begin to race, to know the object of the quest before you set out on it. All I can say is that it didn't work for me. I know because I've tried. I spent the best part of a year trying to figure out the ending to one of my novels – shuffling bits of paper, doing pointless research, staring out of the window. It was my Year of Joyless Mooching. One day I just remembered that what I really liked doing was writing, not planning – sentences not diagrams. So I set off on the *Quest Without an Object*, began *The Race Without a Finishing Line*. And I've never looked back.

If you plan, you get what you plan for. If you just dive in, you get what you never imagined. In chess, if you start the game with a checkmate in mind, you might win. But if your opponent recognises what you're up to, she can stop you dead and leave you defenceless. If you just play the strongest opening, then the strongest middle, by the end you should find you have some choices and you can play the one you like the best. Because writing isn't chess, you can then go back and take out all the dead ends and make your beautiful ending look just as you knew it would all along.

Of course, to make this work you have to be full of hope and faith. So let me give you a message of hope.

People often ask writers about inspiration; you can tell by the way they ask that they see inspiration as the jumping-off point – the spark that ignites the engine. But often the very best ideas come right at the end of the process – after you've slogged your way through months of doubt and failure, after you've accumulated a pile of pages that are OK but . . . You've resigned yourself to the idea that this one didn't quite come off (but at least you tried). Just then, I hereby promise you, often and completely out of the blue a streak of lightning will hit you from a clear blue sky and illuminate some new pathway, some hidden secret spring inside your story. The water you've hauled up from the well will turn to wine. And you'll drink that wine and feel like singing.

Jennifer Donnelly

US author Jennifer Donnelly writes for both teenagers and adults, and is known for her powerful evocations of historical settings. Her Carnegie-winning *A Gathering Light* **was first published in the United States as** *A Northern Light,* **and was awarded many honours there. Recent publications include** *Revolution* **and** *Wild Rose,* **the final part of her Rose trilogy for adults. She lives in New York State.**

I write historical fiction and I was thrilled to be invited to contribute. I was thrilled because I love talking about my work, but to be totally truthful, I was a bit nervous, too. Because it's not every day you get asked to share your own personal insanity with strangers.

And for me, that's what writing historical fiction is. It's a kind of madness, an obsession with the past, a compulsive need to go back – back to the mess and the mistakes and the crimes in an attempt to do them over. To make them right. If only on paper.

For this obsession – and for many other things in my life – I blame my mother.

My mom was my first storyteller. She was the one who tucked me in every night and told me bedtime stories. Sounds sweet, doesn't it? Yeah, well . . . you don't know my mom. The woman was a freewheeling, no-holds-barred kind of storyteller who saw no need to borrow from amateurs like Mother Goose or Walt Disney, thank you. She had her own material and felt it to be more edifying to her offspring than any lessons Mickey Mouse and his colleagues might impart.

My mom is German and she was a child during the Second World War. She grew up in Bremen, a northern port town that was heavily bombed by the Allies. While all my little pals were settling down for the night with stories like *Cinderella* or *Sleeping Beauty*, I was getting a first-person narrative of life during the Third Reich.

One night she might describe how it felt to be eight years old, running for her life to an air-raid shelter. And what it was like to come out again and see that her house was gone. She might tell me about the neighborhood snot-nose, a boy who'd joined the Hitler Youth and who put on his uniform every time he got into trouble. Because when he had it on, he was property of the state and no one – not even his parents – could touch him. Or her friend Herbert, who had cerebral palsy and whose mother had to hide him when Nazi health inspectors came to town to keep him from being taken away. She might tell me how it felt to see the smashed windows of a Jewish shop, to ask where the shopkeeper had gone, and be given no answer.

Some might say that these stories of a war-torn life were not suitable fare for a child, and a few of them were pretty harrowing. I guess I should have been horrified, terrified, unable to sleep. But I wasn't. I was fascinated, sitting up in my bed, asking a million questions: 'Why? How? What happened next, Mom? What did you do?'

My mother's stories made history real for me. They taught me that history isn't only about führers and generals and battles and treaties. It's about us, the ordinary people. It's about my mother. Her friend Herbert. The rotten kid in the uniform. And the Jewish shopkeeper who never came back. It's about how the forces of our world work upon us, how they shape and define us, save us, and sometimes doom us.

The lessons I learned from my mother stayed with me. They made me a reader. They made me a history geek. They made me a lover of museums, archives, libraries, world heritage sites, old cities, fleamarkets, auction houses, ancient ruins, grand estates, cobbled lanes, crumbling towns, shipwrecks, attics full of dusty trunks and boxes, archaeological digs – any place where I can see, feel, and touch the past.

Most of all, my mother's stories made me a writer.

Vivian French

Viv's first job was with the Booktrust (then the National Book League); later she joined a travelling theatre company and began to write plays. She has since published more than two hundred books, including non-fiction, for young readers of all ages. Her talents as writer, performer and storyteller have taken her to countless festivals and other events. She has taught at Edinburgh College of Art, mentoring new writers and illustrators, and has been Writer in Residence at the Edinburgh Festival.

My first books were picture books. I'm basically lazy, and when the wonderful Diana Hendry suggested I had a stab at writing for children it seemed sensible to go for something short. It was while working on those that I had an idea for a collection of stories about a little girl called Zenobia, and Walker Books said fine . . . and I discovered I could manage all of three thousand words. Not long after that I was asked if I fancied writing a non-fiction book. This threw me into confusion; several people told me this could be a mistake, and I should stick to my 'brand'.

So – was I a picture-book writer? A short-story writer? Or a writer of non-fiction? I made a decision. I'd say yes to anything I was offered, just as long as I could find the time to generate my own ideas as well.

It's made for a fascinating writing life, although I've had to modify my response – I did turn down the offer to write a one-thousand-word prose poem about a dead seagull, even though they offered quite good money. And the more I've done, the more interesting things I get to do. Being known as a freewheeler has distinct advantages – you can never be sure what'll happen next, and I like that. An editor has (not once, but twice) rung up at four thirty on a Friday, and asked for a two-hundred-word story (preferably in rhyme) by Monday morning. And it's amazing what can be achieved after a hot bath, and a lot of coffee.

I've had requests for help with illustrators' ideas that just need a little TLC, and I've supplied a text for a picture book that already had twelve full-colour double-page spreads in place. I've woken up with an idea for a non-fiction book about earwigs (sadly, nobody else admires earwigs as much as I do) or horses (that one was a yes). The more usual commissions (early readers in 2,500 words) pop up regularly, but it's the oddball notions that are often best. Rewriting a text from a translation that doesn't match up with the illustrations? Huge fun, as well as a challenge.

And then there are the series. I wrote more than forty *Tiara Club* stories, and I did get slightly bug-eyed towards the end (that's as good a reason as any for avoiding sticking to just one genre), but there's still something very attractive about being able to write about characters you know and love. Gracie Gillypot, Prince Marcus and Gubble, from my *Tales from the Five Kingdoms*, are family. Queen Bluebell is my second self.

Sometimes children ask what kind of books I like writing best . . . and the answer is, I don't really know. I have a love–hate relationship with whatever I'm working on at the moment, but I'd hate to stop.

I think I might ask to be buried with my computer.

Adèle Geras

Adèle Geras has written extensively for readers of all ages. Her work ranges from picture books such as *My Ballet Dream* to adult titles including *Facing the Light* and *Made in Heaven*. As a children's writer she is best known for her teenage novels, including *Troy* (Highly Commended, Carnegie Medal), *Ithaka* and *Dido*, and for retellings such as *Sleeping Beauty* and *My First Ballet Stories*.

If your first published work is a commercial and critical success, then the pressure to continue writing the same kind of book is enormous. My very first story, *Tea at Mrs Manderby's*, was 2,500 words long and meant for newly fluent readers. It appeared with no fanfare whatsoever in 1976 and that meant that I was free to follow my own desires when it came to deciding what the next book would be. I found that I have a low boredom threshold. That's to say, I like writing different kinds of books and my target audience varies from babies to adults, taking in everyone else along the way. If I'm being a fat black cat in one book, and if my main character in that book is a ten-year-old, then it's fun, once that's out of the way, to become a retired ballet dancer looking back at her life and unfolding a story of family tensions and mysteries in a theatrical setting.

I often compare writing to acting. You have to 'become' your main view-point character. You have to find voices for the rest of the cast, too. It's exactly like having a big dressing-up box at your disposal and saying: 'Who shall I be today?' One of the questions I'm often asked is: 'How do you make sure that your story "fits", and is appropriate for, a certain age group?' My answer is: the age of your main characters will dictate the language and the concerns of that book. Six-year-olds, for instance, are not going to be interested in shenanigans in merchant banks, or law firms, nor will they fancy reading about bed-hopping in Hampstead or anywhere else. On the other hand, even the very youngest child is aware of human emotions: anger, jealousy, fear, rage, love and so forth. That's why fairy tales which were meant for an adult audience are so loved by young people even though they're often horrendously violent and distressing. They appeal to our most basic emotions.

Another reason, though maybe a frivolous one, for writing for more than one age group is this: younger children need shorter books and you can't be following one 150,000-word book with another for ever. Or I can't . . . it would wear me out. So it's very pleasant, when you've immersed yourself for over a year in a huge saga with a large cast, to turn to a short picture book consisting of lullabies for the very youngest children.

If I have any advice to give to someone starting out on a writing career, it's to read as much as you can. Read the books you wish you'd written. Read the books your intended audience adores. Try to diversify as much as you can, too, not only for the reasons I've given above but also because in today's uncertain publishing climate it's a good idea to have as many strings available as your personal bow can accommodate. Good luck.

Mary Hoffman

Mary has written over ninety books for children, including the best-selling *Stravaganza* series (six titles so far). An earlier novel, *Amazing Grace*, reached the *New York Times* Best Seller List, and Mary's writing has won numerous awards. She lives in Oxford but travels frequently to Italy, which has inspired much of her work. She has been nominated for the Astrid Lindgren Memorial Award and the Children's Laureateship, a top UK honour among writers for children.

The most frequent question writers are asked takes the form either of 'Where do you get your ideas from?' or 'What is your inspiration?' The odd thing is that I know many writers and none of them ever speaks in these terms. We take it for granted that there is a bottomless well of ideas for us to draw on; the difficult bit is assessing which will turn into books, and then of course the hard work, dedication and professionalism involved in that task.

But there is the concept of a writer's muse and I think I do actually have one. My muse is not an animal, real or mythical, nor yet is it a human source of inspiration. My muse is a country. It began as a youthful crush when I was fourteen and met my muse for the first time, matured into a full-blown love affair when I was twenty, and has been going strong for decades since.

Il Bel Paese (penalty points if your first thoughts were of cheese!) means 'the beautiful country' and is what Italians call Italy. In our family it is known as 'the leg-shaped country' (TLSC) and referred to a great deal because everyone knows how much I would like to have a place to live there. It's not an affordable reality, just a dream – but what a beautiful dream.

Italy was a place of great attraction for all educated and wealthy travellers in the nineteenth century, part of the Grand Tour. It was valued for its art, its music, its literature, the language, the charms of its many different landscapes, its climate and its cuisine and wine. All the things that charm me, in fact. I don't recall anyone ever saying they wanted to go to Italy for the ease of driving and parking, the bureaucracy, the carabinieri or the efficiency of its airport systems.

I find it impossible to be in the leg-shaped country and *not* have ideas for books.

My first ever published book was a long teenage novel called *White Magic* (published by Rex Collings in 1975), set in an imaginary place on the Adriatic coast. And my most recent novel at the time of writing, *David*, is firmly set in Florence, one of my favourite places.

How many books have been inspired by the leg-shaped country? I reckon ten for young adults, plus a novel for adults; that's more than ten per cent of my output so far. And there are signs that the percentage will rise in the coming years. So I reckon Italy counts as a muse, an inspiration and, at least for a tenth of my output, a place where ideas come from. But I didn't set out to find it. I don't think inspiration works like that. The important thing is always you, the writer, who must be receptive and alert to the muse's visits. Good luck finding yours!

Michael Morpurgo

Author of more than a hundred books, Michael was Children's Laureate from 2003 to 2005. One of his best-loved titles, *War Horse*, reached wide audiences as a stage play at London's National Theatre and as a film, directed by Stephen Spielberg. Michael's many awards include the Blue Peter Book of the Year, the Whitbread Children's Book Award, the Nestlé Smarties Book Prize, the California Young Reader Medal, the Red House Children's Book Award and (three times) the Prix Sorcières. With his wife, Clare, he set up Farms for City Children, a charity which enables urban children to experience country life and animal husbandry; there are now three working farms which have been visited by thousands of children.

A writer's ten commandments – and one for luck!

Suggestions may be a better word. Many of these I have not kept but know should be kept.

1. Read widely and often. It's how writers take exercise. Every book is a voyage of someone else's discovery. It is how you learn good and bad technique (useful to know both). It is how you explore the minds of other writers who have faced the blank page, stiffened their sinews, and done it. You can wonder at their achievement, at their mastery, and discover how it is done. Every book you read informs, builds confidence. With every book you read you are subconsciously finding your own voice. The more you read the more the music in words, the rhythm and cadence of a sentence becomes second nature. So read aloud sometimes – listen to literature, don't just read it.

2. Get the habit. Have a notebook handy, a writer's sketchbook – and jot down thoughts and ideas, memories, snatches of overheard conversations, moments of high drama, of quiet reflection. Frequency is important. The more you do it the less inhibited you become; the less you worry about words, the easier the flow comes. The habit takes the fear out of it. Writing becomes as natural a form of communication as speech. From these jottings will emerge the ideas for your stories and poems.

3. Live as full a life as possible, outside writing. Get out there, go places, meet people, experiment, take risks, move outside your comfort zone. Drink in the world around you, fill the well constantly, or else it will run dry. If that happens, then as a writer you are up a gumtree without a paddle – so to speak.

4. Take time, whacks of it, before you settle on the subject of the story you want to write. Read around it, dream around it, research around it, convince yourself you really want to spend months, possibly years of your life roaming around in this idea, developing it, loving it. Don't be in a hurry to decide. But once you've decided don't look back. Your story could turn to stone. And you could too.

5. Live in dreamtime for as long as it takes before you ever set pen to paper. Don't confront the blank page or screen till you've dreamed up the set design, till your players are walking live on your stage, strutting and fretting, till you can see them and hear them, till you know them intimately and the world they live in. You don't have to have decided where they will take you, what the denouement might be – remember that when it come as a surprise to you, it'll be a surprise to the reader too.

6. Be comfortable when you write. You will be tense, and excited and anxious. So arrange yourself so that you don't hurt yourself. Wrists, shoulders, neck, the lower back bear the brunt of writing. Don't hunch over. Don't stay sitting too long. Get up and walk about every half hour. If you dry up, don't sit over it. Go for a walk, put it out of your mind and come back fresh. Do what I do, what Robert Louis Stevenson did, write on your bed, pillows piled up behind you, relaxed, at ease with yourself. Then you can go to sleep easily too – a very useful writing technique I find.

7. Once you begin, finish it. Go through with it to the final full stop. Every abandoned manuscript is a knockback, a huge dent in a writer's confidence. And confidence is the key to a writer's morale. Writers' block is simply a lack of confidence engendered by a lack of sufficient dreamtime.

8. Mean every word you write. What we are asking of a reader is to suspend disbelief. Our technique as writers, our writing voice, can help here. But most important is that we have to believe in the story we're writing. We mustn't pretend, we must mean it. Mean it and they'll read as you meant it and they'll listen. Mean it and they'll be moved to laughter and tears.

9. Rewrite, cut – if in doubt, cut it out! Edit yourself before anyone else does. You are your own best editor. Which is not to say that we don't need a good editor, we absolutely do. But never send it off half done, not right, not truly imagined and thought through. Read it out loud to yourself – feel the rhythm, listen to the music. It's fun and the best fault-finder I know.

10. Forget all about getting published, being famous, being rich. Abandon those dreams if you have them. Excise all such aspirations and ambitions. This is a prerequisite to becoming a writer of truth and integrity – not sure if any other kind of writing is worth bothering about.

And one for luck:

11. Don't sit around waiting for a publisher's or an agent's response to your book. You've done it, done your best. Simply get on with the dreaming up your next one. If the reject letter comes, don't be downhearted. We've *all* been there. You pick yourself up, dust yourself down, and on you go . . .

Beverley Naidoo

Beverley Naidoo was brought up in apartheid South Africa. As a student she was detained for resistance activities, and sought exile in England, where she now lives. After receiving a PhD for research into white teen-age attitudes to literature and racism, Beverley began to write novels which explore themes of apartheid, social injustice and the struggle for independence. *The Other Side of Truth* **was awarded the Carnegie Medal.**

More than once, I've found the hardest part of writing a novel has been the ending. Reason: I've thrown my characters into such challenging, indeed traumatic, situations that it has been extremely difficult to conclude in a way that reflects an element of hope and yet is credible. I spend a lot of time thinking through my plot before I start writing. This is because with my second novel, *Chain of Fire* (sequel to *Journey to Jo'burg*), after six months immersed in research I just started writing. It was like setting off on a long-distance run in terrain that I thought I knew, but making up the route as I went along. However, my characters were in deep trouble before I realised that I was in deep trouble too about finding the ending! It got to nightmares before, one morning, I woke up with the solution. It was an experience that I didn't want to repeat, hence my doing a lot of thinking now about plot, upfront.

With my most recent novel *Burn My Heart*, set in 1950s Kenya, where things end pretty desperately for my two boys, I believe that the element of hope lies in the acknowledgement of the truth. For a while, I tried writing a first-person frame story in which we would see Mathew and Mugo as young men, giving space for possible reconciliation. But it just didn't seem to work well enough and felt too contrived. Nevertheless, I kept some words that had come to me when writing the frame and I used them as a frontpiece, suggesting the voice of an unseen narrator:

'How do I tell you this story? Do I tell you the truth, the whole truth, and nothing but the truth? Do I tell you my side or his? What if I had been born on his side and he on mine? We were both only children . . . '

I suspect it's the challenge of facing the unknown in novel writing that makes it so addictive.

Caragh O'Brien

Caragh O'Brien's debut novel *Birthmarked*, the first in a dystopian trilogy, was published in November 2011. *Prized* and *Promised* completed the sequence in 2012. Connecticut resident Caragh's work has already drawn much attention in the USA, being listed for the Amelia Bloomer, the Junior Library Guild, and the YALSA Best Fiction for Young Adults, among others.

When published writers said, 'Write for yourself,' I used to think they were withholding some hard-nosed secret of publishing and brushing me off with drivel for artsy, dreamy types who couldn't cut it. Yeah, yeah, I thought, but what's the truth? I can take it. I work hard. What's the key to getting over the threshold? As a new, driven writer, I was thinking about publishing as a competition I could win, and it took me decades to realise publishing was merely an ancillary bonus, a distraction at the edge of the real game.

I wrote *Birthmarked*, my debut young-adult novel, with zero expectation of getting it published. Here's what happened. I had become a high school English teacher and I loved my work. I had no time to write, but I did what I could on vacations and I had a fulfilling life, so I no longer cared about publishing. Then my husband and I went on a sabbatical with two of our children, and with the clarity that follows the recent loss of a parent, I decided to spend my free semester writing, just for myself and the pure, twisted fun of it.

I became completely seduced by Gaia's story. I woke up thinking about it. I considered plot twists in the shower. I dropped off the kids at school, came home, and wrote until I realised I was late to pick them up. If I became stumped, I took a walk in the hills, pondering, and came home to keep writing. Soon I had a complete draft of a fast-paced story unlike anything I'd read before, with a teen midwife, missing parents, a code, a divided society, and some serious creepiness. I started revising, and that was even more satisfying than the first-drafting. Writing was all I wanted to do, all the time, and I could, so I did.

I still didn't expect to sell my novel, but I knew any self-respecting writer tries to publish her work even if the chances of success are ludicrous. So I searched for an agent: four offered to represent me. The agent I chose received three offers for my novel: the best was from Roaring Brook Press, which signed me on for a trilogy. A year and a half later, I resigned from teaching to write full time.

Here's what I've learned: writing is what I want to do, all the time, eight or fourteen hours a day. Nothing else can give me the obsessed, fascinated pleasure of being lost in my own mind, as I am when I'm writing. No one can take it away, either. Publishing is never a guarantee – I may be looking for teaching work again some day – but the writing is what matters, and that is within my control. At last, I understand. Writing for yourself isn't whimsy. It isn't the secret to publishing. It's the only thing to do.

Mal Peet

Mal Peet's first novel, *Keeper*, won the Branford Boase Prize, and he went on to win the Carnegie Medal and the Guardian Children's Book Prize, with *Tamar* and *Exposure* respectively. His latest novel, *Life: An Unexploded Diagram*, is a powerful depiction of adolescent love, set against the background of the Cuban Missile Crisis. Mal has also written picture books with his wife, Elspeth Graham.

Tamar was an ambitious book – over-ambitious, perhaps. It was only my second novel, and it was as if, having written a neat little piano sonata (*Keeper*) I thought I was ready to tackle a full-blown symphony. I wasn't. The damn thing nearly drove me crazy; it was like trying to solve a Rubik Cube in four dimensions. I'd solve one narrative problem and thereby create another three.

If the musical analogy above seems pretentious I apologise; but it more or less accurately describes the way I work. I'm more interested in structure, shape, composition, than anything else; in the patterning of loud and soft, fast and slow, light and dark tonalities, major and minor keys. More jazz than classical, though. I start with a few riffs – bits I have in my head, bits I know how to write – and get them down first, trying not to worry how they might join up. I'm not much of a pre-planner; I enjoy the discoveries that improvisation (with luck) creates. They're often the best passages.

But *Tamar* took on a complexity that sometimes threatened to stop me in my tracks. Also, the book is, essentially, an historical novel and I was carrying a burden of research into wartime Holland. (Be wary of research. It's like a helpful passenger with the dangerous habit of trying to grab the wheel.) More than once I lost my way, and tried to draw flowcharts and suchlike that might help me back on track. They didn't. In the end I reverted to my haphazard 'method', switching back and forth between the story's two narrative strands as mood and inventiveness dictated.

The first draft of *Tamar* consisted of twenty-four separate computer files labelled A to X. I wrote down the order in which I thought they should run then asked my editor at Walker Books and Elspeth, my wife, to do likewise. Between us we wrangled out a sequence (a few files got cut altogether at this stage) and I shuffled and stitched them into the book's final form. (Cut-and-paste is God's gift, isn't it?) Then I began the redrafting, starting from page one.

Critics have been kind enough to say that the time and voice switches in *Tamar* are managed so as to seem 'natural'; if so, it's a naturalness that results from hard decision-making and fastidious rewriting.

I would never recommend my flying-by-the-seat-of-your-pants method to anyone else. (The colour drained from Marcus Sedgwick's face when I confessed it to him.) We all need to be our own bespoke tailors.

I like using more than one voice or more than one time-frame. It gives you more colours on your palette, more opportunities for harmonies and counterpoints, more problems to solve. And more opportunities to wind the reader up.

I've pretty much stopped worrying about who my readers might be. The boundary between teenage readers and adult readers is as arbitrary as the borders between African countries. I have a few 'rules', such as: no literary allusions that an averagely well-read teenager might not get; no presumptions about historical knowledge; lucidity is more important than linguistic pyrotechnics. Otherwise, I treat my readers as equals. The greatest vice is condescension; young readers can smell it a mile away.

Helena Pielichaty

Helena Pielichaty was born in Stockholm, Sweden but grew up in York-shire, where she still lives. Her offbeat, irrepressible humour is often in evidence but she nonetheless tackles some gritty topics, including bullying, disability and living with a mentally ill parent. Helena writes for young adults and also for younger readers, with whom her *After School Club* and *Football* series are particularly popular.

HOW TO MURDER YOUR DARLINGS

The scene is a computer screen in a writer's study somewhere in Notting-hamshire, England.

The new paragraph was beautiful. Every word had been chosen with care and every sentence polished to perfection. Satisfied, the writer saved the updated draft and logged off for lunch.

Down in files, the new paragraph peered up at the old one. 'Hello. How are you?' it asked, because not only was it beautiful, it was friendly too.

'Oh, well, you know . . . I've had a few scares but I'm hanging in there. That's as much as you can ask for, isn't it?' was the cautious response.

'I guess,' the new paragraph replied, before enquiring whether its apostrophes looked all right. 'One or two feel a bit misplaced to me,' it frowned.

'Oh, I wouldn't worry about things like that. She sorts all that out at the end.'

'Oh.'

'It's the snip you need to worry about.'

'The what?'

'When she edits, she snips you with the scissors. See? Up there on the icon bar, next to *Copy* and *Paste*. Twice she's used them on me, and it's not nice. It's not nice at all.'

'Oh, she won't use scissors on me,' the new paragraph said with confidence. 'I contain *wow* words and everything.'

The wise old paragraph said nothing.

A few hours later, the writer returned. She rebooted the chapter, read it through and deleted the entire page with one click. Three hundred and fifty-two words; the old paragraph and the new. Just like that.

'What happened?' the new paragraph cried out as it cascaded into the recycling bin.

The old page shrugged. 'The snip,' it sighed.

'What? But I was beautiful! I was perfect!'

'It doesn't matter. Even the most sparkling passages get edited. She deleted forty-eight thousand words, once.'

'What?'

'Uh-huh. That was when she was writing *Accidental Friends*. She'd worked on it for months but the plot wasn't hanging right and . . . well . . . you know.'

'Why did she keep writing, then? Why did she keep polishing? It's cruel, stringing us along then booting us out like this. Cruel and heartless. '

'Don't take it so personally; it's all part of the process. Something she has to go through. If she doesn't do it, her editor will and it's better coming from her, believe me. '

The new paragraph shivered. 'So that's it for us? The end?'

There was a pause. 'I've heard she sometimes changes her mind and puts certain phrases or passages back again.'

'Really?'

'Really.'

'Why didn't you say so?' new paragraph said, and settled down for the night.

Postscript   Sadly, neither the new paragraph nor the old were rescued from the recycling bin this time. What the writer knew from experience was that when you write for children, pace is everything.

Celia Rees

Celia Rees is the author of seventeen books for young adults, including the award-winning *Witch Child* and the celebrated *Pirates!* She tackles very dark, sometimes supernatural themes and in recent times has been highly praised for her well-researched historical settings and intriguing titles, including *The Cunning Man*, *The Vanished*, and *Blood Sinister*. Celia lives in Leamington Spa, not far from William Shakespeare's birthplace.

Writing about then but making it relevant to now: that is the challenge facing anyone who wants to write historical fiction for children and teenagers. Although it has become a popular genre, getting the balance right is a delicate task. Too much detail will make the tale stodgy and stale, an instant reader turn-off. But it is equally wrong to treat the past as some kind of theme park, as a convenient setting for an essentially modern romance or knockabout adventure. When I'm writing historical fiction, I always begin with an idea and a character. They decide the historical period. After I've had that first idea, then this is the path I follow. It works for me. It might work for you, too.

- Planning is the first step. Make an initial plan to explore whether the story is possible. What is going to happen? What do you need to know? Subsequent plans will see where the research is taking you – what else do you need to know?

- Make a timeline – what is happening during the period? What is happening to your characters? Decide how the story will be written – voice, tone and style – then stick to it.

- Your research should find out if the idea is possible and make you familiar with the period. Hunt for 'nuggets' – bits of information which will make the whole thing come alive in the reader's mind. Don't over-research. You are a novelist, not a historian. You don't have to know everything, just enough to get started. The writing is the hard part; fill in the rest as you go along.

- Don't try to put in everything. Research is for *you*, not the reader. Balance what the reader needs to know with what the characters would be thinking and feeling. If the reader needs to know something that the character would take for granted, find ways of including it without unnecessary exposition.

- Don't spend the whole time in the library – visit locations. Even in modern cities, bits of the past remain. Visit houses, 'living museums', museums and art galleries to give you a sense of place, of people's lives. Get in touch with the time through music, ballads, writing, fiction, plays, poetry and paintings created by real people living at the time. Keep a visual record –

take photographs, collect postcards. Keep a scrapbook, collect stuff – do anything to keep the magic alive! Thinking, planning, collecting and visiting places are *not* a waste of time: they are all vital parts of the creative process.

- Once you think that you know enough, give yourself time to mull things over. Allow your story to settle into the research. And always remember: this is fiction. You have to work within the constraints of historical fact but the rest is imagination.

Meg Rosoff

Meg Rosoff was born in Massachusetts but now lives in London. Her first novel, *How I Live Now*, made an immediate impact, winning the Branford Boase Award and the Guardian Children's Fiction Prize, and the Michael L. Printz Award in the United States. Since then she has published *Just in Case*, *What I Was*, *The Bride's Farewell* and *There is no Dog*, as well as three picture books.

You'd think it gets easier to write a book after the first two or three have been published, wouldn't you? Well, it doesn't. Ask any writer – each book throws up a whole new set of problems and headaches and makes you feel as if you've never written anything remotely sensible or insightful in your life.

Sad, but true.

I've published five full-length novels, some short stories, a novella and some picture books, and nearly all of them have been hell to write in one way or another. I console myself with the thought that if writing were easier, everyone would want to do it. After all, it's one of the few jobs you can do without getting out of bed or wearing tights.

The thing I find hardest is plot. Any story arc I manage to squeeze out of my walnut-sized brain is always an emotional arc – protagonist starts off selfish and sad and ends up altruistic and happy-ish, or at least a bit wiser. But as to *how* that happens – to be honest, I don't really care all that much. This is when I need a team of James Patterson-style clone-assistants or James Frey's writing factory drones. 'Fill in the story,' I'd command imperiously, and then go back to sleep.

But they probably wouldn't do it right. Which would make me cranky. And I wouldn't be satisfied with the result. So I'd have to go back and think about it some more, tear my hair out, phone my agent and sound mournful, tell my husband I've lost my touch and we're going to starve, phone up all my writer friends and ask if they have any plots they're not using right now, and eventually, drag some miserable bit of story kicking and screaming into the world, slap it onto the pre-existent emotional arc and pray it works.

A fair amount of cutting, pasting, patching, invisible weaving, and airbrushing comes next, and at the end of months of agonising misery, *voilà*! A book crawls and scrapes and limps its way into the light.

'Wow,' says the sweet guy interviewing me for a literary festival some months later. 'You make it look so easy.'

And I deck him.

Marcus Sedgwick

Marcus Sedgwick won the Branford Boase prize for his first novel, *Floodland*, and the Booktrust Teenage Prize for *My Swordhand is Singing*; he has also been shortlisted four times for the Carnegie Medal. Recent titles for young adults include *White Crow* and *Midwinterblood*. Marcus has spent three years as Writer in Residence at Bath Spa University.

I've been very lucky in my career to date to have had just one editor, and one of the very best, at that. But even early on in our relationship (and a good working relationship is just what you should be looking for) I realised the importance of three things: first, trust; second, respect; and third, honesty.

You are not the best judge of your work. That is a fact, but if you are convinced that you are, at least know that no one else is going to share that opinion. How many famous authors can you name whose books have got longer and, frankly, worse as they became more successful? Have they started believing they no longer need an editor?

You will always need an editor. Therefore, it is absolutely vital that you develop a strong relationship with yours. You need to trust their professional opinion. You cannot be the best reader of your own work. They can be, so let them do their job!

Secondly, linked to that, is the question of respect. If they tell you that that scene with the crocodile pit just isn't convincing, respect that opinion, even if you do not agree with it. They're not saying it to be difficult, they're saying it because they think your book will be better without it. Fight your case if you feel strongly, but fight with doubt in your mind. You might be wrong, they might be right. In my experience, they usually are, but that doesn't mean there aren't times when you need to stick up for something that's important.

Thirdly, be honest. Be honest with yourself, be honest with them. Only if you do this can you establish between you what you're trying to do with this book of yours, and why. If you're honest, your editor can then, hopefully, bring the best out of it, even if that means challenging what you're doing at times.

Of course, all these three things should cut both ways, and a good editor will trust you, respect you and be honest with you too. You are, or you should be, at least, working towards a common goal – the very best book you can write at that moment.

Finally, have fun! Be nice to your editor. Remember their birthday, ask after the children. Remember it's not all about you – you're working on this together, you have different skills to bring to the table, and if you treat this relationship like any other, and know that it's as much about what you do as what they do, you should have the makings of a very fruitful partnership.

Andy Stanton

Fellow author Jeremy Strong once said of Andy Stanton that he is 'far too clever and funny and should be locked away in a very dark place that nobody can find'. A worthy winner of the inaugural Roald Dahl Funny Prize among others, Andy specialises in off-the-wall humour for younger readers, notably the *Mr Gum* series which is set in the fictitious town of Lamonic Bibber.

Funny books for kids sometimes get a bad press. They're 'not educational'. They're 'silly'. They're 'something-else-disparaging-in-quotation-marks'. Well, OK. But as a writer of funny kids' books myself, I'm not going to take that lying down. I mean, what is wrong with making children laugh? You don't hear these criticisms levelled at funny books for *adults*, do you? No, when it comes to *proper books for grown-ups*, being funny is all right. It's all 'comic tour de force' this, and 'hilarious, yet ultimately moving' that. People seem to understand that 'funny' is just another tool at the writer's disposal and that it can co-exist alongside thoughtful reflection, or genuine emotion, or whatever. Yet these same people look at a funny children's book and dismiss it outright, which is nonsense. And not the good man-with-two-pounds-of-carrots-up-his-nose type of nonsense, but the narrow-minded-failure-of-the-imagination type of nonsense.

It's funny, and therefore it has nothing else to offer – that seems to be the thinking. But in fact, writing a funny story for children (or anyone) is a pretty serious business. Any tale which is merely a collection of jokes will become tiresome and very quickly outstay its welcome. So you have to work overtime to build your jokes into the narrative, while ensuring that all the other elements of a good story – character, plot, pacing, etc. – are adhered to. Because the funny is a volatile beast, like a skittish racehorse or a squirrel with ADHD, and it requires careful handling. Otherwise – *ka-boom!* – it will take over completely and dance around for pages on end and make a spectacle of itself and wee off the balcony of a Spanish hotel just to get a laugh, like I did when I was eight or nine years old and it landed on another guest's head and the manager threatened to kick me and my entire family out and – but where were we? Oh, yes. You have to be extremely careful not to let the funny run the whole show, that's all.

So you struggle and you toil and you rewrite and you take out and you put in and you nip and you tuck and you craft and you slave away with exactly as much care as any other writer worth their salt, until your book is a thing of beauty and charm and taste. And there it is, sitting on the shelf in one of those things you used to see tons of on the high street but there's hardly any now, what are they called again? Oh, yes – bookshops. And then someone walks by – possibly a very clever, erudite someone – and they say, 'Hmmph, it's just a funny book. Well, there's nothing to be gained from that; *my* children read Philip Pullman.' And you say, 'No, no, you don't understand. It's not *just* a funny book, I mean, there are all these great characters with real emotions and actually there's all these themes running through it and . . .'

But they've already moved on and are busy trying to remember which of the *Northern Lights* trilogy little Lucy or Jack hasn't read yet. And that's fine, isn't it? I mean, I love Philip Pullman and I even stood near him at a party once. But really, what a shame to throw the baby out just because the bathwater's a bit peculiar-looking, like it might have been coloured in by Dr Seuss. What a shame your children will never get to meet Horrid Henry, or William Brown or Pippi Longstocking. What a shame to miss out on all that fun.

Part 3:
Write on: writing workshop

Writing workshop

Ideas

You must write for children in the same way as you do for adults, only better.[1]

Yvonne   It's one of the most frequently asked questions: where do your ideas come from? The questioner often expects a tale of sudden flashes of inspiration, or waking in the middle of the night and scrambling out of bed. Most of the time, it isn't like that at all. Like many writers I know, I have ideas drifting around in my head all the time, *all the time*. It can drive me crazy, like having the radio tuned to a channel you'd rather not listen to, but you can't find the volume or power controls. No, the problem for me is not *having* ideas, but *using* them: identifying which ones will fly, which ones are going to fizzle out; choosing the right idea for the moment. And accepting that I won't get to them all before I die, because there will not be time. Each book has its own unique moment when the idea takes off and you can really see a story starting to happen, but even the inspirational out-of-the-blue ideas have to be coaxed, nurtured and disciplined with patience and determination.

Cindy Jefferies, author of the *Fame School* series which ran to more than 20 books, says she had 'the germ of the idea' after watching *Fame Academy*.[2] But the idea was followed by 'over a year of hard slog, trying to get the format right . . . I did a lot of research, talking to youngsters who were involved in music at boarding school and a state school, and going to recording studios to meet the professionals, and see how they behaved.'

Contrast this with Linda Strachan's entirely different experience when writing *Dead Boy Talking*:

> . . . a completely random idea. I had an image in my head of a boy lying on his own who has just been stabbed and is thinking, 'In twenty-five minutes I will be dead.' That was all I had and it became the first line of a book. I only discovered what the story was as I wrote it.

Occasionally – very occasionally – a story is delivered, complete. For Rosalie Warren, everyday imaginary conversations with her mother who had died ('Nothing weird, just me making it up . . . I knew exactly what my mother would say') connected with a long-standing fascination with the communication between twins:

> The idea came to me in a flash – suppose a bereaved twin believed her lost sister was speaking to her, was somehow present inside her head? What if the 'haunting' twin got really angry . . . and it became a battle of ownership of Anna's body, for her sanity and survival?

The result was *Coping with Chloe*, a poignant novel about self-image and coping with loss.

There are so many ways to find a story. The time to gather ideas is when you *don't* need them, not when you do. The notebook and the pen are the most essential pieces of equipment a writer can have. I still prefer to write down my ideas longhand, but I guess many emerging new writers will be using technological alternatives much more effectively. I have several notebooks on the go at any one time. The sturdy, hardcover one is built to survive being stuffed into a suitcase or backpack; a small one fits into a jeans pocket or handbag; the ring-bound reporter's notebook is for rough notes 'on the go'. To leave home without a notebook and a pen or pencil would be as unthinkable as leaving the baby behind. In my notebooks are the collections of people, places, random ideas and observations that will become my source books, when I need them, for characters, plots and settings. Some of the pages are filled simply with names and nationalities: Mushtaba Tabatabai from Iran; Betty Puffpaff from Texas; Ejimare and Ozodike Uzoanya from Nigeria; Sophie Sunshine and Sebastian Ponsonby-Smythe from London. These are all real people; I collect them because they, or their owners, are triggers for memories and observations that will be useful, one day.

My notebooks also record snatches of overheard conversation ('So I *gave* him the wrong medicine, Ethel'); words or phrases that will make great titles (what the book will be about, I have no idea); observations and camera-phone pictures of people, landscapes, buildings, events. Real people living in the real world are endlessly fascinating because however boring your life may seem, you are always on the edge of the unknown. At any moment, something – good or bad – can happen that will turn everything upside down.

'What if . . . ?' is the place where ideas and inspiration are born. What if you arrived at your workplace/school/doorstep on an ordinary day to find the police waiting for you, because you are the chief suspect in a crime? What crime, where? What if the evidence against you is overwhelming? What if you know you're innocent, but can't prove it? Why is the evidence over-whelming – what if someone who hates you has planted the evidence? Who would do that? Why? 'What if': it's the match for the blue touch-paper, the stock that simmers your ingredients together.

Don't wait for inspiration: it ain't gonna come on your command. More often, you have to dig for it. Fantasy writer Susan Price won the *Guardian* Fiction Prize for *The Sterkarm Handshake* in 1998, and the novel went on to be one of the Carnegie finalists. The process she describes – frustrating, rather than instant – is a good example of the slow, tortuous birth of a cracking good book:

> *My interest was aroused by reivers[3] after a trip to the Border Country; I wanted to write about them but wasn't interested in writing a historical novel; there was a period of sulking and mulling over how to write an unhistorical story about historical characters; then reading an article about the 'science' of time machines led to an idea about a company seeking to exploit mineral resources from the past – going back to the time of the reivers; still not there; I thought about the mix of modern and historical characters; still, not happy; I wondered what the reivers would make of the modern characters, and decided the reivers would see the moderns as elves. Light-bulb moment! I knew this book would be written.*

Is that a bolt from the blue, or the culmination of much hard graft and subconscious brain activity? Who knows? Who cares? The story is on its way, and that is enough. Frank Cottrell-Boyce's contribution in Part 2 sums it up beautifully: 'The water that you've hauled up from the well will turn to wine. And you'll drink that wine and feel like singing.'

Linda   That perennial question 'Where do you get your ideas from?' often arises, it seems to me, from a misunderstanding about how stories are made. Many people, especially those who are not writers, imagine that a story arrives fully formed in an author's head as a gift from a kindly muse, or that story ideas are somehow different from the other contents of our brains, and come labelled as such. Several times, on school visits, I've been asked, 'Once you've thought of a story, doesn't it get boring just writing it down?' It's a question I could spend some time unpacking, but my usual response is to query that sneaky little word *just*. There's no *just* writing it down. You haven't got a drawing or a painting until you've made the marks on paper, and you haven't got a story until you've written it. And an idea is not a plot; it's the element that sets one off.

Unless you've got ideas for stories, it's unlikely that you'll have read this far. Of all aspects of writing it's the one that no one can really help you with unless you see possibilities for yourself, finding them exciting and intriguing. If that doesn't sound like you, perhaps you'd better find something else to do with your time. If it *is* you, then you've already got an inexhaustible supply of story potential to work with.

Ideas that start off stories don't have to be sensational, fully formed or even particularly unusual. The trick is to hang on to whatever it is that strikes you as offering potential – a place, an interesting situation, a difficulty, a fear – and build on it. This is how stories grow.

Several of my own books (*The Shell House*, *The Sandfather*) have grown from interesting places, real or imaginary: a semi-ruined house, a seaside resort out of season. Gradually I start to think about a character who might live there, or go there, and to gather ingredients for the story. Less frequently, it's the title that occurs to me first (*Catcall*, for instance) and the rest grows from that.

You can make a story out of almost anything by starting with one basic premise, asking yourself questions and telling yourself the answers. As you do this, new questions occur, and new possibilities.

Yvonne's tip is not to wait for inspiration – it won't come on demand. Although I agree with this, my view is that sometimes you *need* to wait; things sort themselves out in that very satisfying right-brained way while you're not looking. Maybe you've got one good ingredient, but feel that your story needs another before it can take off. And that second ingredient is often there already, somewhere in your mind: a memory, an observation, a piece of knowledge, a situation. The trick is, I think, to do the preparation, and to get the thinking started: a sort of revving-up, then a period of idling. The times when you think you're doing nothing can turn out to be the most productive – even before you start.

TOP TIPS

Linda *Don't expect to come up with a complete story idea all in one go. Give it time to develop, time to seem real in your mind and full of exciting possibilities, before you commit yourself to starting. Some ideas that seem brilliant in that first sparking may seem less attractive once they've settled; give time for better ideas to present themselves.*

Yvonne *Try to write something every day. Writing is like playing a musical instrument; a little bit of practice every day is how you become an expert. It doesn't have to be an epic work of fiction. Use your emails, Facebook and Twitter posts, texts, notes and letters (if anyone still writes those) to practise clarity of idea, development of theme, nailing the exact image. If you're moved to write a letter of complaint to your fuel or mobile phone provider, try to get your point across in a way that will grip the poor Customer Service representative, maybe even make her laugh. Mike Berry got a popular, very entertaining book just from baiting scammers,[4] a hobby that developed into a website with ten thousand-plus hits daily before publishing his scam-baiter letters in book form, to great acclaim.[5]*

This may appear to have nothing to do with writing the best-selling children's classic, but writing is about the mastery of words and ideas, and you should take the opportunity to hone your skills wherever it presents itself.

Linda Starting with something as ordinary as a boy setting off for school in the morning, think about these questions and see if you feel a story unfolding:

- The boy is anxious about something in the day ahead. What is it?

- His day didn't get off to a very good start. What happened?

- How old is the boy? What's his name? Who does he live with?

- Was everything at home quite as usual, or was something different? Was someone else staying? If so, who?

- How does the boy get to school (on foot, by bike, by bus?) Does he usually go alone, or with a friend?

- On his way today, does he meet someone, or see something unexpected?

- Does the boy's anxiety about his school day have something to do with the home situation, or is it quite separate?

- Who is his best ally at school?

- Who is the person at school (child or adult) the boy would least like to meet? . . . .

And so on, each answer leading to more questions.

Yvonne Next time you make a longish journey by public transport, or are sitting in a café, pick out one or two people you can observe without being noticed.

(It's very important not to do this obtrusively, and not to 'stalk' or stare at people!) A quick glance with a practised eye can tell you a lot about physical appearance. Take note also of the clothes, the shoes, the luggage or shopping; the way the person moves (graceful, awkward, limping, straight or stooped, etc.) and their mood (anxiously fidgeting, half-asleep, smiling and relaxed, frustrated and angry).

Move on from physical observation to the 'what if?' question. Where is this person going? Are they happy to be going there, or filled with dread? Why? What if something happened during their journey to make it impossible to reach their destination – what would be the consequences?

Your notes may never become a story, your person may never become a character. But I do believe that observation is where the best ideas come from – remember Isaac Newton and the apple?

Making a start – finding the place and time

Yvonne It can be a bit scary, coming out as a writer. Particularly if you have not had anything published yet. The gruesome little gremlin creeps on to your shoulder and starts to whisper in your ear:

You, a writer? What makes you think anyone will want to read anything you've written? Get a grip . . .

Therefore, I think the starting place is a careful, honest look at what, exactly, motivates you. Let's take for granted that you have talent, and you are keen to write a good story. How long have you been writing, and what do you get from it? How important is it to see your work published? What draws you to writing for children rather than adults? How do you feel when you are writing something, and what happens afterwards? Do you destroy it, keep it, or share it? How difficult is it for you to show your work to people? What do you hope writing will give you – will it all be pointless if you don't find fame and fortune?

That last one could be the killer question. If you see being a writer of children's fiction primarily as a route to wealth or celebrity, you're living a fantasy. Most writers do not make a sustainable living from writing alone; they struggle, and may never stop struggling. They are not in it for the money, and success, when it comes, is all the sweeter for being, usually, totally unexpected and frankly quite random. Why this book? Why now? You may never know. And you may never see success again.

If you're full of self-doubt about your ability to make it, but simply have to do it anyway, you're not alone. Being published gives you an enormous boost (however pathetic you believe your work to be, *someone* liked it enough to represent/publish/buy it) but that lack of confidence is a common theme even among well-known, award-winning writers. However good it gets, you are haunted by the knowledge that it could all disappear in the blink of an eye. What if you never come up with another decent story idea? What if people are disappointed that this book isn't as good as the last? What if it bombs so badly that the publisher drops you? And most common of all among the writers I know – what if someone finds out you're a fraud, who's bluffed your way in by replacing talent with bare-faced cheek?

But these doubts don't stop professional writers and they shouldn't stop you. The only way you will find out whether you can write a book that children will want to read is to give it a try. *I gave it my best shot* has to be a better epitaph than, *I always wondered if I could have done it.*

Enough of the rallying cry – how, practically, do you begin? One good opening strategy is to stake your claim. Fix a time that's *your* time and a place that's *your* place. A study of your own is a luxury most people don't have, but maybe the kitchen table is yours between certain hours; maybe you can shut the bedroom door and bag the family laptop; maybe flexitime at work gives you the luxury of saving up for a short working day and a long writing spell a couple of times a week; maybe the library or the café on the corner stays open late and you can hole up there with a laptop or notebook and pen for a while. It's always possible to carve a bit of time and a bit of space if you're determined, though you may run short of sleep and/or social life. Reading children's literature voraciously is also a basic essential, which we covered in Part 1.

TOP TIPS

Yvonne *It will help to have a box, or a cupboard, or a shelf, that keeps everything you need together. Just setting out the pen and paper, or logging on to the computer with your notebook, plot plan and assorted bits and pieces at hand, will signal that this is writing time. Your time. Those around you will get the hang of it in the end, and will notice how much happier you are when you make regular visits to your inner, creative world.*

Linda *Yvonne is absolutely right. This will make you feel purposeful, and feeling purposeful gets you a long way towards starting and completing something. Establish some sort of discipline for yourself, whether it's simply 'Write something every day', or more specific, such as 'Write for an hour between eight and nine in the evening' or 'Write a thousand words every day'. Make your writing routine part of daily life, and you'll feel like a writer.*

Yvonne Writers are often advised to write from what they know, and it's a good start. Think about your own life so far, particularly your childhood, with a view to 'mining' those memories for ideas. Make a note of any you come up with that might spark a story. Draw on your own memories of childhood and adult life: think about people, places, events, passions, hobbies, fears, your own and other cultures.

All of these experiences, happy or sad, have shaped who you are today and may give you a great story or two. If not, reliving those memories will be a good writer's warm-up for the main story that will hopefully come along later. That's one of the things I love about writing – nothing that happens to you, good or bad, is ever wasted!

Linda Give yourself a goal. Not just I'll do some writing, but, for instance, *'I will finish a twenty-thousand word chapter story for seven-to-nine-year-olds within six months.'*

Writing a whole book, especially if it's a longer one, can seem so monumental a task that it can be daunting even to start. Set yourself a target that you'll reasonably be able to achieve, and one that can fit around the demands of your working and domestic life.

Planning and research

Yvonne Like Linda, when I am making a start on a new book it is most often the characters who come first. This is not the same for all writers. Sometimes the plot is the thing, and the characters are developed in order to further the flow of the story. But whether it's the character or the plot that has initiated the writing, there has to be a setting for the characters to interact with, a backdrop for their story: a place, a time, a belief that what is happening, and the people or creatures to whom it is happening, are *real*. So you need to spend some time thinking about where and when your action is going to take place, and getting the details right.

I have already referred to the old writers' axiom that you should always write from what you know. These days, we can travel the world almost as easily as we can travel to the next town or village; we can search the internet for obscure details about the length of a surgeon's knife in the seventeenth century or what is happening in a solar system thousands of light years away. You may not need direct personal experience any more, but you still need the attention to detail that will give your story life.

I rarely step outside the real world for my story ideas, but even in a fantasy world there has to be a sense that everything logically hangs together, that this world *could* be real. This is where planning and research come in. You might be tempted to dive into the story and sort out minor, troublesome details later, but you are unlikely to get your best work without putting in the time before you start.

Cliff McNish, award-winning author of *Breathe* and *The Doomspell Trilogy*, is no stranger to the creation of other worlds. I asked him how he sets about ensuring that the 'other' worlds he creates are credible settings for his stories:

> True fantasy writers make their alternative worlds believable by spending a lot of time just thinking in detail about every aspect of that world – what it looks like, how people behave, what the weather is like, what the stars look like, everything. They do that before they start writing the story . . . .it will not only improve your story enormously, but it will deepen your commitment to it.

The principles – plan, do the research, sweat the details – are much the same for 'real-world' as for fantasy stories. There's no quick fix, but the planning and research stage can be very satisfying. Some writers will even say it's the best bit of writing the book: they get so absorbed in the historical research or the mind game of creating a fantastical kingdom that they are reluctant to leave the research phase and write the story. The trick is in knowing when you've done enough – I reckon if the world (or household, or office, or school, or sports arena or . . . whatever) you have created feels genuinely real to you, it's going to feel real to your reader. But if you have a trusted 'writing buddy', or an enthusiastic supporter, use them as a sounding board: explain your setting and ask them to tell you what mind-picture they have of it – is it the picture you intended? If not, it may actually be a better idea than the one you had; don't worry about this, just use that idea instead. It's my firm belief that inspiration and ideas can come from anywhere, any time, as long as you are open to the possibilities.

Linda   Research can take many forms, from a quick Google search or brief visit to a particular location, to acquiring detailed knowledge of a particular period, or learning a new skill. (Marcus Sedgwick handled and fired guns in order to write *Revolver*; Susan Price spent a week horse-riding in Northumberland before starting *The Sterkarm Handshake*, and Michelle Paver learned traditional Sami survival techniques in Finnish Lapland as research for *Wolf Brother*.) Some books may require extensive research before you can start; for others, you may prefer to write the complete first draft, then check a few points when you've finished.

Many writers know the risk of doing too much research and letting it become an excuse not to start writing. This is especially the case if you're immersing yourself in a topic or a period on which limitless materials are available, such as the Second World War. You could go on reading for ever, as well as watching films and documentaries, visiting museums, websites and significant places, and never start your novel at all. At some point you will have to let go of research and trust your own characters and situations to carry the story forward, knowing that you can read more later if you feel it will help.

To write a story set in another time or place, you need to feel at home there, and you can only really do this by imagining the details of daily life. Vernacular histories are tremendously helpful here, for example *The People's War*, by Angus Calder, which brings together the experiences of ordinary people in British cities and countryside during the Second World War, largely through first-hand accounts.[6]

A quite different but necessary kind of research might be into current slang. This can be a particular problem for writers of teenage fiction, especially those who are some way from their own teenage years and don't have adolescents in the family. Nothing dates a book more quickly than an outmoded idiom (or topical references to music, clothing brands and personal gadgetry) but all the same you will want to make your book seem of the moment, *especially* if you're writing in first person. Certainly it's handy to have young people to ask, bearing in mind that there are regional variations as well as class and cultural differences. If this isn't possible, you can listen to conversations on trains and buses without obviously lurking, and when it comes to writing there are ways of conveying the flavour of idiom without reproducing it too slavishly. If the dialogue in teenage fiction included the full range of expletives used casually in most secondary schools, editors would be kept busy suggesting milder alternatives.

We all have weak areas where our knowledge is inadequate. I feel confident about trees, plants and wildlife – I wouldn't blunder into descriptions of Michaelmas daisies flowering in May or swifts screaming through English skies in October. But my awareness of cars is hazy, and I usually have to ask my partner what model a particular character might drive. For most queries there is help readily available, whether from acquaintances, libraries, message-boards or Google – and of course the internet has made many kinds of research infinitely quicker and easier than they would have been only a decade or so ago.

I've already mentioned the importance of settings in my stories, and that several of my stories have begun with a setting rather than with character or plot. Soon after I begin thinking of (or visiting) a place, I settle on a time of year when the story, or maybe a key episode in the story, will take place. If it's a real location, I try to spend time there alone, wandering around with a camera, absorbing the atmosphere, photographing small details as well as wider views. These pictures will sustain me through the weeks or months at my desk, and take me back to the location of my story. I like to feel that the place in my mind is as real as my physical surroundings at home.

TOP TIPS

Yvonne *Use a box file or something similar into which you can put things that will help you in your planning and making a start. For example: snippets of research, on scraps of paper or in a dedicated notebook; photocopies of documents; photos or drawings of the landscape and people; picture postcards; newspaper clippings or magazine adverts from the time and country you are setting your story in. I also like to include in my box items that help me to create the mood of the setting I am using for my book – shells from the beach, a menu from a restaurant, a train timetable. It can be anything that, as Linda says, takes you back to your story location.*

Linda *You will save time if you're methodical about factual information you collect. Many a time I've had to retrace my steps to re-check a significant date or fact because I didn't make a note of my source on first discovering it. It will help you to feel confident about the background to your story if you know how you know something.*

Yvonne The idea for this exercise is adapted with his permission from one of the excellent information sheets that Cliff McNish offers to schools who engage him for author visits.[7]

Look at a world map (or picture it in your mind). Picture the land, and the oceans. Think about the millions of things that exist and live just on the land: animals, trees, buildings, clocks . . .

Jot down as many of these things as you can think of in two minutes. Now, take your list of things and imagine you lived in a world where just one of these elements of the world is elevated in importance. (For example, Tolkien gave a single ring so much power that everything in the world revolved around the possession of it.)

Once you've chosen, ask yourself how different life would be – for everyone in the world – if this one thing was prized above all others, or was more important, or was considered to be dangerous. How would life change?

Finally, describe one small village or neighbourhood in this newly-angled world: what would be different about it? Would you immediately see signs of the power wielded by the element you have chosen, or would it take you by surprise as you wandered down the street, met people, went into a shop? Let your imagination off the leash, and see if you can create a setting so convincing that you know just how it would feel to live there.

Linda: For a setting you're interested in, make a mood-board (either on an actual board, or if you don't have one, on a sheet of A3 paper). Collect pictures of scenery, weather, objects, buildings; also collect words that conjure the moods and atmospheres in your mind. Each time you look at this, while writing, thinking or when stuck, it will help to refresh your sense of where you want to be.

Characters

Linda   We'll take a more detailed look at viewpoint a little later on, but when thinking about characters there is a big difference between a viewpoint character (with whose eyes you see everything else in the story) and other characters, whether major or minor, who are seen from outside. You may have two or more viewpoint characters, but for the moment let's imagine that there's just one, a fifteen-year-old girl called Amy. We'll use third-person narrative, but the narrative position will always be in Amy's head, so we're as close to her as we would be in first-person.

To start doing this you will need to know enough about Amy to feel at home in her head. There are various ways of building up a character – copious notes on her background, tastes, friends, fears, etc. On writing courses I have a favourite character-building activity which requires everyone present to answer ten questions about the fictional character they are starting to imagine. *What was the best thing that happened to her yesterday? She wakes up – where is she? What is the biggest thing on her mind?* And so on. More and more questions arise from these answers, with the result that paper-thin characters start to flesh out and seem real. They have connections, pasts, fears and doubts, plans and ambitions.

So, back to Amy. *What is the biggest thing on her mind?* If we know that, we're a good way towards knowing what drives her. Depending on the situation we decide on, her main concern could be to stay alive. It could be to get through the day at school without being humiliated. Or she could face some important test or trial, in sport, perhaps.

As soon as we start thinking about character, we're into plot, too (and setting, since it's impossible to imagine characters without providing a background of where and when they live). Carole Blake, in *From Pitch to Publication*, says that any story can be boiled down to these two questions: What does the main character want? And what's stopping him or her from getting it?

So: Amy wants to be a top-class heptathlete (the London Olympics are taking place as I write this). What's stopping her? She has heavy responsibilities at home, looking after a younger brother and sister and a hypochondriac mother, and can't make the training sessions. Add a coach who sees Amy's potential and wants to help . . . a rival . . . an interfering aunt . . . a close friend who resents the amount of time Amy devotes to training . . . possible love interest . . . and we have enough ingredients to get started.

This set-up is not unusual or original, but originality comes from the writing. The story will work if the reader cares about Amy and wants her to succeed – not by winning Olympic Gold, but by asserting her own desires and having the chance to fulfil her potential. It's a difficult line to tread, but Amy needs a combination of spirit and self-doubt if she's to win the sympathy of readers. Nothing is a bigger turn-off than a main character blessed with good looks, athletic qualities, popularity, kindness and cleverness all wrapped up in an improbable parcel. So let's give Amy serious misgivings, as well as the practical dilemmas she has to face. Is she being selfish (as her aunt suggests) to want to devote herself to her training, rather than spend time with the family? In spite of what her coach says, does she really have enough talent? Above all, let's not make her saintly. She must at times be unfeeling or insensitive – we must let her make mistakes. Let's have an episode where she's horrible to her brother or upsets her best friend.

What does Amy look like? Remember, we're inside her head, so unless we want to contrive a scene where she's looking at herself in a mirror, we won't 'see' her. To write such a phrase as, 'Amy's brown eyes widened with excitement as she read the text message' is, frankly, clunky. We have abandoned our position in order to look at her from outside. If we want the reader to be aware of Amy's brown eyes, we'll need a mirror-facing scene, or someone else to comment on them. Or Amy's appearance can be conveyed in, say, a changing-room scene, where she's aware of the athleticism and strength of the other girls and is mentally comparing herself to them.

Usually I don't say much at all about my viewpoint character's appearance. In *The Shell House*, beyond letting the reader know that Greg is quite sporty and at least reasonably attractive to girls, I don't comment on his hair, build or eye colour – because I'm inside his head, and not looking at him. I only 'see' what Greg sees. What I *do* think about is body language. I know how Greg would behave when he feels awkward; I know how he'd enter a room, and I can hear him speak.

Often, when reading, we have such a clear mental picture of a character that it can be surprising to go back and see how little the author has written. Here is K. M. Peyton, introducing Dick in *Flambards*: 'He was a straight, well-built boy, with hair the colour of wheat-straw, and a brown skin, big brown gentle hands and an unhurried way of moving, very quiet and measured, as if the world were full of fractious horses. He nodded at Christina, flushing shyly . . . ' And there we have Dick, physically present in the story.[8]

Yvonne Linda has written about the importance of knowing your viewpoint character as well as you would know any real person. If your character lives and breathes in your imagination, he or she is much more likely to step off the page and into your reader's mind as well.

There is no short cut here, no 'that will do to get started' – not for the viewpoint character nor for any other major players in the story. But if you get it right, sometimes the characters will help you write their roles. Think about someone you know very, very well. If I asked you how that person would react in a given situation, you would probably know. That's how it should be with your fictional characters.

We find out about characters in books from various sources: what the narrator says about them; what they say about themselves; what other characters tell us; their clothes and possessions; their demeanour (the way they stand, move, relax, laugh, show anger, enter and leave a room, and so on). Don't weigh your character down with long and detailed descriptions. Bring him or her to life through action and dialogue.

Names are important. A name which really stands out as unusual or exotic in the culture and time in which your character lives says something about that character's parents. Names have their own context and fashion and place in history. The name Wendy, for example, was very popular when I was a child – there were three of them in my class. But before 1904 there were no children called Wendy – J. M. Barrie invented the name when he wrote *Peter Pan*. Some names have definite religious or cultural connections and you can undermine the believability of a character quite easily by not paying proper attention to the name. You would not want to give a devout Muslim character a Hindu name or vice versa; similarly, in Ireland there are Catholic names and Protestant names. Of course you can go against the stereotypical expectations that get attached to names – but you need to know that's what you're doing, and how it will serve your story.

Once you have written your first draft, it is wise to make one of the elements of your second draft a consideration of the 'realness' of your main character(s). Here is the character checklist I would use as part of my revision process for a novel:

- Have I chosen the right gender/age/family background, or would something else be more convincing to the plot?

- Am I using first or third person – and why? Is the viewpoint consistent throughout the story?

- Is the main character essential to the plot and to driving the action forward?

- Have I got the right number of characters (not too many), and have I made them different enough from each other for the reader to be able to keep a hold on who's who in the story?

- Do I like or dislike my characters? Is that how I want the reader to feel about them?

- Have I given my character(s) a mixture of positive and negative traits (as Linda implies above, every goody-two-shoes has a bad day now and then, and the blackest-hearted villain loves his mum or pets the cat . . .)

- Finally, have I chosen the right name; does it 'fit' the person I have created?

TOP TIPS

Linda *Don't base your characters on people you know – unless very, very loosely. In particular, don't base a fictional character on your son, daughter, partner, ex or parent. It's inhibiting. Making up characters gives you the freedom you will deny yourself if you have a real person in your mind.*

Yvonne *I agree with Linda: don't use family or friends as characters in your books. But a mind-picture of a real person can give you a head start in physical description, because the way people stand, move and enter a room shows something about their personality. As a person gets older, the clues are even stronger – a very happy person will have wrinkles in different places from a grumpy one; a shy, anxious person presents a different body shape to a brash, confident one.*

EXERCISES

Linda Write down the briefest starter sketch of a character, e.g. *Boy, twelve, Eastern European, living in Hackney.*

- Give him a name.

- Now think about these questions: *What does he want?* and *What's stopping him from getting it?* Write down five or six possible scenarios.

- From these ideas, take the one that appeals to you most, and expand it by adding rough details, background, additional questions.

Yvonne For this exercise, you need to know the traditional story of *The Three Little Pigs*.[9] As you may remember, basically you have three piggy brothers holed up in a brick house built by one of them. A big bad wolf is at the door, trying to get in. Here's a snatch of the dialogue:

> *Little pig, little pig, let me come in*
>
> *No, no, by the hair of my chinny chin chin, you shall not come in.*
>
> *Then I'll huff, and I'll puff, and I'll blow your house in!*

You can tell from this short extract that the wolf is not the kind of creature you would invite for tea. But look at that opening line again. Now rewrite that first line – keeping the sense of what the wolf is saying, but without using the letter 'e'. So you can't have 'little', or 'let' or 'me' or 'come'. You will find there are several alternative ways to make the wolf's intention clear, and each variation will change his character. If you want to cheat or get a head start, look at the end note.[10]

Plotting

Yvonne   What would you say if I were to ask, How did last week go? I hope I wouldn't get a frame-by-frame account of every single day:

> *On Monday, I got up at seven o'clock when the alarm went off. I headed towards the bathroom and showered. The shower gel was running out so I had to open a new bottle. I dried myself, put on my clothes, combed my hair and went downstairs. I ate a bowl of cornflakes with a spoonful of sugar, then two pieces of toast with marmalade and butter, and I drank a cup of instant coffee . . .*

Are you gripped? Are you desperate to know what happened after the cup of coffee? I'm guessing not. When I asked the question, I was expecting the highlights of your week, the dramatic bits – the best and the worst. Perhaps there was a theme: it was a traumatic week in which everything seemed to go wrong, culminating in a visit to Accident and Emergency at the local hospital. Or it was a week of celebration with two birthday parties, a wedding and a small lottery win. That's what I want to hear about. That's the plot.

E. M. Forster described a story as 'a narrative of events arranged in their time sequence'.[11] Life in time + life in value = the novel. Life in value refers to that process of picking out the highlights, the things that will grip the attention of your audience, and not the minute details of your everyday experience.

One of the most important things to keep in your head when you plot any novel, but perhaps particularly one for children, is the thread of time. A story has a sequence of events, and it drives forward. This is still true even when the characters are reliving something in flashback. Your readers need to keep a sense of time, or understand clearly why time is being subverted. It is easy to get lost when the person guiding you through the forest does not have any idea where the path might be. Stream of consciousness or abandonment of any sense of time or logical flow might make an enthralling read for an experienced adult reader, but most children struggle with the abstract and will simply be lost and bewildered (or, more likely, will put your story to one side and move on to something more engaging).

The events that form the basis of your plot do have to interest or intrigue the reader, of course, and interesting events should influence, and be linked to, other interesting events. A good example of this kind of linear plot is the soap opera. At any one time, in any soap, there will be a character doing something s/he shouldn't. That event leads on to another – perhaps a lie, or taking action to conceal what has been done. That might lead to a crisis of conscience, and a confession to a trusted friend. The friend might tell someone else, and the deception will come to light. This leads to the reaction of the person who finds out, who may decide to do something . . . and so on. There's a logical flow. You don't know what will happen next, but you have the frame in which the events will happen.

We keep watching a soap because we have come to know the characters; we care about what happens to them, so we keep watching (or reading) to find out. This holds true for a well-plotted children's novel, too. Character and plot come as an indivisible pair.

For me, a good plot plan – a map of the forest, to go back to my earlier illustration – is essential. It doesn't mean you can't leave the path, it just means that you will know where the path is and why you left it. But you need to find the approach that is right for you, and right for your story – it's good to have advice about the tried and tested when you start out, but in time you will find your own way of working, and it might be quite different from mine.

A good illustration of this is the description given by Inbali Iserles, author of *The Tygrine Cat* series:

> I never sit down with a view to inventing a story from scratch as I take my inspiration from the world around me. Stories materialise when I least expect them, like wild things, and I carry a notebook with me in my efforts to ensnare them – that, for me, is the real challenge. For those whose impact lingers, I am struck by the frightening realisation that I must pursue them, wherever they go. I can often picture the first and last pages of their adventures but little in between. I remain, throughout, a hostage to the characters and their conflicting desires, despite my best efforts to set down story arcs. A case in point was my first book, The Tygrine Cat. The idea came to me as I flicked through a book on cat breeds. I started to imagine a rivalry between two ancient feline tribes. I pictured the furious Sa Mau, the cats from the Nile Delta, with their claim to majesty over all modern moggies. But it was the Tygrine who pounced in and out of view, who, for some time, eluded my grasp – one Tygrine in particular – a young cat called Mati, the very last of his kind.

However you choose to pursue your own plot idea, be prepared to be flexible; stories so often take on a life of their own as you start to write.

Linda   Writers vary tremendously in the amount of planning they do. For some, it would be inconceivable to start without first having made a detailed chapter-by-chapter breakdown. Others simply plunge in and see where the story takes them.

The advantage to the first method is, of course, being able to see the complete shape of the novel. The author knows where the key dramatic moments are to fall, and can see how minor episodes are to fit into the whole. The end of the story is known from the start. Because the plot has been worked out, the author is unlikely to crash to a halt in Chapter Eight with no sense of where to go next.

Those who prefer the headlong plunge method tend to relish the freedom of going where the story and the characters take them, and the readiness to be surprised. Writers in this camp would feel over-constrained by having everything worked out in advance. The risk of this approach is that you could spend several chapters finding the real focus of the story, or introducing characters who aren't going to play significant roles. You could lose your way, uncertain which of several plot strands is the central one.

There's a middle path, which is the way I prefer to work. This route consists of having a general idea of how the story will progress, and a sense of how it will end. Patrick Ness has described starting off with an idea of the beginning, the ending, and two or three terrific scenes.[12] Thinking this way, you have a story arc; it's useful to know where and how you plan to leave your characters at the end, and what they will have learned, achieved or experienced by then.

Between beginning and end you can plot your 'stepping-stones', the key scenes which may already have begun to form in your mind. These could be, for example, a revelation or discovery, a dangerous situation, an argument which changes the course of events, a decision.

To me, this way of plotting gives a sense of structure but also leaves space for new ideas to surface through the writing. I think of writing a book as working out a puzzle for myself; having all the puzzle pieces in place before starting would take away the sense of exploration and discovery. Meg Rosoff has a similar view:

> *A book written with an exchange of energy between the conscious*
> *and subconscious mind will feel exciting and fluid in the way that*
> *a perfectly planned and pre-plotted book never will.*[13]

Planning is a logical, left-brain activity; making a plan is different from the immersion in the story that comes only from writing it. Both have their place, but I know that on the rare occasions when I've attempted to write a complete plot, it hasn't been satisfactory – looking back at my proposed outline, I see only scant resemblance to the finished book. This middle way requires more revision than the tightly plotted story produced by the first method – for instance, I returned to the early chapters of *The Shell House* to insert a character I only thought of towards the end of the first draft – but I enjoy revising, and always feel that improvements are made at this stage.

As with so many aspects of writing, you need to find out which approach suits you best: are you a point-by-point planner, a seat-of-the-pants flier? Or, in between, the story grower?

If you're a first-time writer, you may feel reassured by having your plot mapped out. You don't yet have the seasoned writer's advantage of confidence in your ability to complete a novel, or to persevere through difficulties. To start without a plan at all is to risk reaching a dead end, or to get your characters into such serious predicaments that you can find no plausible way of extricating them.

On the other hand, it can be tempting for beginner writers to think that plot is everything, and that once they've thought of a sensational scenario, the job is virtually done. But good writing is about far more than plot. The most promising plot idea will fall flat in the hands of an inept writer; all plots stand or fall according to whether the writer can create interest in the characters.

John Mortimer, author of the *Rumpole of the Bailey* screenplays and novels, says:

> *Plots are essential, but plots are the hardest part; at any rate I find*
> *this to be so. Everything else about writing can be done by turning*
> *up regularly on the empty page and starting the performance. Plots*
> *are notoriously shy and retiring . . . then, as a character begins to talk,*

> *or comes into contact with another, the plot may start working;*
> *because it's important that the characters perform the plot and the*
> *plot doesn't manipulate the characters.*[14]

This is not to underestimate the importance of plot. Our focus is writing for young readers; children and teenagers are unlikely to be impressed by beautifully written but meandering prose, and if they're not gripped, will put the book down and find something else. Young readers are capable of appreciating wit, humour, evocative description, conjuring of atmosphere and all the other things that make up good writing, but plot is what keeps them reading.

The writer for children must find ways of making the child characters active in their plots; they can't merely have things happening *to* them. Of course, children are relatively powerless, their situations determined by adults, but nevertheless a child protagonist must do something which affects the outcome.

Even in situations of extreme oppression and persecution, you must find a way for young characters to be instrumental to the plot. Elizabeth Laird has set novels in a range of settings: *The Garbage King*, about street children in Addis Ababa, *Red Sky in the Morning*, the story of a Kurdish refugee, and *A Little Piece of Ground*, about a Palestinian boy living in the Occupied Territories. Her characters are always more than passive victims of injustice. In *A Little Piece of Ground*, Karim and his friends play football on a patch of wasteland, raising a Palestinian flag as an act of defiance. In the context it's a minor gesture, yet it humanises the situation, giving Karim a small triumph and allowing readers to identify with ordinary aspirations in an unfamiliar (to most) situation.

A plot unpacked

Let's look at Eva Ibbotson's *One Dog and his Boy* to see how the plot is constructed. First, reduced to essentials, what does the main character want, and what's stopping him from getting it? The premise is a simple one; Hal wants a dog, but his parents won't let him have one. If we put this into a rudimentary three-point plan, we have:

- *Boy wants dog*
- *Boy can't have dog*
- *Boy gets dog*

Eva Ibbotson's charming story, somewhat reminiscent of Dodie Smith's *The Hundred and One Dalmatians*, sees Hal finding the dog of his dreams and eventually being allowed to keep it. The resolution of the plot is all in the third point on the plan: *how* Hal gets his dog. It wouldn't be a satisfactory story if this happened too easily, or independently of Hal: if the parents had a sudden change of heart, for example, or a kindly uncle stepped into the story and persuaded them. The plot needs to put Hal centre stage and must depend on his actions and decisions.

So, in more detail: Hal lives in a luxurious London flat, with wealthy, status-conscious parents who won't let him have the one thing he wants: his own dog. His parents lose his trust when, for a birthday present, they let him choose a dog – a scruffy terrier called Fleck – from a dubious outfit called Easy Pets, without revealing that it's only for one weekend. When Fleck is returned to the kennels, Hal is angry and bereft. He takes the decision to steal the dog and to head for the home of his sympathetic grandparents, who live in a Northumberland cottage; he's accompanied by Pippa, younger sister of the kennel-maid, and several more dogs. Along the way they face danger, doubt and difficulties; Hal makes friends, but also meets people who want to thwart him; he takes decisive action, and at one point makes a bad mistake which leads to his capture. By the end, it's Hal who states his terms to his parents, making them respect his wishes and understand that money can't buy everything.

I don't know how Eva Ibbotson – who died in 2010, still writing at the age of eighty-five – planned her novels, but this is a story full of incident and surprises, skilfully holding together several plot strands while never losing sight of the reader's wish for Hal and Fleck to be safely united. It's more than a story of a boy wanting something and then getting it; it's a matter of Hal asserting his own values over those of his parents, prizing love and loyalty and rejecting shallow materialism. As in many a children's story, the child is wiser than the adults, and by the end of the story, through acting independently of them, Hal has gained in confidence and self-awareness. By now we're thinking in terms of both *plot* and *theme*: the plot of the story is Hal's struggle to keep his dog; the theme is the valuing of love and companionship rather than avarice.

Another important question to be asked of any story is *What's at stake?* What does the main character stand to gain or lose? What would be the worst thing that could happen? In Eva Ibbotson's story, Hal looks likely to be parted from Fleck and sent to boarding school; unless things change he will continue to be treated as his parents' possession, his own wishes disregarded.

Knowing the answer to the '*What's at stake*' question, and keeping it in mind throughout, will go a long way towards driving your plot.

Plot and theme

As we've seen above, the **plot** is what happens; the **theme** is the underlying concern of the book. To clarify:

● In a novel about a teenage boy called Sam, the **plot** is about his involvement with friends who lead him into petty crime and the trouble he gets into at school and at home. By the end, something will happen to jolt him out of this way of life.

● The **theme** is the importance of finding values and purpose and rejecting easy popularity at the expense of self-worth.

The **theme** should never be stated: let readers discover it (or not – some readers just don't think that way). If it's too much to the fore, it will dominate the story.

People often ask whether a story has a 'hidden message'. Well, if it's there, it isn't hidden; but I dislike the word 'message' in this context. A book with a message is likely to be obvious and didactic. As the editor David Fickling puts it, aim to deliver a message and 'You appear to know what is right. And then you are delivering not a story but a lecture.'[15] Your readers should experience the events of the story alongside Sam; they shouldn't be told what to think.

Authors often find that the theme emerges through the writing rather than being predetermined; one of the great rewards of writing is discovering, rather than making, patterns and echoes. If ever a story has been accused of having an underlying didacticism, it's *The Lion the Witch and the Wardrobe*, the first of the Narnia series, with its obvious Christian symbolism.[16] Yet C.S. Lewis himself says of it,

> Some people seem to think that I began by asking myself how I could say something about Christianity to children; then fixed on the fairy tale as an instrument; then collected information about child psychology and decided what age group I'd write for; then drew up a list of basic Christian truths and hammered out 'allegories' to embody them. This is all pure moonshine. I couldn't write in that way at all. Everything began with images; a faun carrying an umbrella, a queen on a sledge, a magnificent lion. At first there wasn't even anything Christian about them; that element pushed itself in of its own accord. It was part of the bubbling.[17]

What 'bubbles', of course, for any author, comes from their own values and preoccupations. You can't help but impart your own values when you write; but you can try to keep yourself hidden. You're a storyteller, not a guru, mentor, teacher or therapist.

Plot and structure

Plot is what happens; structure is how the story is told. For instance, will you use a linear narrative – i.e. one thing happening after another, in order? Or will you move back and forth in time? Will you use different time-frames, or include 'flashbacks' in the main narrative?

Structure is also to do with viewpoint, which we'll look at in more detail in the next section. Who's telling the story? An omniscient narrator? A single viewpoint character? Or two, or more? How are these viewpoint sections to be separated – by rows of dots? By chapter breaks?

Aidan Chambers always does something interesting with structure. *Postcards From No Man's Land*, his Carnegie Medal winner, alternates two narratives: in the third person and in the recent present, we have Jacob, a teenager newly-arrived in Amsterdam, alone, to meet members of a family who saved his grandfather during the Battle of Arnhem. In the first person and in 1944, we have Geertrui, nineteen-year-old daughter of that family. The two narratives are linked by the presence of Geertrui in Jacob's 'present' – now terminally ill and about to choose euthanasia to end her suffering. Jacob's stay in Amsterdam will reveal much about his grandfather, the fighting at Arnhem, himself and the possibilities of his life, while Geertrui's narrative allows the reader a fuller experience of occupied Holland, the dangers and hardships faced daily, than Jacob can know. The split narrative allows for potent juxtapositions, poses questions and makes the reader wait for answers.

Many novels use a **framing device.** This is, in effect, starting at the end, often with a first-person narrator (though it doesn't have to be first-person) reflecting on the events of the story, maybe from many years later. Here, for instance, is the opening of Jill Paton Walsh's *Fireweed*:

> *Remember? I can still smell it. I met her in the Aldwych Underground Station, at half past six in the morning, when people were busily rolling up their bedding, and climbing out to see how much of the street was left standing. There were no lavatories down there, and with houses going down like ninepins every night there was a shortage of baths in London just then, and the stench of the Underground was appalling. I noticed, as I lurked around, trying to keep inconspicuous, that there was someone else doing the same. I was lurking because I wanted to stay in the warm for as long as possible, without being one of the very last out, in case any busybody asked me tricky questions. And there was this girl, as clearly as anything, lurking too.*
>
> *I was fifteen that year, and she seemed sometimes younger, sometimes older . . .*[18]

Often the use of a framing device will be more obvious than this; it may be set out as a section on its own, or as a prologue or preface, or can be the whole first chapter (as in Nina Bawden's *Carrie's War*, where Carrie returns with her own children to the remote Druid's Grove). In *Fireweed*, it's just the first two sentences that tell us the narrator is looking back at a memory that has stayed with him very vividly; also 'I was fifteen that year.' We can tell from these phrases that the story isn't happening in the narrator's *now*.

A framing device is like a pair of brackets enclosing the novel. It's a way of creating expectations, of hinting at what will come; we know that that the meeting of boy and girl will be significant. On the final pages of *Fireweed*, we return to the narrator's 'present', the point from which he is looking back:

> *Years later, when the war was over and done with, it occurred to me that she might not have meant what she said . . . I think of it now, leaning on a broken wall, looking at St. Paul's . . .*[19]

And in *Carrie's War*, the final chapter returns us to Carrie's present, thirty years after the main events of the story.

Structure also encompasses the use of letters, diaries, texts, emails, playscripts, recordings of interviews, etc., as a means of telling the story. Frank Cottrell Boyce has written a short story called *Can't You Sleep?* which is told entirely through Facebook updates and comments.[20] Nick Manns, in his supernatural thriller *Control Shift*, framed and interspersed his story with transcripts of interviews conducted by a clinical psychologist with the main character's young sister who, though only five, has been an observant and reliable witness to puzzling events.

Although you don't *have* to decide everything about structure before you start, it helps to decide what your rules are before too long – the rules you make up for yourself about how your story is to be told.

TOP TIPS

Yvonne *I have advocated the linear plot, with a clear chain of linked events moving forward through time. But this doesn't mean you have to write it in a linear way. Start writing at the point you feel most excited about, or the bit of the story where you feel most confident. Doing it that way might help you with the parts of the plot that are a bit sketchy, or questions that have not quite been resolved. Chapter One will almost certainly have to be rewritten, possibly several times, so don't waste too much time and creative energy on it in the first draft. Dive into the story at whatever point most excites you, and find your way back to the beginning later.*

Linda *Often, inexperienced writers feel that their plot is thin – that it won't sustain a whole novel. Padding out a story doesn't work, and will always show, but very different from this is thinking of your characters as rounded people with various aspects to their lives. For instance, if the main action revolves around the youth football team and your character's ambition to be talent-spotted, these scenes can be offset by episodes at school and at home, where there will inevitably be conflicts and demands on the protagonist's time and emotions. Focusing on these will produce a story more satisfying and textured than one that concentrates solely on the football. You will succeed if you can fully engage those readers who have no interest in the sport. I don't know an offside from a penalty shoot-out, but can still be hooked into football stories by skilled writers like Tony Bradman and Helena Pielichaty.*

When working out your plot, whether before or during the writing, keep careful track of the days of the week on which the action takes place, and the date. If you don't do this, and go from one event to another without tracking, you may inadvertently have a week with two Thursdays in it, or no weekend. And if the story spans several weeks or months, there will be seasonal changes. Maybe part of the story coincides with a significant date or festival – for instance, if your story is a realistic one about teenagers, set at the end of October, it's unlikely that they'd ignore Hallowe'en; you could find a way to base an episode around it.

EXERCISES

Yvonne Think about a couple of books for children that you have really enjoyed. Jot down the main elements of the plot in the order they happened, from memory. What drove the story on, and kept your attention? Where were the highlights? What attracted you into the story at the beginning, and why was the end satisfying?

If you are blessed with lots of patience and determination, you can learn a lot about writing by doing this exercise with a really bad book that you hated – but you would have to read the whole thing, and not give in to the temptation to bin it after page twelve.

Linda

- Think of a selection of novels you've read, whether for children or for adults, and reduce them to the basic three-line plot summary.

- Make a simple three-line plot of your own following the pattern that someone wants something and eventually gets it.

- Now start to unpack further, thinking of how the goal might be achieved and some of the difficulties in reaching it.

- Expand this into a 'stepping-stone' outline, so that it has a beginning, an end, and several important incidents. Remember that you don't have to include everything at this stage; your imagined problems don't need solutions. Those can come later.

Voice and viewpoint

Linda   This is part of your thinking about structure, though you're likely to think of viewpoint before much else. Whose story is it? Which character do you want to be closest to? Will it work best to tell the story in first-person, or third-person mode? One viewpoint, or several?

First person or third person?

In first person, the narrator is 'I'. In third person, the narrator is the author, although it's possible for the author to be so close to the character (i.e. inside his or her head) that the identification with the character is as complete as in first person. (This is the kind of viewpoint I use in *The Shell House*, with Greg.)

First, let's consider the advantages and drawbacks of both. First person immediately establishes an intimacy between character and reader, as if the reader is being addressed directly. The voice and language are those of the character. There are a great many teen novels which successfully deploy the 'So I'm like totally wow' kind of address – easy to read, familiar to readers, often humorous, moving the story briskly forward.

First person can show us events from an unfamiliar viewpoint: for example that of a horse, in Michael Morpurgo's *War Horse* and Katherine Roberts' *I am the Great Horse*, which respectively portray the battlefields of the First World War and the exploits of Alexander the Great, or a dog at the time of the peasants' revolt in *Fire, Bed and Bone*, by Henrietta Branford.

The drawbacks are that the viewpoint is limited to that character, and the writer can only use language which that teenager would use. The writer can't suddenly abandon Rosie, or whatever the *totally wow* character is called, to describe a stretch of Cornish coast in painterly terms, unless Rosie herself would think in such a way. Also, anything not known or experienced by Rosie can't be included – for instance, if the plot hangs on the secret revealed by her supposed best friend to her boyfriend while Rosie's away on holiday, the reader can only pick this up as it reveals itself to Rosie. And although we're willing to accept that Joey, Michael Morpurgo's *War Horse*, hears and to some extent understands human conversations, credulity would be strained too far if he were to give a knowledgeable account of the causes of the First World War. The writer of first-person narrative must accept these limitations and work with them, finding ways around them where necessary.

Third person allows more flexibility and a wider range of language, because the author isn't limited to the vocabulary a particular character would use (other than in dialogue, of course). The conveying of information can be easier in third person (in first person, particularly if the main character is supposed to be writing a diary, it's implausible for her to feel the need to say that Robbie is her younger brother and that he's nine years old and has freckles. Many fictional diaries *are* implausible, as they do too much explaining . . . but I won't get sidetracked.) To some authors, third person feels more formal, not allowing the easy address to the reader and instant establishing of rapport that can be achieved with first person.

For many writers, it's a matter almost of instinct, reflecting, perhaps, what they most enjoy reading, or which approach they feel comes more naturally. I generally favour third person, though in *Set in Stone* I used two first-person narratives in alternating chapters.

First person

To see how first-person narrative and voice are indistinguishable, let's look at some early pages from Celia Rees' young adult novel, *This is Not Forgiveness*. Celia uses the viewpoints of three characters: impressionable Jamie; Rob, his embittered elder brother, invalided out of the army; and dangerous Caro, who models herself on the terrorist Ulrike Meinhof. This is the first time we hear from Rob:

> Over in Afghan lots of guys make some kind of statement before they go on ops – especially if there's a chance they might not be coming back, they write an email or a letter or a crap poem, whatever. Or make a podcast, like this one.
>
> I never did that. Asking for it in my opinion.
>
> Inviting bad luck.
>
> Now luck ain't coming into it – I'm doing this because I don't want no misunderstanding. I'm not like those sad-loner no-mates fucks

against the world – there's no chip on my shoulder. Don't be looking to blame anyone – clean up the mess and get on with your lives.

I want you all to know I didn't do it as some kind of personal declaration – I don't have a message.

My only cause is me.

Don't look for reasons because there are no reasons. But people want them, don't they, so take your pick from these:

I was tired of living in Snoreton-on-Boring with no future that I can see.

I was sick of the ordinary and wanted to stir up the ant heap.

I wanted to make people take notice. Nothing concentrates the mind like death and dying, does it?

Don't ask 'Why?' 'cos that's the wrong question.

Better to ask 'Why not?'

It's amazing that this don't happen.

ALL THE TIME![21]

As a dramatic introduction this could hardly be bettered. Such a lot is packed in here. We already know, from the preceding few pages in Jamie's voice, that Rob has died and that Jamie can't forgive him; these two sections form a framing device, of the kind we looked at in the section on structure. Rob is speaking, making a podcast rather than writing. In this extract we can hear Rob's voice, his tone, his mood, his disillusionment. The language and diction are appropriate to Rob, and different from the register used by the other two narrators (a distinction helped by the book design, which uses a different typeface for each of the three voices). We know, or at least think we know, from this and the opening pages, that this is Rob's suicide message, that there was another funeral alongside his, that he's distanced himself from any concern for others and has taken drastic action of some kind. We are left to wonder about his experiences with the army in Afghanistan, and what has led him to this point; whether he succeeded in carrying out his plan, what exactly is the 'mess' he's left to be cleared up, and what will be the effect on his younger brother.

It would be an uncomfortable experience to see the entire book from inside Rob's head or Caro's, but offsetting these two very driven and morally skewed characters is the more ordinary Jamie, caught between them, gradually suspecting what they're planning together and guessing at their motives. As a structural device this creates great tension, because the reader is allowed to see more than Jamie and to foresee the approaching danger.

Third person

Third person can root itself in one character's consciousness or several, or it can stay further back, as if watching them. Often it moves fluidly from one to the other, as in the opening of Philippa Pearce's *The Way to Sattin Shore*:

> *Here is Kate Tranter, coming home from school in the January dusk*
> *– the first to come, because she is the youngest of her family. Past*
> *the churchyard. Past the shops. Along the fronts of the tall, narrow*
> *terrace houses she goes. Not this one, not this one, nor this . . .*
>
> *Stop at the house with no lit window.*
> *This is home.*
>
> *Up three steps to the front door, and feel for the key on the string*
> *in her pocket. Unlock, and then in. Stand just inside the door with*
> *the door now closed, at her back.*[22]

In these few lines we have moved fairly unobtrusively from looking at Kate, being told about her family situation, to being with her, standing there, in effect, with the door at our own back. We are not meant to imagine that Kate is actually thinking, 'I am first to come, because I'm the youngest of my family,' but by the time we reach 'Not this one, not this one, nor this . . . ' we are sharing Kate's perceptions.

Philip Pullman takes a similar narrative position at the start of *Northern Lights*:

> *Lyra and her daemon moved through the darkening Hall, taking care*
> *to keep to one side, out of sight of the kitchen. The three great tables*
> *that ran the length of the Hall were laid already, the silver and the*
> *glass catching what little light there was, and the long benches were*
> *pulled out ready for the guests. Portraits of former Masters hung high*

> *up in the gloom along the walls. Lyra reached the dais and looked*
> *back at the open kitchen door and, seeing no one, stepped up*
> *beside the high table. The places here were laid with gold, not silver,*
> *and the fourteen seats were not oak benches but mahogany chairs*
> *with velvet cushions.*
>
> *Lyra stopped beside the Master's chair and flicked the biggest glass*
> *gently with a fingernail. The sound rang clearly through the Hall.*
>
> *'You're not taking this seriously,' whispered her daemon. 'Behave*
> *yourself.'*
>
> *The daemon's name was Pantalaimon, and he was currently in*
> *the form of a moth, a dark brown one so as not to show up in the*
> *darkness of the Hall . . .* [23]

We are with Lyra, but not directly sharing her thoughts – for example, she has no need to tell herself what her daemon's name is, and probably wouldn't use the word dais, be able to identify mahogany, or pause to notice such detail of furnishing and table setting. We are aware of an author showing us these things, whereas with first person the author is completely hidden behind the character. The effect here is that we're given a sense of a story unfolding for us, and a setting and atmosphere being conveyed in a more textured and leisurely way than is likely with a first-person narrative. We move into Lyra's thoughts when the occasion requires it; when she is disturbed and has to hide under an armchair, our perspective is hers, down there on the floor:

> *Lyra could see his legs, in their dark green trousers and shiny black*
> *shoes. It was a servant . . . and then the Master's feet became visible*
> *too, in the shabby black shoes he always wore.*

A crucial difference between this kind of narrative and the first-person direct-ness used by Celia Rees, above, is that we can believe what the narrator of *Northern Lights* tells us, whereas we have no way of knowing whether to trust what Rob says. Why would Philip Pullman lie about whether or not the chairs are made of mahogany, or who is shown in the portraits? If he says so, as omniscient narrator, then it *is* so. With Rob, we are apparently listening to his suicide message, but maybe he's deluded, pretending, playing a role – we can't tell. And although we know that he's dead, we can't be certain that he carried out his plan; he could have died in some other way, shot by police at the scene, for instance.

The reading experience is very different: with Philip Pullman there is the sense of setting off with a trustworthy guide, whereas with the unreliable narrator, or a narrator we don't know whether to believe or not, we're on shifting sands. (This doubt and the tendency of readers to make assumptions can be used to astonishing effect. For a masterpiece of reader-tricking and wrong-footing, try Robert Cormier's *I Am the Cheese*.)

When close to a single character, third person can work in much the same way as first person. In *Troy*, her novel of the Trojan war, Adèle Geras stays with the viewpoint of whichever character is central to an episode. Here is the opening:

> *'They'll be here later on,' said Charitomene. 'You may be sure of it. It'll be a fierce battle today, and we must be ready for the wounded, poor creatures. Put that pallet over there, Xanthe, where it's cooler.' Xanthe did as she was told. Please dear Gods on Olympus who see everything we mortals do, she thought, help me now. Please keep Boros away. Please let it be other men who bring us these bodies. She shivered. Since the day when he'd first approached her, his words (What's a frisky little filly like you doing all alone here? I've seen you before, haven't I? . . .) went round and round in her head, and with them a vision of his face, with its thin, lipless mouth and his eyes the colour of phlegm set too closely together in his enormous head. She tried very hard not to think of him and most of the time she succeeded . . .[24]*

This immediacy helps ease the reader into an unfamiliar situation, one that may at first glance seem to be peopled by goddesses and classical heroes rather than by recognisable humans. The close identification with Xanthe (and, in turn, with her sister Marpessa and with Alastor, a young soldier) makes the strangeness seem approachable. Here we have Xanthe, a girl doing her best to be obedient, intimidated by a predatory and physically repellent older man. (Adèle Geras has said that, although the Trojan war is her subject, she approaches it via kitchens and bedrooms.)

Problems with viewpoint

In each of the above extracts you can see, I hope, how the writer makes use of the chosen narrative position, exploiting its potential. Not every writer is so sure-footed. On writing courses, I frequently read stories where the writer has begun a story or even written a whole book without considering viewpoint. A typical piece might resemble this:

As she approached the cottage, Matty felt nervous. Would they let her in? She thought of going back – but no, she'd come all this way. She wasn't going to give up now.

Inside, Josiah was getting out the oak box with runic symbols painted on it. He hoped he would remember the spell; it was so easy to get muddled. Oliver was watching, his stomach clamped tight with jealousy. He should have been the one to say the potent words. It was typical of Josiah to take everything for himself.

When there was a knock on the door, everyone jumped. It was Edwina who moved first. She had been watching the stew-pot, sniffing the aroma of meat and herbs, wondering what Oliver had put into it. Now her heart was thumping as she slid back the bolt. Was it Klaus? He'd promised to come, but then Klaus had disappointed her before. She couldn't bear it if he let her down today, of all days.

Matty stood on the doorstep, looking in at the dimly lit room. Slowly her eyes focused on Edwina's pale face and green eyes. She could hardly speak.

'I'm Matty. Er – Klaus told me to come,' she stammered, wishing now that she'd thought of bringing a gift – flowers or fruit, anything rather than arrive empty-handed.

'Klaus? How do you know Klaus?' Edwina narrowed her eyes and surveyed the newcomer from head to foot. She looked like a timid little thing, but Edwina had learned not to judge by appearances.

Klaus, at that moment, was trudging through the snow. He had walked for many a mile and was tired and hungry; he would have found a place to shelter for the night, but for his promise to Josiah . . .

Whatever's going on here, one thing is obvious – we're all over the place in terms of viewpoint. We start inside Matty's head, then leap to Josiah's, Oliver's, Edwina's, back to Matty, Edwina again, then to Klaus. It's unsettling; reading it, we are floating above them all, not anchored anywhere in particular. We can't tell whose story it is. There is such a thing as an omniscient narrator – i.e. a narrator who has the freedom to go anywhere and know everything. But the narrator shouldn't resemble a restless flea, hopping about at random, with the reader obliged to scuttle along behind.

Almost always, when this is pointed out, the writer is surprised. This viewpoint-hopping isn't intentional; she or he hasn't realised. My suggestion would be to choose one of the characters and stay inside that person's head – for instance Matty, the new arrival. Everything will then be seen through Matty's eyes; she can work out the relationships and the tensions among the others.

There is a difference between viewpoint-hopping (as above – shifting viewpoint from paragraph to paragraph, even from sentence to sentence), and *multiple* viewpoint. Many a story is told from more than one viewpoint; as we've seen with Celia Rees's and Adèle Geras's novels. In both, the changes of viewpoint are clear, and are demarcated by section or chapter breaks. The point is that it must be controlled, used to effect and not by accident. You should always know where you are in terms of viewpoint; if *you* don't, your reader will have an uncomfortable ride.

As bad as viewpoint-hopping is a story told almost entirely from one character's point of view which takes an unexpected dive into someone else's head when it suits the author. For instance this, in a novel that's so far used Joel's viewpoint:

> *Joel banged the door behind him and slumped into his chair. It had been an awful day, and Maths last lesson was more than he could face. It was hot and stuffy in the Maths room and any minute now he'd have to hand in the homework he'd forgotten about till break, and barely started. God! When would it be over? He couldn't wait to be outside, running.*
>
> *'Shall we try that again, Joel?'*

>Joel had tuned out, as he usually did. His seat at the back of the room let him hide behind Jamie Dobson's bulk. It took a few moments before he realised Mr Haynes was talking to him.
>
>'What?'
>
>Someone giggled.
>
>'I said shall we try that again, Joel? Coming into the room without slamming the door or kicking chairs?' Mr Haynes was weary. He'd had a stressful day and had lost his free period to cover year nine science. Now the tightening at the back of his neck and the blurring of his vision warned of approaching migraine. The last thing he wanted was a confrontation – and with Joel Riley. It would have to be Joel Riley
>
>'Oh, for God's sake,' Joel muttered, as he heaved himself to his feet. What was it with teachers? Why couldn't they get off his back?

The excursion into the teacher's thoughts gives the reader a jolt and takes us away from Joel. The author may want to include these details in order to give the sense of escalating tension – but Joel can't know about Mr Haynes' stressful day, his migraine and the loss of his free period. If the reader is to get a sense of Mr Haynes' weariness, it would be better shown through speech, body language, or an overheard conversation with another adult, and through Joel's eyes and ears.

There are no rules apart from the ones you make for yourself, but you should break those only knowingly, and for good reason. If the narrative position you're taking is inside Joel's head, you shouldn't nip out and take a tour of the room when it happens to suit you.

TOP TIPS

Linda *At the early stages, it's worth experimenting. Do you want a single viewpoint, dual, or multiple? Try writing in short bursts from the point of view of two or three characters – remembering that this, now, is just for you. None of it need appear in the final draft unless you want it to. If nothing else, this is a good way of developing a feel for the characters, their voices, their priorities, their behaviour.*

Yvonne *Voice can be passive* (The door was shut and the toys hurriedly packed away) *or active* (She shut the door and hurriedly packed away the toys). *Active is almost always a better choice. It makes a more immediate contact with the reader and describes what's happening more vividly. For younger children (as for many adult readers) the passive voice is more difficult to keep up with.*

EXERCISES

Linda Continue the Joel story, above, for another page or so. Aim to show the teacher's mood as well as Joel's, while staying firmly in Joel's viewpoint. Or, write the whole episode from the point of view of a girl in the class – maybe a girl who despises Joel, but rather likes the teacher.

Also, try creating the sense of a speaking voice by making up a recorded message, like Rob's podcast. For instance, a teenage girl leaves a voicemail message for her family, saying why she's run away.

Yvonne Staying with a school theme, read this teacher's report on a wayward pupil: 'Sam is a very lively, humorous boy who could achieve a lot more if he made the effort to concentrate on his studies rather than cultivating a reputation as the class clown. He is undoubtedly able, but has yet to learn that the admiration of classmates provides transient satisfaction, while a good education can set him up for life. Neither his coursework, nor his homework record, reflect his abilities.'

It's a fairly typical report format, with that underlying tone so beloved of teachers who have to rein in their true feelings in the interests of being 'professional'.

Sam's doting mum is going to read this report, and then tell her sister what the teacher said. In the staff room, the teacher is going to chat to a colleague about the frustrations of teaching this 'lively' boy. And Sam himself is going to read the report and tell his friend about it.

Rewrite the report from the viewpoint of one or more of these three people. Keep the content, but use another viewpoint to broaden the picture. What does the teacher really think of Sam? How will Mum interpret the report? What are Sam's thoughts on the matter? Write in first or third person; try both, and see if it makes a difference. Which viewpoint feels the best to engage the reader?

Dialogue: coming off the page

Linda Good dialogue carries a story, transforming it into drama. When it's done well, you *hear* it rather than read it; sometimes you forget you're reading words on a page rather than overhearing a conversation. Bad dialogue drags its feet, drawing the reader's attention to the shortcomings of the writing.

Crucially, dialogue must sound alive and convincing when read aloud. It's important to read *all* your work aloud, but particularly the dialogue. If you can't physically get the words out, if you trip and falter or tie your tongue in knots, your dialogue isn't working (unless that's the effect you wanted). If you can't hear each character's voice, the dialogue is bland and lifeless. To paraphrase Elmore Leonard: if it sounds like writing, rewrite it.[25] We've already talked about *voice*, and in dialogue we need to hear those voices, individually and distinctively. With voice goes body language, tone – so much more than the words spoken. Good dialogue conveys a great deal without needing to explain.

Much is said about *said*. Children in primary classrooms are routinely taught to avoid *said*, and encouraged instead to use other speech verbs like *questioned, muttered, protested, insisted, complained*. This is one of the things you need to unlearn when you write for reasons unconnected with SATS tests. The eye skims over *said*, but snags on the pompous intrusiveness of *asseverated, interpolated*, as in:

> 'Where were you?' Jenny demanded.
> 'What business is it of yours?' Jim grunted.
> 'You're always like this when you're in the wrong,' Jenny complained.
> 'Since when?' Jim questioned.
> 'Every day of the week,' Jenny hissed.

It's distracting, isn't it? – and suggests that the writer doesn't trust the reader to pick up the tone of the exchange, reading grumpiness, irritation or outrage into the words spoken. Also (one of my pet peeves) it's impossible to hiss words that don't include sibilants; and anyone who writes 'Why?' he questioned' or 'Sorry,' she apologised' would do well to try saying things just once.

I'm not suggesting that verbs other than *said* should never be used, but if scattered all over a page they will draw attention to themselves and away from the speech itself. *Let the dialogue do the talking* is a good rule of thumb. Often, especially if there are only two people talking, you don't need speech attributions at all, or only intermittently. Some authors write whole pages of nothing but dialogue – which can, however, be irritating if the reader loses track of who's saying what, and has to return to check. But if someone is shouting, or complaining, or objecting, or whingeing, that should be clear from the words said, and needn't usually be underlined by *he shouted* or *she objected*.

Yvonne   Linda is quite right when she says that dialogue must sound alive and convincing when read alone. Curiously, though, dialogue in a story will sound much more convincing if you do *not* write it in a true-to-life way. Do you know what I mean, like? Because, um, you know, when we, like, talk to each other (especially, like, *kids*), we . . . they . . . you know. They, like, talk in circles and there are, you know . . . . pauses, so you have to, like, um, guess what . . . It's easier face to face, you know? You don't, um, notice, sort of, how . . . well, um, how boring speech can be. And I absolutely haven't, um mentioned, you know, all the swearwords lots of people . . . and the, um, sort of verbal tics people have; you know, the way they say, like, 'absolutely' all the time. So, um, what we aim for is, like, pretended reality. Right?

There's a similar problem with accents. It is tempting to try and render, on the page, a perfect Bradford accent for your Yorkshire lad, born and bred. But it can be very irritating for the reader. I remember being very intrigued, as a ten- or eleven-year-old, by Dickon's accent in *The Secret Garden*, still one of my favourite children's books. Frances Hodgson Burnett transcribed the boy's speech very carefully; lots of apostrophes and missing letters. For a short while, I delighted in trying to read it, thinking that I was learning a true Yorkshire accent. But it soon became too slow and irritating; it interfered with the story and I was impatient to know what happened. So I skimmed over what Dickon said, in order to get on with the story.

It is usually better, particularly when writing for children who are relatively new to the finer complexities of punctuation, to convey accent more subtly.

Make a reference to the character's origins, and choose a few words or expressions that are typical of the character's region or country. Go for the rhythm and inflexion of the dialect, or have your foreign character consistently use titles in his or her native tongue (Senor/Monsieur/Herr). But don't overdo it.

'I've lived on these moors since I were no more than a lad' conveys a local accent without requiring a Yorkshire dictionary – which, by the way, you can obtain. (Teenage slang, swearwords, text-speak, cockney rhyming slang, body language – you name it, there's probably a dictionary for it.)

TOP TIPS

Linda *Always read your dialogue aloud. Your ears are alert to things your eye skims over.*

Yvonne *Think carefully about using swearwords. It may be realistic to have your inner-city urchins swearing like troopers, but you have to get your book past the gatekeepers who have the money to buy it. You should not be intimidated, but you will almost certainly have to defend your choice of words during the editing process, so be ready.*

Linda Try writing a page of dialogue without any speech verbs at all. When someone is speaking, either leave the dialogue unattributed or use body language or actions to indicate what he or she is doing.

Yvonne In your writer's notebook, try to remember and then faithfully record short snatches of conversation you have heard around you when out and about: buses, trains and assorted queues are good for this. Include the verbal tics and repetitions, the pauses and the expletives – this will help you tune your ear to the wide variety of accents, patterns and vocabulary we all live with and among. When you have gathered a good sample of one particular accent or age group, try to write the 'pretended reality' version, that makes the character sound authentic without driving the reader to distraction.

Pace and suspense

Yvonne You will hopefully have some instinctive sense of pace and suspense – it comes along with the ability to see and shape a story in your mind's eye. But it is easy to be diverted into over-relishing one part of a story at the expense of another, and this can lead to a slow or uneven pace. Once the plot stops driving forward, it is more likely that the reader will find the book slow, or boring, and give up. There are technical tricks that can help you to keep an eye on your pace and introduce a thread of suspense that will hopefully hook your readers and keep them reading.

Pace and mood are closely linked. If your character is thinking over a big decision – whether to run away from home or stay and face up to something they've done wrong, for example, or which to believe when two friends are giving completely different accounts of an event – we will need to share what's going on in the character's head. The mood may be edged with fear, or self-loathing, or excitement, but essentially it will be reflective.

Length of sentences can convey mood, and influence pace at the same time – action, danger and excitement – by short, stripped sentences:

> *She stopped. So did he. She crossed the road. So did he. She looked down the deserted street. No lights in any of the houses. No passing cars. Only darkness, and Jane, and the man.*

For a reflective mood use longer, flowing sentences:

> *She leaned back in the boat and lazily trailed her hand through the water, watching small fish dart and scatter as the oars dipped and pulled. Overhead, birds drifted, hitching a ride on the thermal; bees hovered over the clover on the river bank, unhurried, gorged with nectar.*

Another way to keep up the pace and create suspense is to switch scenes at a crucial moment and leave your reader hanging; just as a character is about to open the box, perhaps, or enter the underground chamber. This is particularly good when you want to build a sense of fear or danger. Jack's day on the beach takes a menacing turn when he finds himself on a rocky outcrop, trapped between a fast-rising tide and a sheer cliff face. Meanwhile, back at the hotel, Mum and Dad are settling down for afternoon tea and wondering where Jack is. They were expecting him back by now. Back at the beach, Jack is sizing up the cliff and realising there's no chance. His feet are starting to be washed by the tide. He climbs as high as he can on the rocky outcrop, and starts to shiver with cold and fear. Back to the hotel, and little sister says she saw Jack heading for the rocky outcrop. The waitress bringing scones overhears and turns pale. Perhaps she slams down the scones and calls for the manager. She knows the dangers of the tide on that part of the beach . . . The alarm is raised, but is there time to save Jack?

And so on. As with all techniques, don't overdo scene change or the effect will be more like a stream of paparazzi camera flashes than a sense of building terror.

You can also build suspense by slowly layering clues, creating an air of expectation that something is about to happen: you follow a pawprint on a muddy track through the woods; another set of prints join the trail, showing a larger, heavier animal; further on, the freshly killed and half-eaten carcase of the smaller animal lies across your path. There's a rustle in the undergrowth; you stand frozen to the spot: silence; breath of relief, move on; a sudden low growl from behind you just as you realise there is no escape.

I talked earlier about driving the action. There needs to be a clear sense of direction, but now and then, where the characters choose a course of action, let them make an unexpected choice that will surprise the reader and perhaps change the pace. Note the word 'surprise', as opposed to 'stun'; don't make your characters do something completely off-the-wall and alien to their personalities. Your reader will lose faith in your ability to make a story 'real'. A random sprinkling of shocks and surprises that have no relevance to the character or story you have set up is high on the list of no-no's for a successful author, along with the 'and it was all a dream . . .' ending and using the story as a mouthpiece for your own personal moral campaign. Instead, set up clues that make the surprising choice, when it comes, credible.

For example, Lucy – a sensible girl – loves heights. We know this because she likes to go rock climbing and often walks to the top of the local church tower. She explains that climbing up high helps her to calm herself and face down her fears when she is upset. But Lucy is aware of the dangers, and is always careful about where she climbs. Later, it will make sense that when a traumatic event occurs, and there is nowhere else to climb, Lucy starts to ascend the dangerous electricity pylon – not a sensible choice for sensible Lucy, and therefore surprising. But understandable. Will she come to her senses and realise what she's doing? How does the helpless friend feel, standing on the ground, unable to stop Lucy from climbing? How will it all end? There's your suspense.

Suspense is not just for serious stories, though. Light-hearted and humorous tales also benefit. Comedian Rowan Atkinson's *Mr Bean* character illustrates how well suspense works in comedy. We watch him bumbling along, teetering on the edge of disaster, just missing the cliff edge or the plate glass window or the banana skin on the pavement. But we know that each time Mr Bean smiles smugly at having avoided a hazard, he is moving one step closer to the final, hilarious disaster which will inevitably take him completely unawares. Keep the reader (or the viewer, in Mr Bean's case) waiting for the dramatic climax; they know something big is going to happen, but they don't know when, or how, so they have to stick with you and pay attention.

Humour, used carefully, also plays its part in pacing a book. It can actually heighten the sense of despair or foreboding in a serious situation. We grip our seats, we freeze motionless in our chairs in suspense or fear for the character as we read, because we have no idea what will happen next. With tension so high, a momentary release that makes us laugh unexpectedly gives a helpful respite and relaxes us a little. So when the next, horrifying thing happens, it pulls us back into the story like a whiplash, sending us straight back into the fearful situation with an even higher sense of shock or foreboding because of the brief respite that made us feel everything was under control. Shakespeare used this technique in his tragedies by introducing jesters and fools in comic interludes, interrupting the action and relaxing the tension by encouraging the audience to laugh before dumping them right back into the murder and intrigue. (Note for those of you with awful memories of badly taught Shakespeare in school: I promise you, people really *did* laugh at that stuff in the sixteenth century.)

It is important for the writer to stay in control as the story develops, judging and monitoring its pace and manipulating the reactions of the readers to create the mood that the story needs. The character's loss of control is also a useful device for creating suspense: being trapped, being forced to do something against your will, losing the path on a snowy moor; not being able to discern whether someone is lying or telling the truth; all of these plot devices are good vehicles for suspense.

Finally, try this to judge the pace of a novel that you have finished in first draft, or which feels 'stuck'. Summarise each 'scene' in the plot on to a postcard or similar-sized note; where there is a significant event that moves the action on, use a different coloured paper or pen. Now lay your cards out across the floor in a line, or in a circle. Look at the pattern; you should be seeing regular splashes of the 'action' colour across your line, with an extra splash or two towards the end, when you reach the climax of the story. Where there are long stretches of the non-action colour, your pace is likely to be uneven.

Yvonne Bearing in mind the suggestions above for creating pace and suspense, take an ordinary, everyday activity - for example, walking home at the end of the day; leaving a note for someone to find; revving up the courage to ask someone on a date; climbing the stairs. Write a few sentences to create a leisurely, happy mood where it's clear all will go well. Now take the same situation and introduce a sense of menace and uncertainty, changing the mood completely. Finally, if you can, create suspense in a humorous description of the same situation.

Linda Look at pace and suspense by making a tension graph.

- Choose a book you know well and have to hand.

- On a sheet of A4 paper, landscape, draw a horizontal axis labelled Chapter One, Chapter Two, etc; across the page. Label the perpendicular axis Tension, and mark out a scale of 1 to 10.

- Plot the rise and fall of tension throughout the novel. If the main character is running for his life in Chapter One, the tension will be somewhere near 10. If she's almost dozing off during a very dull assembly, the tension will be closer to 1. Mostly, though, it will be somewhere in between.

- Look at the peaks and the lows across the graph you've made. Notice that even in action-packed stories full of excitement and danger the tension can't stay at the same pitch throughout.

- Where are the highest points of tension? Look especially at how tension is managed towards the end of the story. The climax is rarely in the last pages, unless the author has contrived a cliffhanger ending leading to a sequel (which, in my view, is cheating the reader); it's more likely to be in the last-but-one chapter or earlier, followed by a drop in tension towards restoration of normality, or some kind of assimilation of what's happened.

- You could try this with different kinds of stories, and then with your own.

- In your own graph, is there enough tension? Enough variation? Have you written three consecutive chapters where the tension is low? Or six in a row with unremitting excitement?

TOP TIPS

Linda *Look closely at moments in your story when something dramatic is taking place – the high points in your tension graph. Have you given these moments enough importance? Have you rushed the reader through them? Paradoxically, the split-second moments in an action sequence are the points at which the narrative needs to slow down. See, for instance, the episode in* Postcards From No Man's Land *in which Jacob is mugged at an Amsterdam café, and gives chase,[26] or the killing of Hector's baby son Astyanax in Adèle Geras'* Troy.[27]

Yvonne *My tip comes originally from either Wilkie Collins or Charles Reade – opinions differ on its source. But it was passed on to me by Julia Jarman, author of* The Big Red Bath *and many more titles, who is skilled in the art of pace and suspense even for very young readers:*

'Make 'em laugh, make 'em cry – but above all, make 'em wait.'

Titles

Linda   Look at the face-out displays in shops and think about which books catch your attention, and why. Of course the cover design is crucial, but what about the titles? Do some sound particularly intriguing? Are there others that just don't interest you?

When you're writing, it's good to have the title in mind before you start, but that doesn't always happen. You may have a title in mind without being quite sure that it's right; maybe you're hoping for a better one to come along while you're writing. (Many a contract has been issued for a book with a *working title*, to be changed at a later stage – author, publisher and agent at least know which piece of work is being referred to.) Perhaps a phrase you've written will strike you as suitable, or the friend to whom you entrust your first draft will come up with something you prefer to your own effort. But it can feel unsettling not to have a title at all.

Sometimes a publisher will decide against your favoured title, and ask you to change it. This happened to me with a young teenage novel I wanted to call *Marbles*; I liked that, but my editor thought it sounded like a much younger story. After a lot of thought, I came up with *The Sandfather*, which is much better for this book. (I still like *Marbles*, though – maybe it will start another story.)

Publishers at present favour 'high-concept' books – stories with a gripping central idea that can be summed up in a sentence or two – and some titles reflect this: for instance *The Hunger Games* by Suzanne Collins, *Wolf Brother* by Michelle Paver, and *My Sister Lives on the Mantelpiece* by Annabel Pitcher. On the other hand, many recent teenage books have rather abstract, one-word titles, such as *Breathe, Fallen, Gone, Starcrossed, Bloodchild, Stolen, Holes* and of course *Twilight*. These titles are more allusive than explanatory, depending on atmospheric cover artwork or photography to suggest what the story is about. Titles for younger readers are generally more explicit. Do you want yours to convey excitement, mystery, fantasy, humour, domestic drama? If you've written a series, all the titles can start with the same word or phrase, as in Mary Hoffman's *Stravaganza* sequence, beginning with *Stravaganza: City of Masks* and going on to *Stravaganza: City of Stars,* and several more.

Picture books and humorous stories for young readers often have rhyming titles, such as Julia Jarman's *Class Two at the Zoo* and Nick Sharratt's *Shark in the Park,* or alliteration – for example Andy Stanton's *Mr Gum and the Biscuit Billionaire,* Steve Voake's *Hooey Higgins Goes for Gold* and Dave Shelton's *A Boy and a Bear in a Boat.* Titles such as *Ratburger* (David Walliams), *The Toilet of Doom* (Michael Lawrence), *My Brother's Hot Cross Bottom* (Jeremy Strong) and *Morris the Mankiest Monster* (Giles Andreae and Sarah McIntyre) share a kids-only, adults-keep-out factor which is guaranteed to get the books into the hands of young readers, particularly boys.

Unusual titles can command attention, such as *The Curious Incident of the Dog in the Night-Time* – not everyone will pick up the reference to the Sherlock Holmes story, but the title is intriguing enough without that. *A Monster Calls* (Patrick Ness), *The Secret Diary of Adrian Mole Aged 13¾* (Sue Townsend) and *Before I Die* by (Jenny Downham) are also arresting. I've already mentioned one of my favourites, *Bambert's Book of Missing Stories,* a title I find as irresistible as *The Ostrich Boys* (Keith Gray), *This is All: The Pillow Book of Cordelia Kenn* (Aidan Chambers) and *A Midsummer Night's Death* (K. M. Peyton). Each of these would make me pick up the book to find out more, regardless of the author's name or the cover design.

Your ideal title will stand out, stay in people's minds once they've heard it, and also give the flavour of the book. Finding it will help give you confidence in the story you're telling; but if you can't, don't panic. Here are some things to try:

Linda

- If the title just won't come, get a large sheet of paper and write down every word that has something to do with your story. 'Brainstorming' may bring something to the surface, or show how words could combine in unexpected ways.

- Try also brainstorming sayings, proverbs and even clichés to see if they provide a title (like my *Set in Stone*). A small twist to a familiar saying can give a shift of meaning. An example of this, for an adult thriller rather than a children's book, is Sophie Hannah's *The Other Half Lives*. We're all familiar with the saying 'how the other half lives', but omitting the first word gives a different emphasis, and a title that immediately makes us question what the book could be about, contrasting life with death rather than the original opposition of poverty and wealth.

- Chapter titles aren't obligatory, but I include them more often than not because of the scope they offer to alert attention and provide links and contrasts. If you try giving a title to each chapter, one of them may prove to be the one you need for the whole book.

Yvonne Develop an ear for disjointed snippets of speech overheard from conversations, TV and radio that sound intriguing (*'Don't come any closer'*, *'something of the night'*, *'dogs wear jumpers, too'*, *'and the laughing stopped'*) and write them in your notebook – you never know when they will come in handy.

TOP TIPS

Linda *Although I've advised keeping your book to yourself until it's ready, the title is something you could try out on a range of people. Once you have their immediate response, ask what kind of story they'd expect it to be.*

When you've settled on a title, go to the Amazon website and enter it to see if there's already a book with that name. If so, it doesn't necessarily mean you have to change; there is no copyright on titles. But if there's already a children's book with your title, you'd better think again, especially if it's a recent one or by a well-known author.

Yvonne *It's great if a title comes early on, but don't worry about it until the end, when you're ready to submit. Start with a working title that sums up something about the story or format or audience; some of the working titles for my books have included 'the pink book', 'rain and bully', and 'the school teen book' – never destined to make it to the final mix, but enough to keep me going until a proper title came along.*

Beyond the first draft: becoming a self-critical reader

Yvonne So you have finished the final draft and the story has come alive – it's a good feeling. You have invested a lot of time and creative energy in this book, so it's important not to let it down at the final hurdle. Now is the time to focus on the technical details, the fine-tuning that will help the reader absorb the story just as it appeared in your imagination when you were writing it down. Editing looks at the story as a complete package: the big picture (plot, structure, characters, voice, narrative thread and so on) and the detail (accuracy or otherwise of facts, contradictions in the story, words or expressions that jar or will be censored, questions that remain unanswered for the reader). The final job of editing is a careful, technical proof-read for misspelling, typos, poor grammar – things of that detailed nature.

But you are not at this stage yet. Many writers, myself included, feel that the first essential step in editing is to do nothing, for at least a month if possible. Do something else entirely – start a new story, plan a fishing trip, visit relatives, whatever will keep you away from the story. When you return, you will be looking at it with fresh eyes, and you will be surprised at what you see this time around. When you come back to your draft, read it aloud from a hard copy. Reading and re-reading on a computer screen is not the best way to edit (or to re-draft), as your brain helpfully accommodates to make your eyes see what you meant to say. Reading aloud, which uses a different part of your brain with slightly different connections and pathways, helps you to look afresh. Better still, get a trusted friend or writing buddy to read it aloud to you – they can only read what is actually there, not what you meant to say, and you will hear how differently the story is being interpreted by listening to the emphases and inflexions a first-time reader of the story uses.

Paeony Lewis, who with illustrator Penny Ives created the internationally successful picture book *I Will Always Love You*, is very clear about the need to walk away for a time:

> 'Sometimes there's a vague niggle whispering at the back of your mind, but you want to ignore it. You've already spent an incredibly long time on the manuscript and your friends seem to like it, so what's the problem? Ho hum, the problem is something's not quite right and you don't want to admit it . . . so you're getting tired of editing and revising and decide 'That will do'? Imagine you had to invest £1000 of your own money in the publication of this book. Would you do it? Or would you want to improve it further? Be honest with yourself!'

TOP TIP

Yvonne Try to adopt a professional distance from your work for this part of the writing process: if this was someone else's story and you were asked to review it, what would you say? What strengths and weaknesses would you be considering? It's important to consider both halves of that question, not get sucked into the self-doubt and lack of confidence that dogs many talented people.

EXERCISES

Yvonne Edit this wandering, flowery paragraph below to make it a more succinct, interesting insight into this character's thoughts:

The thing is, when I think about what it might be like to ride the surf of a huge wave or climb to the summit of a mountain or write an epic best seller, it makes me feel small. All I can feel is how impossible it would be to do it, for someone like me. It's not as though I am clever or daring or even very sporty, and I don't know if life, so far, has taught me anything that it would be worth sharing with the rest of the world and maybe the only interesting things that have happened to me are things I wouldn't want to share anyway. I look at all the people who do everything better than me and I wonder what the point is of trying when the chances are you won't succeed anyway.

Linda As Yvonne says, reading your manuscript aloud is essential, and should be done before you even think about submitting your work. With a longer book, this may take place over several days, so that you can give it your full attention. Reading aloud will highlight any clumsy phrasing, accidental tongue-twisters, repetitions, involuntary rhymes. It can help you to hear, rather than see, that an action-packed scene is over too quickly or that a descriptive passage is too long, and sounds indulgent. When you find yourself getting tired and losing concentration, stop. This stage shouldn't be rushed.

Revise, cut, edit

Yvonne   When I talk about redrafting to school students on author visits, I sometimes ask how many of them have been told by teachers that they must do a rough draft, then revise and redraft it before handing it in. Almost all hands go up. Then I ask the teachers to look away, and ask the students how many actually *do* more than one draft; I never see more than about three hands raised. So when I tell them that the book they are asking me to tell them about went through three, four, six drafts before I was happy with it, they are amazed. Several budding writers change their career choice immediately.

It is a truth universally acknowledged among writers – of any kind – that your first draft is not going to be your best work. For me, this knowledge is both a joy and a curse. It means I can write the first draft with complete abandonment to the moment. Not sure if this idea will work? Maybe there are too many characters? This page is descending into a rant and ramble that won't contribute to the story? Never mind – write it all in anyway. You don't need to decide on whether it's working right now; you know there is a long process of revising, redrafting and editing to come, and you can sort it all out then. I enjoy the freedom of being able to dive straight into the story, letting my creative puppy off the leash to chase whatever scents prove enticing, before hooking collar back on to lead and regaining the path.

The curse is knuckling down to the re-draft. Linda enjoys the redrafting and revision process; for me, it is a mixed pleasure. Knowing that I have the complete story hidden in that first draft is satisfying, exciting even. The expedition to dig out the story from the creative dust and sand I have thrown over it in the process of the first draft can be tedious, though, and sometimes painful. Occasionally you will get away with only a couple of major re-drafts, and a few more read-throughs where you are tinkering more than re-drafting. But be prepared for more. After more than twenty published books and a string of 'still in process' ones, I have learned never to try and timetable how much redrafting will be needed for any manuscript. Like a child, each story is unique and individual, making its own demands. And like children, some are clingier, pickier, or need a bit more attention than others.

In conclusion, love it or hate it, re-drafting is as important to the success of your work as the incarnation of the idea and the first draft. One word of caution: it is possible to do too much re-drafting, getting sucked in to an addictive cycle of perfectionism and self-doubt that can keep you endlessly reading, changing, editing and picking away at minor points. When you find you are making very minor changes, to punctuation or paragraphing, for instance, then it really is time to let go. Hand it over to your constructive critic, or put it away for a while and get on with something else. There is as much art to the recognition of when a book is finished as there is to re-drafting itself.

Cutting

Yvonne Writers often liken their books to children: much loved, precious, sent forth in hope and joy but not without fear. Cutting is like deliberately maiming this much-loved child, or submitting her to a major operation in order to cure her sickness and maximise her life opportunities. To others, relinquishing pages of inspired prose that – at the time – you thought were essential to your lovingly crafted novel feels like cutting the love and joy from the relationship you have tenderly nurtured with your characters.

You may understand the necessity of it without feeling any wish to be involved in the doing of it. But if you cut wisely and well, you will see your new improved work emerging like a phoenix from the ashes. I tend to do very extravagant and wordy first drafts; this suits my need to abandon myself to the story without worrying about repetition, contradiction and poor style. My first draft is therefore a sprawling mess of good, bad and ugly writing. This approach relies on the ability to be ruthless when it comes to the second and subsequent drafts.

Let's say that I believe pages 34 to 40 comprise some of my best ever writing: insightful, engaging, using exactly the right image and metaphor to get my point across. But what if that beautiful writing is actually a diversion from the story's path, or is holding back the action, or simply doesn't fit? It has to go. Sigh over it, mourn it, bury it with full honours, but get rid of it.

My first book was written in notebooks, longhand, and on a typewriter. This made cuts even harder, as I was physically crossing out whole pages that I had spent quality time composing, leaving a blood-trail of red ink across my slaved-over manuscript. I was constantly retyping whole chapters because of changes I'd made to one or two paragraphs. Computers were in their infancy then, and very expensive. Thankfully, most of us can now delete or move the superfluous piece without leaving a blodge of eraser fluid or oddly spaced pages.

Like Sue Purkiss, author of *Emily's Surprising Voyage*, I keep a folder on my computer for the offcuts from drafted novels and non-fiction books and papers. You never know where or when you might have just the right place for it. As Sue says:

> *It's like a security blanket. You'll be a lot more ruthless if you think you can retrieve your precious words if you change your mind. In fact, you very rarely will: pruning is essential for a healthy plant!*

TOP TIPS

Yvonne *To cut or not to cut? Don't over-think: if you are not sure whether to cut a passage/character/event from your manuscript, just do it (saving it on computer or on a written note, if you are not using a computer). See how the story flows without it. You can always put it back in, after careful reflection.*

Linda *Almost every piece of writing can be improved by cutting. At each stage of revision, right up until the final proof-reading, look for redundant words. Adverbs, especially when attached to speech verbs, can often be dispensed with.*

Linda Have a careful look at your first three chapters and see if you can make them into two by cutting out anything redundant. Look in particular at 'unpacking', by which I mean filling in background detail. I try to do the barest minimum of unpacking in chapter one, where I want the reader to be hooked into a character or a situation.

For instance, in chapter one you might have your main character, Tim, desperately searching for his dog on a clifftop in the dusk. How Tim chose the dog from Battersea Dogs' Home after a soul-searching choice, and that the dog has enormous importance to Tim because Tim's father died when he was ten, can wait to be unpacked in chapter two; in the opening scene it would be easy enough to show Tim's love for the dog, and his dread of losing it.

The unpacking you do in chapters two and three may turn out to be too much, especially when considered in the context of the finished book. If Tim has gone off the rails at school as a result of losing his father, this can be shown, not told. The link between Tim's behaviour and his father's death doesn't need spelling out to the reader. How Tim's mother struggles to cope with him as well as working full-time for not much money can be shown through their interactions.

Often, the details you put in at this stage of a story are really part of your 'warm-up' – things it's useful to know for yourself, but that needn't appear in the revised draft.

Yvonne The following paragraph is 110 words long. Rewrite it, keeping the sense of what is happening but using as few words as possible. The record to beat is the 32-word version which I have included as an endnote so that you can compare it with your – much better – one.[28]

She wondered why she had bothered to come, after so many previous disappointments; there didn't seem to be any point any more. She had travelled a very long way. She had needed to travel on three buses and a train. The journey usually took over four hours, which was bad enough without the C61, the second bus that ran from the city centre to the train station, being more than half an hour late. When she had arrived at the hospital, she had walked up to the ward. But, just like so many other times before, her gran didn't even know her name, and thought she was a complete stranger.

Learn to love criticism

Yvonne Handing over your finished manuscript to anyone, even a close friend or member of the family, is a daunting prospect. There are many secret writers who write compulsively, sometimes long into the night. They may be turning out great stories, beautiful poems or heart-catching memoirs, but we will never know; their work is hidden away or destroyed as soon as it is finished. I have come across secret writers in author visits at schools and libraries and in creative writing workshops, and I have tried, sometimes unsuccessfully, to persuade them to share their work.

When I ask what holds them back, the answer is usually to do with fear of finding out that the story or poetry collection that has absorbed and delighted them in the making, is worthless. Sometimes it's a fear of being laughed at, and occasionally people talk about not wanting to let the work go, like a parent who has to face the day when the child insists on walking to school alone.

Fiction is a story told and received; it goes nowhere without an audience, regardless of whether it is published or not. The confidence to hand over your work to be assessed by someone else is an essential element of the writer's life, because it's the only way you will get feedback, and improve your writing. On the other hand, entrusting your work to someone who has a real talent for sarcasm, negativity and 'taking people down a peg or two', or someone who doesn't read much, is clearly both unhelpful and downright daft.

So, you need to find an honest, constructive and supportive source of criticism. First, prepare yourself. You are taking a risk that your work will not please, that comments will come back that you don't like or don't agree with. If that's going to lead to you throwing your cherished work into the fire and never taking up your pen or laptop again, writing is not the career for you. You have to develop a professional approach; all opinions are subjective, and not all opinions are helpful or right. But a reasoned, considered review and assessment can throw up questions and flaws that you haven't seen, or spark ideas for making a weaker part of the story come to life, or encourage you that you are on the right track and your story really has merit.

You may decide, after careful reflection, that you do not agree with the opinion expressed and that you do not want to follow it; the important thing is to have understood the criticism and considered it dispassionately. It is easy to allow yourself to be over-sensitive, and to take any negative views of your work as wholesale, personal rejection. But with practice, you will feel the hard-bitten professional veneer begin to form a shield between your inner soul and the work you are offering for criticism. Your story represents many beautiful, ethereal things, but if you want to be published you are going to have to learn to see it as a product. If part of a farmer's crop has been blighted, you don't expect him or her to throw all his crops away and give up farming. You expect a careful consideration of what has gone wrong, some work to put it right for next time, and then a resowing of the field. And so it is with the professional writer and the next book.

Usually, you would hope that constructive criticism would highlight the things that are going well and also ask some pertinent questions about parts of the story that are not working or which need more work. A good critic will not only point out the weaker bits, but be part of the discussion about how they can be improved. Choose your critic carefully, particularly the first few times when you will inevitably be struggling with confidence levels. Your immediate loved ones and closest friends may seem the natural choice, but will they be honest, or will they worry about hurting your feelings? Have you ever watched one of the reality television talent shows where the contestant delivers an audition so shockingly awful that the judges are momentarily speechless, before launching a savage attack? It doesn't help to hear from those contestants that their mum/grandad/best friend/partner has encouraged them to follow their dreams because they have a huge talent.

This is where the 'writing buddy', a creative writing course, or the writers' group, comes into its own. You will never have more supportive critics, because everyone there is on the same mission: to write, and find an audience. They are struggling with the same issues of confidence as you, and they know that in due course, they too, will be counting on that same audience to give them a fair, constructive hearing. You are never far away from an evening class, a residential course or a group of aspiring writers who meet regularly. You can take along part of the story to hear the views of others, or a knotty problem or passage that isn't working, for help in 'unsticking' it. You can also develop your own ability to criticise constructively – handy for a sideline in book reviewing, once you are an established writer.

TOP TIPS

Linda *Commenting on someone else's work can be much easier than appraising your own. Coming to a story fresh, rather than from the hours of work you've invested in it, allows you to see both the flaws and the qualities; to see what a story might be, and what it isn't yet. This is one of the benefits of attending a writing group, or course. As Orange Prize winner Ann Patchett says, 'You can learn more, and more quickly, from other people's missteps than from their successes. If we could learn everything we needed to know about writing fiction by seeing it masterfully executed, we could just stay in bed and read Chekhov.'* [29]

Also from this you'll learn how to both give and receive criticism, and how to evaluate the comments on your own writing. Some may give you the insight you need to transform your work; others, as Yvonne has said, you may decide to ignore. Taking in criticisms you don't agree with may be frustrating, annoying, disappointing – but they can help to confirm your sense of why you've written the piece in the way you've chosen, and to show whether or not it's working for a range of readers.

Yvonne *Never share your first draft, because you will always want to make changes, regardless of other people's views. Wait until your story is in final draft and you feel satisfied with it before handing it over. That way, your critic will approach your work fresh.*

EXERCISES

Linda When your first draft is complete, put it aside for a week or at least a few days before re-reading it. As you read, try to forget that you wrote it yourself. (Yes, this is hard, but one thing I find helpful is to email the text to my Kindle and read it in e-format, where it looks like any other book. Reading on a computer screen doesn't give you the required distance. If you haven't got an e-reader, it's probably best to print out a copy and read that.)

Then write a full and honest review of your own book, being sure to comment on its good points as well as on any flaws you see. Be tough, but also be generous. Then put that review aside for another few days and see how you feel when you next look at it.

Do you agree with yourself? Have you been too harsh / too lenient? Have you highlighted flaws which can now be addressed?

Yvonne Set aside some time to look at the websites and online blogs and tweets of children's authors whose work you admire. Some authors include workshop-style discussions of a piece in progress, or invite comments on their work. By contrast, look at professional reviews of books online or in newspapers and magazines – how constructive are they? Do you get a sense of the book, and how the reviewer feels about it? Develop your own sense of what 'constructive' criticism means, and how it is different from a critic who is more interested in showing off his/her own prowess with language than in giving a genuine account of the book. This will help you recognise and use constructive criticism when it comes along.

What makes a story stand out?

Linda   What is good writing? It's easy enough to point to some of the features of *bad* writing: clunky dialogue, overuse of adverbs, clichés, random viewpoint-hopping, etc. – some of the things we've been looking at. Good writing is more difficult to analyse, but is unmistakable when you see it.

Several times I've been a judge, for awards for published books or for short story competitions. I found it revealing and instructive to put myself into a role similar to that of an editor looking at submissions. It showed me how crucially important the first page is; in fact the first sentence. By the time I'd read half the first page of any entry, I'd almost made up my mind whether the book or story deserved serious consideration; so many disqualified themselves almost instantly. And with more than one of the story competitions I've judged, the winner introduced itself to me within two sentences, and didn't disappoint as I read on.

Tutoring courses, I've seen a great deal of more-than-competent, publishable work. I've had one typescript in my hands that announced itself as the work of an exceptional writer from page one, and gave me the tingle down the spine that an editor must feel on discovering a new talent. It wasn't half-formed or tentative. It wasn't showy. It wasn't trying to be a crowd-pleaser. It had intelligence, promise, the sureness of living in the moment with all senses engaged. It was *The Traitor Game*, by B. R. Collins.

So what is it, that hard-to-define something that marks out good writing from merely workmanlike?

David Fickling, of David Fickling Books, often says that good writing 'sings'. To Jon Appleton, Editorial Director at Hodder, 'a fresh treatment of familiar ideas can be as arresting as totally innovative content, and more satisfying. I want to know that the writer has thought about the reader, so that meaning isn't obscured by clumsy repetitions or awkward imagery or careless spelling or punctuation. Overall, I want to feel as though I'm in safe hands − that I trust the writer and want to engage in whatever it is they want to tell me. That's the mark of a gifted writer − you will follow them anywhere, whether it's into the familiar or the unknown.'

For me, what stands out is *authority*. Good writing says, from the very first sentence, 'Come with me. I'm in charge here. I won't let you down. It will be worth your while.'

TOP TIPS

Linda *If you want to be a better writer, revise, revise, revise. Enjoy revising. Know that the really important work is done there.*

Yvonne *Don't try to write a story you don't really believe in yourself, hoping to cash in on a market trend. It is unlikely to work, and readers will see through the cynicism and fail to engage with it.*

Yvonne It is a well-known theory that there are only a limited number of story themes in the world. What these themes might be varies, but my favourite is Christopher Booker's theory that there are seven:[30]

- Overcoming the monster
- Rags to riches
- The quest
- Voyage and return
- Comedy
- Tragedy
- Rebirth

What do you think?

Consider the following questions before you start to write, and return to them after your first draft.

- Am I truly, genuinely, excited by this story idea? If so, why? And if not, why am I writing it?]
- What is its main theme? Will the reader recognise it?
- Can I identify three to five powerful images that hold the story together?
- Have I 'thought about the reader', as Jon Appleton says: do I know what I want to inspire in the reader?
- If someone asks me what the story is about, can I answer clearly and concisely?
- Are there some twists and turns, some surprises that nonetheless fit into the story?
- Am I in charge – do I know where the story is going, and have I laid clues and details that will help my reader follow me through the story?
- Is the ending satisfactory? (If everyone has died, or it has all been a dream, think again!)

> **Linda** Take ten or more novels, for any age group, and read just the first page of each. Put them into three categories: those you could put down now, those you'd be willing to continue with, and those that make you want to read on immediately. Now concentrate on the best ones. What is it that's grabbed your attention? Finally, read your own first page (if you already have one) and compare it to those you've just read.

Writing a synopsis

Linda A synopsis is an outline of your book which you send to a publisher or agent, together with your letter and sample chapters (see next section). Writing an effective synopsis is an art in itself, and you should write several drafts in order to convey the strengths of your book as well as you can.

To clarify: a synopis is not the same as the 'blurb', or cover copy, that appears on the back or inside cover flap of a published book. Nor is it the same as a detailed plan you write for yourself (if you do). Unlike the blurb, a synopsis can mention the ending. Unlike a plan to work from, it doesn't cover every plot element or mention every character.

The idea of a synopsis is to give an agent or editor assessing your submission an idea of whether you can shape a plot and hold it together. Without reading the whole book, they will be able to tell whether or not they're likely to be interested in it. Also they can see at a glance if it's too similar to a book they are already publishing, or to the work of another author the agency represents. With children's books, too, it can show whether or not you have a realistic idea of readership and the market.

Although some prospective authors send in sample chapters with no synopsis, or even whole manuscripts, literary agent Carole Blake says, 'I won't read chapters from a prospective new client unless I also have a synopsis . . . initially I can't commit myself to the many hours of speculative reading that a whole manuscript would entail. Having a synopsis makes it much easier to analyse the use of characters in the plot, the pacing and the tension.'[31]

Done well, the synopsis will make the agent or publisher want to read the story. A good synopsis alone won't sell your work, but it can show that you are professional, that you have a grasp of plotting and what will interest a reader.

The synopsis should convey the main thrust of the plot, say something about the characters, and address that important question of *what's at stake* as well as how the main dilemmas are resolved. It should not be a simple listing of plot points; nor should it include self-praise such as 'brilliantly written' or 'unputdownable' – the agent or editor will quickly decide that for herself.

Whole books could be written on the subject of selling your book to an agent or editor, and indeed have been. As there's no room to give more than brief details here, we can do no better than refer you to *Dear Agent* and *Write a Great Synopsis*, both by Nicola Morgan, full of clear, practical advice.

Yvonne   My daughter once sent me a postcard when I was working away from home.[32] It was an economic summary of some of the great classics available in the English language, including:

Moby Dick: *Ahab chases whale. Whale chases Ahab. Whale Prevails.*

Romeo and Juliet: *two teenagers fall in love and then they die.*

Gone with the Wind: *Scarlett's a yuppie. The South falls. Rhett legs it.*

I wouldn't advise sending such a short synopsis to a potential publisher, but it shows it can be done . . .

A synopsis is a hateful thing, and once you are an established author you may – I repeat, may – be able to get away with *not* telling your agent or publisher in advance what the book is about. But Carole Blake, whom Linda has quoted above, is not alone in relying heavily on a synopsis to show the merits of a prospective new client's work. Until you reach those heady heights, your synopsis is going to be crucially important to getting your story past the first base. It is your sales pitch, your advertisement, your invitation to come inside and learn more. It shares this in common with poetry: every word counts, and if you waste words, or you do not communicate your ideas clearly, you destroy the desire to read more.

It is important that you pay attention to the requirements of any agent or publisher you are planning to approach. Many of them will have guidelines for submissions stipulating whether they want the whole manuscript or just the first few chapters, and what length the work should be. Invariably, there will also be a request for a synopsis, sometimes with a recommended word length. If none is indicated, aim for no more than five hundred words. Within this limit you need to communicate the central idea, and the identity and circumstances of the main character. I don't think you always have to reveal the ending, particularly if it is supposed to be a startling twist, but you do need to show that you understand pace, plot and the necessity for an interesting character in a situation that will engage the reader. In writing for children, you also need to convey that you have understood the audience and written appropriately for the age range you have identified; that you have not written a 'brilliant, one-size-fits-all story for everyone from nought to ninety'.

Basically, you want the agent or publisher to read the synopsis and then feel inclined to read the longer sample chapters, or the whole manuscript. A hint of mystery, for example posing a question that is left hanging, can be quite enticing if you can convey an assurance that you do know where the story is heading. Here's an example:

> Leila has a secret that will blow her family apart – she was the one who anonymously tipped off the police about her brother Benji being involved in a local bank robbery where a cashier was badly injured. She has told no one what she did, but the feelings of guilt are hard to handle. Now Benji has pleaded 'not guilty' and the police are trying to track down the anonymous caller, who is a vital witness. On the estate, opinion is divided about Benji's involvement in the robbery. Leila's parents accept that he has fallen in with the wrong crowd lately, but firmly believe he is innocent. They see Leila's avoidance of public support as a betrayal; they have no idea that Leila actually witnessed the getaway and knows Benji was involved.

Everyone is asking who shopped Benji, including the rest of the gang, who are doing their best to find and silence the potential witness. The gang leader, Donny, is someone Leila has always dreamed of noticing her. But when he appears, at last, to be taking an interest in her, Leila is frightened of him and wonders if he suspects her secret. As the investigation proceeds and Leila's family struggle to come to terms with the press intrusion and the shame of having their family circumstances laid bare in the robbery's aftermath, Leila has to make the hardest decision of her life: does she have the courage to go public with what she saw, and help to send her brother to jail for what she knows he has done, or will she continue to cover her tracks and never tell? Leila knows that whichever option she chooses will come at a painful price.

When a frightening encounter with Donny's gang forces her hand, Leila makes her decision and prepares to face the consequences.

This is a short synopsis (about three hundred words) that would accompany the first three chapters of Leila's story. It is not much longer than a blurb (the snippet of information that traditionally goes on the back of a book jacket), and it would usually be sufficient, unless you have been specifically asked for more. Sometimes the agent or publisher will ask for a longer summary, perhaps chapter by chapter. A chapter summary is a good idea to have to hand in any case – if you do it as part of your revision process, it will help you see the structure and pace of the story, and give you a point of reference for discussion with anything the agent or publisher wishes to raise.

The synopsis can also be adapted to form the blurb for the book's cover. If I were doing this for the story outlined above, it would probably go something like this:

Leila has a secret – she was the anonymous witness who told the police about her brother's gang committing a violent crime. Now Donny, the gang leader, is taking an interest in her – but does he suspect what she's done?

TOP TIPS

Yvonne *I find that the synopsis is best left until near the end of the writing process, when the story is firmly embedded and unlikely to change.*

Linda *Be aware that writing a synopsis for an agent or publisher is very different from writing the story, and requires the skill of an advertising copywriter. You may feel that this is not you – but work and work and work at it. Prune, cut and refine until it's as lean and sharp as you can get it. There's no room for padding.*

EXERCISES

Linda I hate writing a synopsis, and rarely do – certainly not one that follows the rules we've suggested. So I'm relieved that Yvonne wrote the one above, and I didn't have to. However, I can see what a good job she's made of it. So many words and phrases in the longer version pack an emotional punch. There are high-octane words such as *secret – blow her family apart – anonymously – tipped off the police – bank robbery – guilt – vital witness – suspects – betrayal – struggle – decision – courage*. And so on. We can tell from this outline that the story has the potential to be full of drama and tension.

One thing I've found helpful is to convey the flavour of a story in a few such words. *Set in stone*, for example. *Love and possession. Art and immortality. Convention and defiance. Ambition and desire.*

Try a similar pairing of ideas for Yvonne's outline on the next page, for stories you know – and for your own. Once you've got this distillation, you can try expanding to fifty a hundred, three hundred words, never losing sight of where the emotional charge of the story lies.

> **Yvonne** Just for fun, and to exercise your creative mind, look back at the postcard examples above. Can you summarise, in less than fifteen words, some of your favourite children's classics? Here are a few to get you started, if you know them:
>
> *The Lion, the Witch and the Wardrobe*
> *The Cat in the Hat*
> *Twilight*
> *Anne of Green Gables*

Approaching agents and publishers

Linda There's nothing to stop you from approaching a publisher directly rather than finding an agent; it's how both Yvonne and I started. But, back then, we knew nothing, and with hindsight would certainly have approached agents first.

It's not obligatory to have an agent, and some writers and illustrators in the children's book world function very well without one. This may particularly suit authors who have established a long and satisfying relationship with one publisher and editor. Specialists in short stories and educational publishing are less likely to have agents than those who write mainstream fiction, partly because there is less room for manoeuvre over advances and terms in these areas. Some writers take the line that they don't want to pay commission to an agent when they can handle the contractual side themselves.

However, publishing has changed in the years since I got my first contract. It's become harder and harder for an author unrepresented by an agent to get the attention of an editor; many publishers won't even look at unsolicited submissions. If you set out on your own, not only will it be hard for your work to get beyond the slush pile; if you *are* offered a deal, it's unlikely that you'll know whether or not it's a good one.

An agent not only has a thorough knowledge of the book world and how it operates; she (or he, but I won't keep saying that) has contacts with many publishers, has a good idea what they're looking for and knows what kinds of books succeed. She knows what sort of advance you can reasonably expect, and will almost certainly get a bigger one than you'd manage alone. She goes to all the big book fairs and talks to foreign publishers; she will negotiate all the details of the contract, and will talk to editors about how your work is to be promoted. In return she will take commission on your earnings; generally this is 15 per cent on homes sales, 20 per cent on overseas and translations. (*The Writers' and Artists' Yearbook* gives details, as do agency websites.) In the light of the difference she is likely to make to your earnings, this is worth paying – *and*, when you're preparing your tax return, agent's fees can be put down as a tax-deductible expense.

Whether you're approaching a publisher or an editor, the following details of how to submit your work will be relevant.

How to find a publisher or editor

Your first stop should be *The Writers' and Artists' Yearbook*, an up-to-date edition (or find it online). More specifically there is the *Children's Writers' and Artists' Yearbook*, in which you can find listings of publishers and agents, with details of what they publish or who they represent, and submission guide-lines. You will avoid wasting time if you study these carefully before deciding whom to approach. For example, there is little point in sending your picture-book text to a publisher that doesn't produce them, or your fantasy trilogy to a specialist in non-fiction and educational books. As well as reading the listings, you should look at publishers' websites to be sure of sending the right book to the right place. Look at the authors they publish; if you've written a contemporary teenage thriller, then you will want to know that their list includes young adult authors you admire.

Most of the publishers and agencies listed in the *Yearbook* specify how to submit – for example:

- 'Will consider MSS [manuscripts] either by post with sae [stamped addressed envelope] or by email. Send covering letter, synopsis and up to three sample chapters. Allow twelve weeks for response.'

- 'No email submissions and no unsolicited material without preliminary letter.'
- 'No unsolicited MSS. Will only consider MSS via agents.'

It makes sense to do exactly what's stated, rather than imagine that the publisher or agent will be so overwhelmed by your brilliance that they'll make an exception for you. If they ask for a letter, send a letter. If they specify email, do it that way. As you see, you will need to be flexible and not expect to use the same approach for everyone.

Most will ask for sample chapters (usually three, or they may give a word limit), not the entire book, unless it's very short. If interested, they will then ask to see the whole. So obviously you should have completed it before making your approach. Send the first three chapters, not random pages or samples from different stages of the book.

Whatever you're sending, it must be conventionally presented, on loose A4 sheets, one side of the paper only, with double or 1.5-line spacing. Pages should be numbered. Don't be tempted to send fancy folders, bindings, ribbon trims or the like, and don't include illustrations unless you have the intention of illustrating your own book. Check spelling, punctuation and sense *very* carefully; it's part of being professional. Weak spelling, slapdash punctuation and missing words won't impress, and you don't want to tip the scales in favour of rejection.

We've already looked at how the synopsis should show the strengths of your book. The letter should say something about yourself, and indicate that you're serious about your writing. I have it on good authority that at least one agency has an 'idiot board', where they display, for general amusement, letters written by people who appear to be delusional, illiterate or barking mad. These will include:

- Claims to be the next Tolkien/Dan Brown/Jacqueline Wilson, or all of them combined.
- Promises that the enclosed book will enable both author and agent to retire to the south of France.
- Confident expectations of film deals and Oscar triumphs.
- Letters which demonstrate the writer's inability to form a coherent sentence.

Do you want to get farther than the 'idiot board'? Yes. So don't write letters like those. Neither should you say, 'I will phone next week to arrange a meeting' or 'I expect to hear back from you with a firm offer within two days.' Confidence is one thing; arrogance is another, and will only annoy. It's for the agent to decide whether to arrange a meeting or make an offer.

Your letter should give a brief idea of your book, its subject, genre and length, and what age group it's for. You can mention any writing courses you've been on, and anything else that suggests commitment. Carole Blake says, 'I, and most agents I know, want to represent writers who are planning a career. I never take on one-off fiction.'[33] So if you already have a second novel under way, mention that.

Pat Shepherd has recently set up Orchard Publishing Consultancy after years of experience in the marketing department of a major publisher. As her agency is 'small and focused', she will only take on 'authors I absolutely believe in. The hairs need to go up on the back of my neck as I read the submission and the story has to talk to me. The words have to spring off the page with no help from packaging. It's very difficult to quantify – it just happens.' The letter should give her the sense that she wants to read that author.

You may have been struck by 'allow twelve weeks for response', which wouldn't be unusual. Twelve weeks is three months. If you send your work to four publishers, and they each take three months to reject it, a year will have passed and you'll be no farther on than when you started.

So: is it reasonable to send work to more than one publisher or agent simultaneously? Yes, I think so, as long as you make it clear. An agent will be annoyed if she devotes hours to reading your complete typescript only to find that you've accepted representation elsewhere. If you state that you have also approached X, Y and Z, she may either reject you swiftly or, if she's impressed, move your submission to the top of her reading pile in order not to be pre-empted.

If an agent shows interest, the next step is to arrange a face-to-face meeting. If you're lucky enough to get that far with more than one agent, meet them all. It's likely to be a long relationship, and you need to know that you can get on well together. At this stage, ask whether or not the agent gives editorial advice – some do, some don't, some are flexible, according to the author's needs.

Fostering a professional approach

Linda   We've already talked about some of the misapprehensions people tend to have about writers and writing. Here's another, variously phrased as: 'I suppose you have to feel inspired before you can write?' or 'Presumably you can only write when you're in the mood?'

No, no, no. It's wonderful to feel inspired, but unless you're very lucky, and very unusual, inspiration won't carry you joyfully through a book of fifty, sixty or ninety thousand words. To be a professional writer, you must train yourself to work whether or not you feel like it. As the American writer Peter de Vries put it, 'I write when I'm inspired, and I see to it that I'm inspired at nine o'clock every morning.'[34] Also, those exhilarating moments when the writing seems to take flight tend to happen once the work is under way; they have to be earned.

The idea of 'inspiration' can be misleading, too. No one expects a dentist, electrician or teacher to wait for inspiration before they embark on their highly skilled, exacting work. A teacher can't slump in the staff room, claiming not to be in the mood for Year Nine; a dentist doesn't fling down his or her implements and walk out, complaining that inspiration won't come today. Applied to writers the term can be misleading, making you think that you're only really functioning when you're creating something of outstanding brilliance. Great, if you can – but it's also helpful to think of writing as a job of work, and to know that if you simply get on with it, you'll finish. It's often fear of failure that inhibits us, but you don't have to get everything right at the first try. So much important work is done at the revision stage, as we've said.

I've already mentioned the importance of routines. Most writers I know have some kind of structure or discipline, whether it's working at regular hours or producing a certain number of words each day; I don't know of any who wait until they're in the mood. In fact, most will confirm that keeping to a routine *helps* them to feel ready to write. Nothing is more dispiriting than fidgeting around the edges, like someone hesitating on the edge of a swimming pool, afraid that the water will be cold, or not wanting to get wet. You will feel far more positive if you plunge in and start swimming. And if you make it your daily routine you won't waste time dithering.

Another aspect of being professional is finding the ability to continue when things aren't going smoothly, and – more than that – to accept it as part of the job. Writing a book is running a metaphorical marathon. Distance runners face times during the race when their knees ache, their lungs hurt and they struggle to keep going. Do they give up? No, unless forced to by injury. They know from experience that if they keep running they'll find a burst of new energy, enough to complete the distance. Very few marathon runners find the experience a complete pleasure from start to finish, but they keep running regardless. They start with the firm intention of finishing, and so must you. There will be days when your writing feels like stodge, your plot is falling apart, your characters might be made of cardboard – times when the whole project feels pointless, and you feel like abandoning it. You must get through days like this; in fact you must expect them. You must find solutions, and with experience will come the confidence to know that you will. Like the marathon runner, you will get through the barrier and find your second wind.

We've talked about being self-critical, and about presenting your work to a writers' group for a response. Along the way to publication, there will certainly be other times when you'll receive criticism, and you must listen and take it in. When you've worked hard on a piece of fiction, and believe that it's as good as possible, it can be deflating to learn that it's not finished yet, or even that you need a major rethink. But – especially if you have a good relationship with your editor and/or agent – this is your opportunity to develop as a writer, very probably in ways you can't see for yourself.

This criticism may come in the form of a rejection letter or email. Some rejections use fairly standard terms, such as 'not right for our list' or 'we just didn't feel strongly enough about it to want to publish'. Editors and agents haven't the time or inclination to enter into further correspondence, so don't ask. But if you receive four rejections all saying that your characters aren't engaging, or that your plot flags, you should definitely take them seriously and have another hard look at your work.

Criticisms from editors, on first submission, may not be rejections: the publisher may be prepared to look at the work again if you revise it in line with their advice. Or the comments may come at a later stage. Particularly with established writers, the work may have been commissioned and will definitely be published, but the editor is now trying to help the author to capitalise on strengths and iron out weaknesses. Although you don't have to take up every suggestion, you should certainly be willing to consider every point that's made. Being professional doesn't mean being precious, insisting that your work is already perfect and refusing to change a single thing. As Carole Blake says,

> Writers should be greedy for criticism . . . It's a smart writer who listens to several sets of editorial criticism and then distils the best of them into a rewrite that turns a good book into a superb book. Who wouldn't want to improve characterisation, tighten plot, increase pacing and deepen motivation, along with adding impact to the opening and the climax? If you can do all that by listening to criticism and then take credit for it all by putting your own name on it, again: why not?[35]

TOP TIPS

Yvonne *One of the greatest joys of writing for a living is the choice it gives you to work flexibly; this is also one of the greatest drawbacks.*

When you are writing, you are working. If you were going to a job on the other side of town, you would not be at home to answer the telephone, mop the floor or open the post. So try to behave just as you would if you were working for an employer outside the home. Turn off your mobile, resist the temptation to browse the internet unless you are researching something genuinely relevant; train friends and family to understand that when you're working you will not be available except in an emergency.

Linda Don't put off starting. Nothing is easier than to find reasons not to start – perhaps you'd better deal with all your emails first, or confront the ironing or weed the garden – but don't let yourself. The world is full of people who don't write; you can very easily be one of them, if that's what you choose. But presumably you want to be one of the people who do write, or you wouldn't be reading this.

So much of writing is about commitment. You can't do it in a half-hearted way. I've lost count of the number of people who've told me, 'I've always thought I might write a novel one day.' I know that most of them won't; one day, more often than not, means never. It won't happen unless you make it. Books don't write themselves. So, if you want to write – write.

EXERCISES

Linda Keep a record of your word count. This may sound petty, but it's one of the things I do to keep myself motivated. Each morning, I make a note of how many words I wrote the day before, and of the total. As I tend to write about 1,200 words a day – on a really good day, maybe 1,500 – an average weekly output adds up to almost 10,000 words. As the days go by, this mounting total becomes more and more encouraging, and working at that rate would produce a 60,000-word first draft in less than two months.

I'm lucky to be able to make my writing the main focus of my day, fitting everything else around it. But even with a full-time job you can give yourself a writing discipline. The word count is only one way of doing that, but if you decide, say, to produce 100 words a day, you'll have 700 words in a week, 3,000 in a month – and a real sense of progress.

The crucial thing is to do some writing every day, even if only for half an hour. Then it becomes part of your life.

Yvonne Buy yourself a small, sturdy notebook, of the size that would enable you to write one decent paragraph per page. At the end of each day, write one paragraph about how your writing has gone. Handwrite it, and don't allow yourself to cross out anything or redraft – this will make you think more carefully about what you want to record. Use your paragraph to sum up your day's work. You might simply log that you made progress on research into boot factories in nineteenth-century Northampton, or the completion of Chapter Five of *Great Gatsby Junior* went very well, or your frustration at your characters being stuck up a tree and insisting they won't come down without a rewrite of the plot . . . The point is not so much what you write, as the pause to reflect on the process and sum it up simply and clearly, without gushing or wallowing.

And when you feel yourself sliding into the oblivion of self-doubt because you've stared at an empty screen or notepad and achieved nothing, you can look back and see there were other days like these, and you dusted yourself off and started afresh. That's what professionals do.

Courses, consultants and competitions

University courses for writers

Linda   Many universities now offer undergraduate and postgraduate courses up to PhD in Creative Writing – full-time or part-time – and some specifically offer courses in writing for children and young adults. As well as producing and refining their work, students develop the working habits which will sustain their career, and are also introduced to the business side of publishing through visits from editors, agents and other professionals.

If other commitments don't allow you to take a full-time course, numerous institutions offer day and evening classes in writing – for example the City Literary Institute (City Lit) in London offers a taster day on Writing for Children.

Short residential courses for writers

Linda   A number of organisations run weekend courses – for instance the Faber Academy and the Masterclasses organised by the *Guardian* newspaper, and many others outside London. Several literary festivals – Oxford, Brighton and Cheltenham, for instance – regularly include writing workshops in their programmes, and courses are also offered through Adult Education, Continuing Education and, for older people no longer in full-time employment, the University of the Third Age (U3A). A Google search for writing courses in your area will probably bring up an extensive list.

The Arvon Foundation and Ty Newydd in North Wales run residential courses specialising in various aspects of writing, children's fiction and writing for teenagers among them. Both organisations run their courses along similar lines – two tutors, a midweek guest, workshops and one-to-one tutorials.

Consultancies

Linda   Although an editor or an agent might think your work could be improved to the point of being publishable, only in exceptional circumstances will they offer to mentor you – they simply don't have time to spare from the authors they publish or represent. However, there are other ways of getting the advice you need. Many writers use editorial consultancies to refine and revise their work before submitting it. Investing time and money at this preliminary stage can greatly increase an author's chance of securing a contract.

Such consultancies can be found online, or in advertisements in the pages of writing magazines. (A search for 'literary consultancies' or 'manuscript assessment' will bring up a list.) They may offer the choice of paying a fee for a short assessment of your work, or a rather larger sum for a full appraisal. Some consultancies offer to approach agents on your behalf if or when they think your work is saleable. If you're thinking of trying this, you should feel confident that you'll be spending your money well. Before signing up with a literary consultancy, find out who will be reading your work and what their qualifications are for advising you. Have they been successfully published? Does this consultancy handle or specialise in children's fiction, and does it list the names of authors it has guided to publication?

This is not meant to imply that editorial and literary consultancies are dubious – just that you should be quite clear that what appears to be a consultancy is a genuine one, and can give sound and knowledgeable advice. There are many well-regarded consultancies such as TLC (The Literary Consultancy), Gold Dust (whose mentors include Sally Cline and Carole Angier, the editors of this series), the Writers' Workshop and Cornerstones. All these list the names and publications of their editorial team, have many success stories, and are clear about what they offer. Some offer longer-term mentorship programmes, or additional services such as copy-editing and proof-reading.

Successful children's authors who took the consultancy route to publication include Jenny Downham, Katherine Langrish, Gillian Philip and Ellen Renner.

Writers' groups

Linda There are writers' groups all over the country – you can probably find details online or from your local library. These vary tremendously, and before committing yourself it might be wise to attend as a guest to meet the members and to see if the group will provide the stimulus you need. You may find, for example, that the group consists mainly of retired people who meet to share reminiscences and poems; although of course there's nothing wrong with this, you won't get the robust criticism you need if your eventual aim is publication. Another group could be more targeted and experienced, including published writers or people with knowledge of the book world. So it may be worth exploring beyond your immediate area in search of a group to suit you.

Writing buddies

Linda If you're lucky, you might be able to team up with another writer whose tastes you share and whose opinion you value. This can be one of the most effective ways of getting a response to your work. I'm never sure of the value of exposing your work to a larger group, since the aim of writing can't and shouldn't be to please everyone. But if you can find the *right* person, someone who likes your work and your aims and genuinely wants to help you to improve, and for whom you can do the same in return, you will both gain from the experience.

What's needed is a balance between encouragement and constructive criticism. For most of us, it's easy to consult a kind relative or friend who will say, 'That's brilliant,' or 'I really liked it,' but how helpful is that? Another writer is likely to see possibilities you've overlooked yourself, and also to be tactful enough, knowing the difficulties of writing as well as the rewards, not to give a high-handed dismissal.

There are plenty of internet forums, too, on which you can air your work in progress, and invite responses from readers. One example is Writing Forums (www.writingforums.com), where you can if you wish post your novel chapter by chapter, and which does seem to attract detailed and thoughtful responses. The idea of exposing your work to strangers may be alarming, and you might decide at once that it's not for you. On the other hand it may be an attraction – an unknown person, unlike a friend or family member, doesn't need to humour or flatter you, and is engaging with your story through choice and interest, not because you've asked a favour.

Competitions

Yvonne My professional writing career started with a competition that I entered on the spur of the moment. My local London radio station, Capital Radio, ran a short story competition, giving a title that exactly fitted a story I had written when I was fourteen and never shown anyone. I retyped it, using Capital Radio's title; to my astonishment, it won. I spent the book-token prize on a couple of creative writing textbooks, and started writing stories for a range of magazines. I discovered that what I really wanted to write was children's fiction, and I've never looked back. I still have a great fondness for competitions, although as a professional I am barred from most of those for children's writers. I will occasionally enter a festival poetry or essay competition, for example, just for the joy of doing something different and trying my hand at, say, romance, or science fiction (usually unsuccessfully). A variety of writers' magazines (*Writer's Monthly*, *Writers' News* etc) also offer regular competition opportunities, and the magazines themselves are full of useful tips and techniques, as well as news of what's going on in the publishing world.

If you simply type 'writing for children competition' into a search engine, you will come up with a variety of opportunities online. Below are three that were available at the time of writing (Autumn 2012) and are likely to be around in the future; type in the title to get the latest news on each one.

Mslexia magazine regularly runs competitions to find new, female writers' voices. In 2012, and possibly again in 2014, these opportunities involved a novel for children. The entry fee in 2012 was £25.

The Academy of Children's Writers runs an annual story for children competition (the entry in 2012 was £3, $10 or €10). You can submit a short story, or the first two thousand words of a longer work.

Finally, every February, the Amazon Breakthrough Novel competition (open to all comers, amateur and professional) searches for a new work of fiction in adult and young-adult categories. The prize is publication by Penguin (and the usual razzamatazz of a prizegiving awards celebration). Entry is free, and there is a lively online forum for those who have entered as the competition goes through its longlisting and shortlisting process.

There are many more one-off competitions in magazines, and for festivals, promotional campaigns and so on. If you win, your work will be published and may come to the attention of agents and publishers. At the least, it will give you an enormous confidence boost. Sometimes, you pay a fee to enter the competition, sometimes not. In some, shortlisted entrants are offered workshops or mentoring, or entrants are given very valuable feedback on the work they have entered. Always be careful to read the competition rules and stick to them exactly, or your entry is unlikely to be read.

Making a living from writing for children

How do authors get paid?

Linda When a publisher wants to buy your book, they will offer you an advance. For the purpose of illustration, we'll say that this is £5,000. This is usually split into thirds: one part to be paid on signature, one on delivery of the complete typescript; the last on publication. Some advances are split into four parts, with parts one and two as before, part three on hardback publication, and part four when a paperback appears.

From this you can see that you probably won't get all your money in one financial year, because a book may not appear until a year or more after the contract is signed.

Your contract will specify what royalties are to be paid. A royalty is a percentage of the selling price, usually 7½ per cent, which will be paid only after a book has earned back its advance. So, if your book sells at £5, the royalty on each copy will be 37½p on copies sold at full price. You will receive royalty payments once the book has earned the full £5,000 advance – in other words, when it has sold 13,333 copies, which may take some time, or may never happen. And many books are not sold at full price, as you'll know from looking in bookshops, on the Amazon website and in catalogues offering discounted books, so the total sold would need to be higher.

You may never 'earn out' your advance, in which case you won't have to give anything back; but the publishers will have worked out what to offer you on the basis of what they think your book will earn. If your book sells well (or your advance is very low) it will soon have 'earned out', and you will then receive a royalty payment twice yearly.

As we've already indicated, many children's writers need to find ways of supplementing their income. Very few authors for children can earn a living purely by writing; a survey for the Society of Authors[35] showed that most earn less than the minimum wage. Because we so often read of new authors being paid six-figure advances for their dazzling debuts,[36] it's tempting to imagine that getting a book deal will immediately make you rich and enable you to give up the day job, but this applies only to the exceptional few. Most authors who make their living by writing have worked hard at it for years, Yvonne and myself included.

Even if you do succeed in earning enough to live on, authors' earnings are unpredictable: you may find that one year you sign three contracts and are paid signature advances, whereas the next you're waiting for publishers to decide, your books aren't earning royalties yet (or, farther down the line, have gone out of print) and you earn almost nothing. Being an author is unlikely to make you financially secure, especially at first. If you're supporting yourself or a family it's advisable not to burn your other boats until you feel confidently established. Perhaps not even then.

The unpredictability of authors' incomes isn't always negative: you may sometimes earn money for doing nothing, e.g. if your publisher or agent sells translation rights to your work, an audio company buys it, or an educational publisher wants to use an extract. And there is Public Lending Right (currently under review) which pays authors a sum of money every February. Under this scheme, authors are paid a small sum (at the time of writing, 6.05 pence) every time their book is borrowed from a UK public library. On first publication, you must register yourself with the Public Lending Right Office, then remember to add each new title or edition by the last day of June in the year it becomes available. You can't claim in retrospect, so if you forget you will have lost the money you're entitled to. The maximum that can currently be earned in a year is £6,600, and there are many children's authors whose loans earn this amount, particularly those who have published numerous titles for younger children, as those books tend to go in and out of libraries very frequently. One of the benefits of the PLR scheme is that books that have gone out of print can continue to earn money from library loans, often for many years.

If you're looking for ways of supporting yourself as a writer, consider:

- Writing for a different age group, either under your own name or under a pseudonym

- Writing for an educational publisher

- Writing for Working Partners, Hothouse Fiction or other book packagers

- Writing features for magazines or journals (not covered in this guide)

- Giving talks and running workshops in schools and libraries

- Tutoring writing courses for adults

Author visits to schools and libraries

Linda If your local authority is lucky enough to have a Schools' Library Service (sadly, they are diminishing fast) you should make yourself known to them. Also, find out the name of the children's librarian for the public library service. These contacts may lead to valuable experience in schools and libraries, and possible inclusion in holiday reading schemes and the like.

Contact with local bookshops can lead to school visits. Although visits organised in this way will almost invariably be unpaid, and should be treated as promotional work rather than educational, they can be a good way of raising your profile locally and introducing your books to children. They can take place in the bookshop – owners or managers may see it as a chance to bring children into the shop who don't otherwise visit – or, more likely, given the organisational complexities of taking children out of school, in a classroom or assembly hall. The bookseller will, of course, want to sell books, and will often ask the school to send a letter or email to parents in advance, to maximise sales.

For promotional visits like these, you would expect to do just one session. For paid days in school, though, you may be asked to do three, four or more talks, for different age groups. Paid school visits are usually arranged through a librarian, teacher or sometimes a governor, and there may be specific requests, for example to talk to the children about plotting, or research, or to fit in with the theme of a Book Week.

The Society of Authors issues guidelines about fees and what you can reasonably be expected to do. I think it's important to distinguish between paid visits and promotional ones. If the school is paying you £300 or £350 for the day, then an intensive sales pitch is not appropriate, and you should fit in with their requirements (as long as they're reasonable, of course). Book sales *may* happen: some authors insist on it, sometimes taking stocks of their own books, or arranging for the publisher to send them. Many schools have good links with a local bookseller, who will bring books and take care of the selling. Occasionally a school decides not to have books on sale, because it makes a distinction between those children whose parents can afford books and those who can't. In such cases it's worth suggesting that the school buys a few copies for the library, and giving them at least one signed copy.

If talking to groups of children is an unfamiliar experience for you (i.e. if you don't have a background in teaching!) you could consider offering a one-off promotional talk, free of charge, to your local primary or secondary school, depending on the age range of your book, in order to give yourself a trial run and see how you feel about it. It's rather an assumption that every author can hold the interest of a group of children for up to an hour. Maybe it comes naturally to you – and maybe it doesn't. One way of preparing yourself could be to ask a local bookseller, library or children's book group if there's an author visit you could sit in on, or preferably more than one; that's a good way of seeing what works and what doesn't.

A warning here, though – some of the authors on the circuit are almost stand-up comedians (it's a male thing, I've noticed). This can be daunting for those of us who aren't extroverts or natural performers, but do remember that it's not essential to get children rolling on the floor. You're there because you can write, not because you're a comic turn – a head teacher told me recently that a visiting poet had all the children laughing hysterically at toilet jokes, but hadn't really conveyed much about writing. You're there to enthuse children with ideas and the love of creating stories. You can find your own ways of engaging an audience.

Children aren't used to sitting passively in class for long periods; if they're bored, they will soon show it. You need to find ways to involve them, through question and answer, activities, quick changes, or the showing of PowerPoint images. Primary children can usually be counted on to be interested and enthusiastic, but if you've written a teenage novel, Year Nine can be a very different matter, and there's nothing more off-putting than a row of blank faces, or teenagers openly yawning or texting while you're trying to engage them. The deadliest thing to do is to read aloud for more than a few minutes; keep readings short, and have something to fall back on. Above all, be flexible: rather than sticking doggedly to your planned presentation, it's more effective to adapt to the audience in front of you, and change tack if necessary.

There are various listings for authors available to give talks, readings and workshops. One such site is Contact-an-Author, where, for an annual fee, you can set up and maintain your own page, updating as often as you wish with new books, testimonials, etc. Through this website, interested parties can contact you directly.

There are agencies which handle author visits, such as Authors Abroad and Authors Aloud UK (website addresses can be found at end of this section). For published authors, these agencies deal directly with schools to arrange talks, workshops and residencies.

Going it alone: self-publishing

Linda Anyone can publish a book – that is, anyone can pay for it to be printed and bound. This isn't what we mean in this guide by being published, though it does work well for certain kinds of book – for example, local histories, reminiscences or walking guides which are unlikely to be of interest outside the author's own region.

In the last few years, e-readers such as the Kindle have had major effects on the publishing industry, and no one can be sure how things will develop. For authors, an interesting aspect of this is that anyone can now make an electronic book available, free of charge, through Amazon Kindle, Smashwords or other such programmes. Many authors are relishing the unwonted freedom of choosing their cover and price, promoting their own books and knowing that anyone in the world with an e-reader can buy and download a copy.

So: the good news about e-readers is that anyone can publish a book.

But the bad news is also that anyone can publish a book.

If you're a first-time author, the drawback is that you won't have the satisfaction of knowing that a publisher considered it worthwhile to invest in your work. In a saying attributed to the late Gore Vidal, 'It is not enough to succeed. Others must fail.'[37] – but, with e-publishing, no one need fail. Anyone who has passed the first and only test of assembling enough words to constitute a 'book' can make it available for sale. The risk is that the market will be swamped by indifferent, badly produced, badly written, unedited, even illiterate books. How is the unwary reader or buyer to tell the difference?

Some professional authors are taking the opportunity to reissue out-of-print titles on their own initiative, having asked for the rights to be reverted. This kind of e-publishing works, because the author already has a reputation and a following; also, crucially, the books will have been professionally edited before first publication. It is quite possible for a freelance author to engage the services of a professional editor, and it's advisable to do this if you want your novel to be as good as it can possibly be before making it available. Many first-time writers have strange ideas about the setting out and punctuation of dialogue, too, which will make your work look amateurish if you allow it to go on sale uncorrected.

The practicalities of e-publishing are surprisingly simple. If you have your text as a Word document, you can upload it at the click of a mouse – though it is as well to check the formatting very carefully before you do so. Nothing looks worse than an ebook with random line spacing, inconsistent layout and inexplicable jumps in the text.

If you're writing for younger children, it will be harder to reach them via e-publishing, especially as you'll be in competition with professionally produced apps, with animations and sound effects.

It has to be said, too, that self-produced e-books will not sell without a great deal of promotional activity on your part – using Twitter, websites, Facebook and the like. Some self-published authors (and some conventionally published ones, too) seem to spend more time promoting than they spend on writing. If this is what you're good at, it may work for you – there have been stories recently of astonishing successes with go-it-alone e-publishing, such as the notorious *Fifty Shades of Grey* by E.L. James, which sold in its millions before (and after) being conventionally published.

Yvonne   The rise of the ebook and e-publishing has raised the levels of interest in self-publishing of all kinds. No agent takes a commission, no editors exert pressure to make changes, no publishers argue with you about covers, titles, and how to make your book fit their lists. Above all, there are no long waits for decisions about your manuscripts, and no rejection letters. You are in control, and your royalties are much, much higher on any books sold. What's not to like? Yet mainstream publishers have not been driven out of business in droves, which gives the clue that it's not quite so simple.

The fact that anyone can publish anything they want, without having to meet any defined standard, has positive and negative aspects. On the one hand, in a hugely subjective marketing environment, it enhances the opportunities for genuinely talented authors to find their readers. I hope it will lead to many fresh, new and exciting writers being discovered who have not made it through the conservative, risk-averse attitudes that can suffocate imaginative publishing deals before birth.

On the other hand, for any writer, whether or not s/he is established, the collaborative creative journey undertaken with a good editor can result in a much better, more satisfying and more marketable book. Agents and editors are not infallible, but they have a lot of experience in the way market trends are going. Publishers are often very cautious, but the resources they are able to put behind a book and its author are considerable, and the costs of producing and promoting the book are risked by the publisher, not by you, if the book fails to sell.

Readers are quickly becoming aware that choosing and paying for a book that has not gone through the traditional publishing hoops is a risky business. 'There's so much rubbish out there now!' wailed a friend who was trying to gather some holiday reading for herself and for her children. 'You read half the book and find out the writer doesn't know how to develop the story, or end it, and it all descends into gibberish!' I would hazard a guess that those who buy books for children will be especially cautious about investing in a self-published, unknown author, because a book that fails to deliver on a promise to a child may well lead to a young reader becoming disillusioned about books and reading generally. The input from an experienced, objective eye during the agent–editor–publisher process doesn't guarantee this won't happen, but it makes it much less likely. Many who have spoken to me about the wealth of strange imprint names on the books they browse online or in shops are wary of trying a title whose author they have never heard of who does not have a recognisable publisher.

Linda has commented on Kindle, which has particularly fuelled the self-publishing market by offering the attractive option of an ebook published under the auspices of the mighty Amazon brand quickly, easily and for free. Many of the titles are ebook versions of works that are also available in traditional paperback or hardback versions. Both Linda and I have reissued titles on Kindle in this way. The boundaries between self-publishing, e-publishing and mainstream publishing are definitely shifting, and it will be fascinating to watch the impact on books and reading habits over the next few years in these fast-moving markets.

There are many smaller operators advertising on the internet and in writers' magazines who offer print-on-demand services, sometimes with promotional and marketing packages attached. Some e-publishers will take your document and convert it into a format that can be downloaded onto e-readers, laptops, mobile phones and desktop computers; for Amazon Kindle you simply upload your own document. But print-on-demand offers the option of paying to have good quality paper copies of your book produced from the documents held electronically. You can request just one or half a dozen copies, or a run of a hundred or a thousand – the more copies, the cheaper the unit price. The books are yours to promote, sell or give away.

Some print-on-demand publishers offer extra services to provide technical assistance with covers, presentation and so on. I found print-on-demand very useful when two of my titles went out of print with their mainstream publishers, and I had letters from individuals and from English departments in schools who nonetheless wanted to purchase copies or sets for use in libraries and classrooms.

My advice to a new writer would be always to try, try and try again to get a good agent behind you when you start out. Don't close the door on e- or self-publishing, but try the more traditional route first, particularly while you are finding your way. I know that there are writers who have found huge success via the self-publishing route, and others whose books have been taken up by mainstream publishers after coming to notice as self-published form. But these writers are very few and far between, and you need boundless time and energy (not to mention self-confidence) to devote yourself to the promotion and marketing of yourself and your work. If you are going to self-publish, research the options well and gather up-to-date information and opinions – it's a very fast-changing landscape at the moment.

Finally, a word of caution. The most important thing to grasp about self-publishing is the difference between self- and vanity publishing. Make sure you understand what you are getting into. Vanity publishers advertise in places frequented by aspiring authors. They usually present themselves as seeking new authors, inviting submissions of novels, plays, poetry collections or short stories. That's your first warning sign – no bona-fide publisher needs to advertise; they are unable to keep up with the unsolicited manuscripts hitting their desks every single day. Your submission will, of course be successful – no author is ever refused by a vanity publisher, because you will be paying all the costs of production and providing an extra profit on top for the company. What you get in return is often poor quality, and assurances of promotional links between these companies and sales outlets are unlikely to come to anything. The majority of booksellers, and reviewers too, will not deal with vanity publishers. So, be clear: if a publisher is expecting you to 'contribute towards' (i.e. pay for) the costs of production, and it is not a publisher with whom you have engaged in the full knowledge that you are dealing with a vanity publisher, then steer clear.

> **"** *If I were you, I wouldn't be starting from here . . .* **"**
> (traditional Irish)

Get the book written!

Yvonne   Where does this leave you, the aspiring children's author, with that story burning in your imagination, waiting to be shared? How are you supposed to navigate the choppy waters of raging debates about what should and shouldn't influence a children's book, competing definitions of 'child' and so on? I am sometimes asked for my top tips for writing children's fiction, so here they are:

- Take your eyes off the best-seller lists. Write the story you want and need to write, and have faith that it will find its way.

- Know your audience – even more crucial for children's books, I believe, than for adult novels. Haunt your local library, look at which books children cluster around, which books they glance at and reject. Make friends with the children's librarian, if such a noble creature exists once the current global financial crisis is over. They can be valuable sources of information and support.

- Read voraciously. Read as many children's books as you can get your hands on: not just the kind of books you want to write, but the whole range. If you can, read with and for children. Read to your own children and their friends; help out at the local school (also useful for when you get that first book published, and need a bit of 'author visit' practice). You'll get an idea of what real children look like and what real children read, from that first 'taste and see' – literally – book for babies through to the young-adult novel that will blow your granny's socks off.

- Finally, GET THE BOOK WRITTEN! Whatever it takes, however daft and useless a task it seems, there is no substitute for simply sticking at it and getting it finished. How many people talk about the book they have within them? The book they will write one day when the bills are paid, the children are more independent, the garden stops growing and the demands and restrictions of the outside world have all gone away? These things will never happen, so don't waste time waiting. Write the book now. Make a start, now. Only pause to read this book, because Linda and I spent a long time writing it and we think it might be useful.

Notes

1. Widely quoted, attributed to Maxim Gorky.
2. *Fame Academy*, shown on BBC TV for the first time in 2002, was one of the early 'talent-spotting' concepts, combining reality TV and live entertainment where the TV audience voted for their favourite singer. The show was developed from the original Spanish version, *Operación Triunfo*.
3. Reivers were horse-mounted raiders and fighters who roamed the border between Scotland and England from the fourteenth to the seventeenth centuries. Many became mercenaries or were forced into military service.
4. Mike spent five years pretending to be seriously interested in the propositions being put to him in scam emails. Sometimes he would engage for weeks or even months, seeking revenge on behalf of our general society and scamming back. He has claimed to be Del Trotter Antiques and Inspector Morse, among other fictitious characters, getting the scammers to waste hours of time answering his queries, in making expensive journeys, and in one case tattooing his (fake) religious sect on to their flesh. His website is www.419eater.com
5. Mike Berry, *Greetings in Jesus Name!*, Harbour Books, York, 2006.
6. Angus Calder, *The People's War*, Jonathan Cape, London, 1969.
7. See www.cliffmcnish.com for more details of Cliff's work in schools.
8. K.M. Peyton, *Flambards*, Oxford University Press, Oxford, 1967, p. 49.
9. This first appeared in 1886 in James Orchard Halliwell's *The Nursery Rhymes of England*, but the best known version was probably first published in Joseph Jacobs' *English Fairy Tales* in 1890.
10. For example, write 'Small pig, small pig, allow my admission to your building,' and the wolf is transformed into an old-fashioned charmer. But if he says, 'Oy, pig! I'm

coming in!' he becomes a thug with no manners at all. Now stop cheating and have a go yourself . . .

11. Forster gave a series of lectures in 1927 that were published as *Aspects of the Novel*, republished Penguin Classics, London, 2005; also available on Kindle.

12. Patrick Ness, speaking at the London Book Fair, 2012.

13. Meg Rosoff, 'Who Are You Really?' in *The Guardian* and *The Observer* supplement 'How to Write'; see www.megrosoff.co.uk/2012/11/11/how-to-write

14. John Mortimer, 'Plot Luck', in *The Agony and the Ego: The Art and Strategy of Fiction Writing Explored*, ed. Clare Boylan, Penguin, London, 1993.

15. David Fickling, in a talk to the Scattered Authors' Society, Oxford, 2004.

16. See Philip Pullman, 'The Dark Side of Narnia', first published in *The Guardian* in 1998. The article is online (at the time of writing) at The Cumberland River Lamp Post, www.crlamppost.org/darkside.htm

17. C.S. Lewis, *Of Other Worlds: Essays and Stories*, Geoffrey Bles, London, 1966, p. 36.

18. Jill Patron Walsh, *Fireweed*, Macmillan Education, Oxford, 1978, p. 9.

19. Jill Paton Walsh, ibid., pp. 126–7.

20. Frank Cottrell-Boyce, 'Can't You Sleep?' in *Next*, ed. Keith Gray, Andersen, London, 2012.

21. Celia Rees, *This is Not Forgiveness*, Bloomsbury, London, 2012, pp. 5-6.

22. Philippa Pearce, *The Way to Sattin Shore*, Kestrel, London, 1983, p. 7.

23. Philip Pullman, *Northern Lights*, Scholastic, London, 1995. p. 3.

24. Adèle Geras, *Troy*, David Fickling Books, Oxford, 2000, p. 1.

25. Elmore Leonard, quoted in 'Ten Rules for Writing Fiction', *The Guardian*, 20 February 2012: 'If it sounds like writing, I rewrite it.' He isn't referring specifically to dialogue, but the point is especially relevant here.

26. Aidan Chambers, *Postcards From No Man's Land*, Bodley Head, London, 1999, pp. 11–13.

27. Adèle Geras, op. cit., pp. 325–7.

28. 'It took nearly five hours, on three buses and a train, to reach the hospital to visit Gran. She got the usual response: 'Who are you?' She wondered, what was the point?'

29. Ann Patchett, *The Getaway Car*, 2011, Kindle version location 264.

30. Christopher Booker, *The Seven Basic Plots*, Continuum, New York, 2005.

31. Carole Blake, *From Pitch to Publication*, Macmillan, London, 1999, p. 33.

32. Hallmark Cards reference 20HZA 314-5 No. 11.

33. Carole Blake, op. cit., p. 18.

34. Source unknown, but attributed to Peter de Vries and widely quoted

35. Carole Blake, op. cit., p. 34.

36. The media love nothing more than a dazzling debut. 'Author writes book' is not a story, but 'New (and preferably photogenic) young author tipped to be the next J.K. Rowling' is. On closer examination, the 'six-figure advance' may not be what it seems. The six figures (say £100,000) may have been offered for a seven-book deal, one book to be delivered each year. That would be a good advance, even when divided by seven (many children's authors can only dream of five figures, let alone six) but it can result in the author being tied to a contract which obliges her to keep producing the books even after the first one has had a disappointing reception and low sales – not good for morale or creativity.

37. Gore Vidal, quoted by Gerard Irvine, 'Antipanegyric for Tom Driberg', memorial service for Driberg, 8 December 1976.

Reference

Some useful websites and organisations

Organisations

Booktrust www.booktrustchildrensbooks.org.uk

The children's division of Booktrust. Appoints the Children's Laureate and administers the Blue Peter Book Award and the Roald Dahl Funny Prize. The website includes news, reviews and listings.

Children's Book Council www.cbcbooks.org

Website includes reviews of books published in the USA, news and author profiles.

The Federation of Children's Book Groups www.fcbg.org.uk

Organisation comprising individual book groups from around the UK, for anyone with an interest in children's books: parents, teachers, librarians, authors and illustrators. Administers the Red House Children's Book Award, judged entirely by children, and hosts a yearly conference. Linked to *Carousel* magazine. Members can join as individuals or through a local group.

IBBY (International Board on Books for Young People) www.ibby.org

A non-profit-making, international network of people committed to bringing children and books together. IBBY hosts a biennial conference, publishes a journal, and administers the Hans Christian Andersen Awards for writing and for illustration.

SCBWI (Society of Children's Book Writers and Illustrators) www.scbwi.org

A professional organisation for both published and unpublished writers and illustrators. Runs conferences and other events, advises on all aspects of publication, and produces New Voices yearly – an anthology featuring work from new writers.

The Society of Authors www.societyofauthors.net

The authors' trade union, for published writers only. Includes specialist sections such as CWIG (Children's Writers and Illustrators Group) and Educational Writers. Advises on all aspects of publication, and holds regular meetings for members and guests.

Writing courses

The Arvon Foundation www.arvonfoundation.org

Details of residential writing courses held at four centres in England and Scotland.

Faber Academy www.faberacademy.co.uk

Details of weekend and longer courses and online opportunities.

The Guardian Masterclasses www.guardian.co.uk/guardian-masterclasses

A range of day and weekend courses covering various aspects of writing and publishing.

Ty Newydd www.literaturewales.org/ty-newydd

Details of residential courses at the National Writers' Centre of Wales.

Consultancies and mentoring schemes

Cornerstones www.cornerstones.co.uk

Consultancy, editorial agency and scout for literary agents, specialising in fiction for children and young adults.

Gold Dust www.gold-dust.org.uk

Consultancy for authors of fiction, biography and screenplays which offers one-to-one mentoring over a period of several months. Tutors include Sally Cline, Carole Angier, Midge Gillies, Michele Roberts, Andrew Miller, Tim Pears and Romesh Gunesekera.

TLC (The Literary Consultancy) www.literaryconsultancy.co.uk

Mentorship scheme called Chapter and Verse offers tutoring by writers including Su Box, Jane McNulty, Tim Clare and Miranda Miller.

News and reviews

Armadillo http://sites.google.com/site/armadillomagazine

A quarterly online review magazine, for which Linda Newbery currently edits the teenage section; Yvonne Coppard is one of the reviewers. It has an associated intermittent blog, covers all ages from picture books to young adults, and includes author interviews and news from the book world.

ACHUKA www.achuka.co.uk

The website of Michael Thorn, independent reader and reviewer. Includes news, reviews and recommendations.

The Horn Book www.hbook.com

The Horn Book magazine is a leading US review magazine specialising in books for children and young adults. This website features reviews and recommendations.

Lovereading4kids.co.uk

Online children's bookstore, with reviews, selections and features. Guardian review editor Julia Eccleshare is a regular contributor.

Stroppy Author: Book Vivisection http://bookvivisection.blogspot.co.uk

This website is not for reviews, but contains detailed analysis of how picture books work, hosted by writer and academic Anne Rooney.

Teen Reads www.teenreads.com

Lively US website specialising in young adult fiction.

UKYA http://ukya.co.uk

A website specialising in young adult fiction by UK authors. Listings by genre, reviews, competitions, polls.

Blogs

Individual author blogs are not listed here, but can be found via Google searches or author websites.

ABBA (An Awfully Big Blog Adventure)

www.awfullybigblogadventure.blogspot.com

A daily group blog by members of the Scattered Authors' Society, which covers all aspects of writing and the children's book world.

Authors Electric http://authorselectric.blogspot.com

A daily blog by UK authors of e-books for Kindle and other devices. Among children's writers who contribute are Susan Price, Pauline Fisk and Dennis Hamley; others write adult fiction or non-fiction, and there are regular guest posts. All are professionally published authors who have independently made one or more books available electronically.

GirlsHeartBooks http://girlsheartbooks.com

A daily blog aimed at book-loving girls aged from eight to fourteen.

The History Girls http://the-history-girls.blogspot.com

A group blog by writers of historical fiction, including Mary Hoffman, Michelle Lovric, Caroline Lawrence, Celia Rees and Adèle Geras. Covers all aspects of writing historical fiction: voice, research, chance finds, fascinating facts.

PictureBookDen http://picturebookden.blogspot.co.uk

A group blog hosted by UK writers and illustrators of picture books.

Writing in the House of Dreams http://jenalexanderbooks.wordpress.com

Author Jenny Alexander's website about writing, inspiration, dreams, writing methods and motivation

Author listings

Authors Abroad www.authorsabroad.com

Agency handling author visits to schools.

Authors Aloud UK www.authorsalouduk.co.uk

Agency handling author visits to schools.

Contact an Author www.contactanauthor.co.uk

Links to authors offering work in schools and libraries.

The Word Pool www.wordpool.co.uk

A website for parents, teachers and writers. Includes listings, resources and an author database.

Select bibliography and further reading

Novels and series for children

Almond, David, *Skellig*, Hodder, London, 1998

————, *My Name is Mina*, Hodder, London, 2011

Awdry, W., *Thomas, The Tank Engine*, Edmund Ward, Leicester, 1946 onwards

Baum, Frank L., *The Wonderful Wizard of Oz*, George M. Hill, Chicago, 1900 (first title in a 13-book series)

Bawden, Nina, *Carrie's War*, Gollancz, London, 1973

Berg, Leila, *Nippers*, series including *Fish and Chips for Supper*, Macmillan, London, 1968 onwards

Blyton, Enid, *The Little Black Doll*, first published 1935, World Distributors, 1965

Blume, Judy, *Blubber, Macmillan,* London, 1974

Brahmachari, Sita, *Artichoke Hearts*, Macmillan, London, 2011

Branford, Henrietta, *Fire, Bed and Bone*, Walker Books, London, 1997

Carroll, Lewis, *Alice's Adventures in Wonderland*, Macmillan, London, 1865; Appleton, New York, 1866

Chapman, Linda, *Skating School* series, Puffin, London, 2010; *Unicorn* series, Scholastic, London, 2007

Coolidge, Susan, *What Katy Did*, Roberts Brothers, Boston, 1872

Coppard, Yvonne, *Simple Simon*, Red Fox, London, 1992

————, *To Be a Millionaire*, Barrington Stoke, Edinburgh, 2000

Cotterill, Jo, *Sweet Hearts* series, Red Fox, London, 2010 onwards

Crompton, Richmal, *Just William*, Macmillan, London, 1922

Crossley-Holland, Kevin, *Storm*, Heinemann, London, 1985

Dahl, Roald, *Charlie and the Chocolate Factory*, Allen and Unwin, London, 1967

Daniels, Lucy, *Animal Ark* series, Hodder, London, 1996 onwards

Edwards, Monica, The *Romney Marsh* stories, beginning with *Wish for a Pony*, Collins, London, 1947

Edwards, Monica, The *Punchbowl Farm* stories, beginning with *No Mistaking Corker*, Collins, London, 1950

Fforde, Jasper, *The Last Dragon Slayer*, Hodder and Stoughton, London, 2011

Fine, Anne, *It Moved!*, Walker Books, London, 2006

Garner, Alan, *The Owl Service*, Collins, London, 1967

Garnett, Eve, *The Family from One End Street*, Frederick Muller, London, 1937

Gleitzman, Morris, *Two Weeks with the Queen*, Piper, Australia, 2001

Grahame, Kenneth, *The Wind in the Willows*, Methuen, London, 1908

Hartnett, Sonya, *The Ghost's Child*, Walker Books, London, 2008

Higson, Charlie, *Young Bond* series, Puffin, London, 2005 onwards

Hodgson Burnett, Frances, *The Secret Garden*, Heinemann, London, 1911

————, *A Little Princess*, Scribner, New York, 1905; Frederick Warne, London, 1905

Hoffman, Mary, *Stravaganza: City of Masks*, Bloomsbury, London, 2002

————, *Stravaganza: City of Stars*, Bloomsbury, London, 2003

Horowitz, Anthony, *Alex Rider* series, Walker Books, London, 2000 onwards

Ibbotson, Eva, *One Dog and his Boy*, Marion Lloyd Books, Scholastic, London, 2011

Johns, W.E. *Biggles* series 1932–62, beginning with *The Camels are Coming*, John Hamilton, London, 1932

Jung, Rheinhardt, *Bambert's Book of Missing Stories*, translated by Anthea Bell, Egmont, London, 2002

Kemp, Gene, *The Turbulent Term of Tyke Tiler*, Faber and Faber, London, 1978

Kinney, Jeff, *Diary of a Wimpy Kid*, Puffin, London, 2006

Kipling, Rudyard, *The Jungle Book*, Macmillan, London, 1908 (first published as magazine stories, 1893–4)

Laird, Elizabeth, *The Garbage King*, Macmillan, London, 2003

————, *Red Sky in the Morning*, Piper, London, 1989

————, with Nimr, Sonia, *A Little Piece of Ground*, Macmillan, London, 2003

Lawrence, Michael, *The Toilet of Doom – a Jiggy McCue Story*, Orchard, London, 2006

Lewis, C.S., *The Chronicles of Narnia*, Geoffrey Bles, London, 1950–6

Lofting, Hugh, *The Voyages of Dr Dolittle*, J.B. Lippincott, Philadelphia, 1922

Magorian, Michelle, *Goodnight Mr Tom*, Kestrel, London, 1981

McCombie, Karen, *Ally's World* series, Scholastic, London, 2010 onwards

Milne, A.A., *Winnie-the-Pooh*, Methuen, London, 1926; Dutton Children's Books, Boston, 1926

Morpurgo, Michael, *War Horse*, Kaye and Ward, London, 1982

Muchamore, Robert, *Cherub* series, Orchard, London, 2007 onwards

Munro, Rona, and O'Connell, Mabel, *Janet and John* series, James Nisbet, London, 1949 onwards

Naidoo, Beverly, *Journey to Jo'burg*, Harper Collins, London, 1999

Naughton, Bill, *Goalkeeper's Revenge and Other Stories*, Harrap, London, 1961

Newbery, Linda, *Lob*, David Fickling Books, Oxford, 2010

————, *The Sandfather*, Orion, London, 2009

Paver, Michelle, *Wolf Brother*, Orion, London, 2004

Pearce, Philippa, *Tom's Midnight Garden*, Oxford University Press, Oxford, 1958

————, *The Way to Sattin Shore*, Kestrel, London, 1983

Peyton, K.M. *Flambards*, Oxford University Press, Oxford, 1967

Pitcher, Annabel, *My Sister Lives on the Mantelpiece*, Orion, London, 2011

Pullman, Philip, *The Firework-Maker's Daughter*, Doubleday, London, 1995

————, *Northern Lights; The Subtle Knife; The Amber Spyglass*; Scholastic, London, 1995–2000

Ransome, Arthur, *Swallows and Amazons*, Jonathan Cape, London, 1930

Roberts, Katherine, *I Am the Great Horse*, Chicken House, London, 2006

Rowling, J.K., *Harry Potter* stories, beginning with *Harry Potter and the Philosopher's Stone*, Bloomsbury, London, 1997

Sachar, Louis, *Holes*, Farrar, Strauss and Giroux, New York, 1998

Serraillier, Ian, *The Silver Sword*, Jonathan Cape, London, 1956

Shelton, Dave, *A Boy and a Bear in a Boat*, David Fickling Books, Oxford, 2012

Simon, Francesca, *Horrid Henry* series, Orion, London, 1994 onwards

Smith, Dodie, *The Hundred and One Dalmatians*, Heinemann, London, 1956

Snicket, Lemony, *A Series of Unfortunate Events*, HarperCollins, London, beginning with *A Bad Beginning*, 1999

Stanton, Andy, *Mr Gum and the Biscuit Billionaire*, Egmont, London, 2007

Strong, Jeremy, *My Brother's Hot Cross Bottom*, Puffin, London, 2009

Sutcliff, Rosemary, *The Eagle of the Ninth*, Oxford University Press, London, 1954

Sykes, Julie, *Fairy Bears* series, Macmillan, London, 2009

Townsend, John Rowe, *Gumble's Yard*, Hutchinson, London, 1961

Updale, Eleanor, *Montmorency*, Scholastic, London, 2003

Voake, Steve, *Hooey Higgins Goes for Gold*, Walker Books, London, 2012

Walliams, David, *Mr Stink*, 2010; *Gangsta Granny*, 2011; *Billionaire Boy*, 2011; *Ratburger*; HarperCollins, London, 2012

White, E.B., *Charlotte's Web*, Hamilton, London, 1952

Wilson, Jacqueline, *The Story of Tracy Beaker*, Yearling, New York, 1992

Young adult fiction

Angelini, Josephine, *Starcrossed*, Macmillan, London, 2010

Blackman, Malorie, *Noughts and Crosses*, Doubleday, London, 2001

Blume, Judy, *Forever*, Dell, New York, 1991

Blundell, Judy, *Strings Attached*, Scholastic, London, 2011

Bowler, Tim, *Bloodchild*, Oxford University Press, Oxford, 2009

Burgess, Melvin, *Junk*, Nadersen Press, London 1996; as *Smack*, Henry Holt, New York, 1996

————, *Doing It*, Andersen, London, 2003

Cassidy, Anne, *Looking for JJ*, Scholastic, London, 2004

Chambers, Aidan, *Breaktime*, Bodley Head, London, 1978

————, *Dance on my Grave*, Bodley Head, London, 1982

————, *Now I Know*, Bodley Head, London, 1987

————, *The Toll Bridge*, Bodley Head, London, 1992

————, *Postcards From No Man's Land*, Bodley Head, London, 1999

————, *This is All: The Pillow Book of Cordelia Kenn*, Bodley Head, London, 2005

————, *Dying to Know You*, Bodley Head, London, 2012

Christopher, Lucy, *Stolen*, Chicken House, Frome, 2008

Cleary, Beverly, *Fifteen*, HarperCollins, London 1956

Collins, B.R. *The Traitor Game*, Bloomsbury, London, 2008

Collins, Suzanne, *The Hunger Games*, Scholastic, London, 2008

Cormier, Robert, *After the First Death*, Pantheon, New York, 1979

————, *I Am the Cheese*, Gollancz, London, 1977

————, *Heroes*, Hamish Hamilton, London, 1998

————, *The Rag and Bone Shop*, Hamish Hamilton, London, 2001

————, *Tunes for Bears to Dance to*, Gollancz, London, 1993

Donnelly, Jennifer, *A Gathering Light*, Bloomsbury, London, 2003; in USA as *A Northern Light*

Downham, Jenny, *Before I Die*, David Fickling Books, Oxford, 2007

Geras, Adèle, *Troy*, David Fickling Books, Oxford, 2000

Grant, Michael, *Gone*, Egmont, London, 2009

Gray, Keith, *The Ostrich Boys*, Random House, London, 2008

Haddon, Mark, *The Curious Incident of the Dog in the Night-Time*, David Fickling Books, Oxford, 2003

Higson, Charlie, *Young Bond: SilverFin, A James Bond Adventure*, Puffin, London, 2005

Hoffman, Mary, *David*, Bloomsbury, London, 2011

Hooper, Mary, *Fallen Grace*, Bloomsbury, London, 2010

Hunt, Peter, *Going Up*, Julia MacRae, London, 1989

Kate, Lauren, *Fallen*, Corgi, London, 2010

Manns, Nick, *Control Shift*, Hodder, London, 2000

McGowan, Anthony, *The Knife That Killed Me*, Delacorte, New York, 2008

McNish, Cliff, *The Doomspell Trilogy*, Orion, London, 20

————, *Breathe: A Ghost Story*, Orion, London, 2007

Meyer, Stephanie, *Twilight* series, Little, Brown, New York, 2005 onwards

Ness, Patrick, *The Knife of Never Letting Go*, Walker Books, London, 2009

————, *The Ask and the Answer*, Walker Books, London 2009

————, *Monsters of Men*, Walker Books, London, 2010

Newbery, Linda, *Run with the Hare*, Armada, London, 1988

————, *The Shell House*, David Fickling Books, Oxford, 2002

————, *Set in Stone*, David Fickling Books, Oxford, 2006

Nicholson, William, *Rich and Mad*, Egmont, London, 2009

Peet, Mal, *Tamar*, Walker Books, London, 2005

————, *Life: An Exploded Diagram*, Walker Books, London, 2011

Peyton, K.M., *A Midsummer Night's Death*, Oxford University Press, Oxford, 1978

Price, Susan, *The Sterkarm Handshake*, Scholastic, London, 1998

Rees, Celia, *Witch Child*, Bloomsbury, London 2000

————, *The Fool's Girl*, Bloomsbury, London, 2010

————, *This is Not Forgiveness*, Bloomsbury, London, 2012

Suzuma, Tabitha, *A Note of Madness*, Bodley Head, London, 2006

Townsend, Sue, *The Secret Diary of Adrian Mole Aged 13¾*, Methuen, London, 1982

Ure, Jean, *See You Thursday*, Kestrel, London, 1981

——————, *If it Wasn't for Sebastian*, Bodley Head, London 1982

——————, *The Other Side of the Fence*, Bodley Head, London, 1986

——————, *Plague 99*, Methuen, London, 1989

Walsh, Jill Paton, *Fireweed*, Macmillan, London, 1969

——————, *Goldengrove*, Macmillan, London, 1972

——————, *Unleaving*, Macmillan, London, 1976

Warren, Rosalie, *Coping with Chloe*, Phoenix Yard Books, London, 2011

Young, Moira, *Blood Red Road*, Simon and Schuster, London 2011

Other fiction

Alain-Fournier, *Le Grand Meaulnes*, Emile-Paul Freres, Paris, 1913

De Larrabeiti, Michael, *The Provençal Tales*, Pavilion Books, London, 1988

Dickens, Charles, *David Copperfield*, Bradbury and Evans, London 1850

Donoghue, Emma, *Room*, Little, Brown, London, 2010

Dunn, Nell, *Up the Junction*, MacGibbon and Kee, London, 1963

Frayn, Michael, *Spies*, Faber and Faber, London 2002

Golding, William, *Lord of the Flies*, Faber and Faber, London, 1954

Hartley, L.P., *The Go-Between*, Hamish Hamilton, London, 1953

Hoban, Russell, *Riddley Walker*, Jonathan Cape, London, 1980

Hosseini, Khaled, *The Kite Runner*, Riverhead Books, 2003

Hannah, Sophie, *The Other Half Lives*, Hodder, London, 2009

Huxley, Aldous, *Brave New World*, Chatto and Windus, London, 1932

James, Henry, *The Turn of the Screw*, Heinemann, London, 1898

Lee, Harper, *To Kill a Mockingbird*, J.P. Lippincott, Philadelphia, 1960

McEwan, Ian, *The Cement Garden*, Jonathan Cape, London, 1978

Sagan, Françoise, *Bonjour Tristesse*, Rene Julliard, Paris, 1954

Sebold, Alice, *The Lovely Bones*, Little Brown, New York, 2002

Shelley, Mary, *Frankenstein*, Harding, London, 1818

Tolkien, J.R.R., *The Hobbit*, 1937; *The Lord of the Rings*, Allen and Unwin, London, 1954–5

Tremain, Rose, *The Way I Found Her*, Sinclair Stevenson, London, 1997

Walker, Alice, *The Color Purple*, Harcourt Brace Jovanovich, San Diego, 1982

Short story collections

Blackman, Malorie (compiler), *Unheard Voices: An Anthology of Stories and Poems to Commemorate the Bicentenary Anniversary of the Abolition of the Slave Trade*, Transworld, London, 2007

Bradman, Tony (compiler), *Skin Deep*, Puffin, London, 2004

Bradman, Tony (compiler), *Under the Weather*, Frances Lincoln, London, 2009

Gray, Keith (compiler), *Next*, Andersen, London, 2012

Sedgwick, Marcus (compiler), *The Truth is Dead*, Walker Books, London, 2010

Picture books

Andreae, Giles, and McIntyre, Sarah, *Morris the Mankiest Monster*, David Fickling Books, Oxford, 2009

Blake, Quentin, *Clown*, Jonathan Cape, London, 1995

Bradman, Tony, and Browne, Eileen (illustrator), *Through my Window*, Methuen, London, 1986

Browne, Anthony, *Gorilla*, Julia MacRae Books, London, 1983

Bush, John, and Paul, Korky (illustrator), *The Fish Who Could Wish*, Oxford University Press, Oxford, 1991

Burningham, John, *Mr Gumpy's Outing*, Puffin, London 1978

Carle, Eric, *The Very Hungry Caterpillar*, World Publishing, New York 1969

Crowther, Robert, *Robert Crowther's Most Amazing Hide-and-Seek Alphabet Book*, Walker Books, London, 1999

————, *Robert Crowther's Amazing Pop-Up House of Inventions*, Walker Books, London, 2000

Donaldson, Julia, and Scheffler, Alex (illustrator), *The Gruffalo*, Macmillan, London, 1999

Durant, Alan, and Gliori, Debi (illustrator), *Always and Forever*, David Fickling Books, Oxford, 2003

Hughes, Shirley, *Dogger*, Bodley Head, London, 1977

Hutchins, Pat, *Rosie's Walk*, Bodley Head, London, 1968

Jarman, Julia, and Chapman, Lynne, *Class Two at the Zoo*, Hodder, London, 2008

Jarman, Julia, and Reynolds, Adrian (illustrator), *Big Red Bath*, Orchard, London, 2005

McBratney, Sam, and Jeram, Anita (illustrator), *Guess How Much I Love You*, Walker Books, London 1994

Potter, Beatrix, *The Tale of Peter Rabbit*, Frederick Warne, London 1902

Sendak, Maurice, *Where the Wild Things Are*, Bodley Head, London, 1967

Seuss, Dr, *The Cat in the Hat*, Houghton Miffin, Boston, and Random House, London, 1957

Sharratt, Nick, *Shark in the Park*, Corgi, London, 2007

Varley, Susan, *Badger's Parting Gifts*, Andersen, London, 1984

Waddell, Martin, and Benson, Patrick (illustrator), *Owl Babies*, Walker Books, London, 1992

Graphic novels

Appignanesi, Richard, and Leong, Sonia (illustrator), *Romeo and Juliet: Manga Shakespeare*, SelfMadeHero, 2007

Briggs, Raymond, *The Snowman*, Hamish Hamilton, London, 1978

Goscinny, René, and Uderzo, Albert (illustrator), *Asterix the Gaul*, Dargaud, Paris, 1961; first UK publication, translated by Anthea Bell, Brockhampton, Leicester, 1969 (first published in French in serial form in *Pilote*, 1959–60)

Haggarty, Ben, and Brockbank, Adam (illustrator), *MeZolith*, DFC Library, David Fickling Books, Oxford, 2010

Hergé (Georges Remi), *The Adventures of Tintin*, Editions du Vingtième, Brussels, 1930 (first published in serial form, 1929 onwards, in *Le Petit Vingtième*, a supplement of the Belgian newspaper *Le XXe Siècle*).

Higson, Charlie, and Walker, Kev (illustrator), *Silverfin: The Graphic Novel* (*Young Bond*), Walker Books, London, 2008

Horowitz, Anthony, Jonston, Antony, and Yuzuro, Kanako (illustrators) *Stormbreaker: Stormbreaker the Movie*, Walker Books, London, 2006

Selznick, Brian, *The Invention of Hugo Cabret*, Scholastic, London, 2007

Shelton, Dave, *Good Dog Bad Dog*, David Fickling Books, Oxford, 2010

Spiegelman, Art, *Maus*, Pantheon, New York, 1991 (first published in serial form in *Raw*, a graphics magazine produced by Spiegelman and Françoise Mouly)

Reference, criticism and commentary

Dixon, Bob, *Catching Them Young 1: Sex, Race and Class in Children's Fiction*, Pluto Press, London, 1977

————, *Catching Them Young 2: Political Ideas in Children's Fiction*, Pluto Press, London, 1977

Hunt, Peter, *An Introduction to Children's Literature*, Oxford University Press, Oxford, 1994

Hunt, Peter, *Understanding Children's Literature*, Routledge, London 1999

Leeson, Robert, *Reading and Righting*, Collins, London, 1985

Townsend, John Rowe, *Written for Children*, 1965, revised edn, Penguin, London, 1987

Other

Blake, Carole, *From Pitch to Publication: Everything You Need to Know to Get Your Novel Published*, Macmillan, London, 1999

Boylan, Clare (editor), *The Agony and the Ego: The Art and Strategy of Fiction Writing Explored*, Penguin, London, 1993

Brande, Dorothea, *Becoming a Writer*, Harcourt, Brace, 1934; reissued with foreword by John Braine, Macmillan, London, 1983

Cameron, Julia, *The Artist's Way*, Souvenir Press, London, 1994

Calder, Angus, *The People's War*, Jonathan Cape, London, 1969

The Children's Writers' and Artists' Yearbook 2012, Bloomsbury, London, 2011

Chambers, Aidan, *Booktalk*, Bodley Head, London, 1985

Goleman, Daniel, *Emotional Intelligence*, Bloomsbury, London, 1996

King, Stephen, *On Writing*, Hodder and Stoughton, London, 2000

Lewis, C.S., *Of Other Worlds: Essays and Stories*, Geoffrey Bles, London, 1966

Morgan, Nicola, *Write to be Published*, Snowbooks, Oxford, 2011

————, *Write a Great Synopsis*, Crabbit Publishing, Kindle, 2012

————, *Dear Agent: Write the Letter that Sells your Book*, Crabbit Publishing, Kindle, 2012

Newman, Sandra, and Mittelmark, Howard, *How Not to Write a Novel*, Harper Collins, New York, 2008

Patchett, Ann, *The Getaway Car*, Byliner, San Francisco, 2011.

Acknowledgements

We would both like to thank

- Sally Cline and Carole Angier for the invitation to be involved in this excellent series, and for enthusiastic and positive encouragement from the sidelines.

- Rachel Calder, the series agent, and David Avital at Bloomsbury, for a light, but clear, steer when necessary.

- Anne Fine, for kindly agreeing to write the Foreword.

- Our twenty-one guest contributors for their informative and entertaining writing.

- Friends and fellow writers who offered suggestions and ideas.

- Editors and agents who generously responded to our queries.

- Trevor Arrowsmith and Reg Quirk, who between them make one hell of a great proof-reader.

In addition

Yvonne   Of course I have to say how wonderful it has been to work with a co-author of such calibre as Linda, and how thoroughly I have enjoyed our discussions and exchange of ideas. I have to say it, but it doesn't have to be true. Well it is, absolutely. Thanks, Linda.

Linda   It's been a privilege to work with Yvonne, a gifted writer herself and with a wealth of knowledge and experience which has been both invaluable and reassuring. Thank you, Yvonne, for asking me to be your co-author. It's been more rewarding than I could have guessed.

Index